How To Establish
A Successful Business
In Thailand

How to Establish a Successful Business in Thailand
Copyright ©2007 by Philip Wylie
All rights reserved

Paiboon Publishing
582 Nawamin 90
Bungkum, Bangkok 10230
THAILAND
Tel 662-509-8632
Fax 662-519-5437

Paiboon Publishing
PMB 256, 1442A Walnut Street
Berkeley, California 94709
USA
Tel 1-510-848-7086
Fax 1-510-666-8862

info@paiboonpublishing.com
www.paiboonpublishing.com

Cover design and typesetting by Douglas Morton
72 Studio, Chiang Mai, Thailand
72studio@gmail.com

Printed in Thailand
ISBN 1-887521-75-8

Edited by Rich Baker

Contents

Foreign Ownership Of Limited Companies; Foreign Ownership Of Land; Visa Regulations

Introduction; Management; Capital; Legal Structure; Thai Partner (Or Representative); Premises; Employees; Product Concept; Summary

Start-Up: Buy Or Franchise?; Using Business Brokers; Premises: Rent Or Buy?; Business Location; Business Development; Type Of Business; Legal Ownership; Do You Need A Work Permit?; Establishing An Investment Budget; Timing: The Best Time To Start

The Key Determinants Of Business Valuation; Total Investment; Business Valuation Methods; Adjustment To Net Annual Profits; Lease Terms; Location; The Seller; Morale; Asset Sale; The Reason For Sale; Due Diligence; Business Evaluation Checklist; Property Prices

The Stages Of Buying A Business; Completion; How To Deal With Sellers; Finding A Lawyer And Accountant; Forming A Thai Limited Company; The Treaty Of Amity And Economic Relations; Business Licenses; Trademarks And Patents; Opening A Bank Account; Transferring Money To Thailand; Looking For Suitable Premises; Visas; Work Permits; Labour Law; The Board Of Investment (BOI); Leasing Land; Are You Ready To Make An Offer? (A Checklist)

Introduction

This guidebook is the result of collaboration with a group of successful businesspeople in Thailand, all of whom stress the importance of extensive research before investing hard-earned money. It will provide you with all the necessary information and local knowledge to enable you to establish a successful business in Thailand.

The word "successful" is not measured only in Thai baht or US dollars. Personal fulfilment can never be quantified, and even seasoned entrepreneurs will be surprised by some of the stories here.

This practical business guide clarifies key issues that affect foreign businesspeople in Thailand; issues that are commonly misunderstood or misinterpreted. Jargon has been left out and both sides of the story are covered—including successes and tales of tribulation—so that you might avoid the latter.

This book is for anyone (including Thais) considering investing in or starting a business in the Land of Smiles. It is intended to serve every type of businessperson including overseers, investors, managers, partners in a joint venture or company directors.

You may be investing only 3,000 US dollars in a restaurant or starting up a multi-million dollar manufacturing facility using a Thai Board of Investment (BOI) company, but business is done differently in Thailand, at all levels, so it's essential to understand the rules of the game before you start. To be successful, you must know the 'lay of the land' and the numerous unwritten rules.

In many ways, successful people in Thailand enjoy a better quality of life than they would in the USA or Europe. The main advantages of doing business in Thailand are greater freedom and fewer regulations, more quality time away from work and less stress and—if you do it right—more fun. After all, what's the point of working so hard to be successful if you can't enjoy your rewards?

This book will prepare you for doing business in Thailand in two ways. First, it outlines the established formula for success, based on a survey of successful businesspeople. Then it lists the most common pitfalls and explains how to avoid them.

Some tips in this book are so critically important, they are highlighted in bold. Ultimately they could save you thousands of dollars, many hours of time, and a lot of headaches. There are also numerous money-saving ideas and practical business rules of thumb.

The information in this book has been compiled from numerous sources including lawyers, accountants, local researchers, governmental organizations and Internet research. This information has been supplemented by subjective feedback from successful businesspeople, professional advisors and people who have learned from their mistakes.

Rules and regulations are constantly changing in Thailand, and legal professionals often interpret the law in different ways. The relationship between you (or your lawyer) and the government officer dealing with your case is sometimes as important as the relevant regulations.

This book is not intended as a legal guide book. **Information that is current and correct at the time of going to press might eventually be superseded, so please double check all details before acting upon them. Always instruct a professional lawyer to review all legally binding contracts.**

We hope you will enjoy this book and, of course, benefit from the information and experience provided by the contributors. We welcome your feedback and suggestions so we can improve and enhance the next edition and complementary publications. Please send comments and feedback to Philip using the contact form on www.advisaweb.com.

Establish your business successfully, with confidence, and enjoy the journey. May Buddha grin with you and bring you good fortune in the Land of Smiles.

Essential Website Addresses

Category	Details	Website Address
Airlines	Flight information	www.aviation.go.th
Business Registration	M.O.C. D.B.D	www.moc.go.th www.dbd.go.th
Chambers of Commerce	International directory of chambers	www.worldchambers.com www.iccwbo.org
Exchange Rates	Currency Calculator	http://www.x-rates.com/calculator.html
Investment	Board of Investment	www.boi.go.th
Land	Land registration and valuation	www.dol.go.th
Radio	Radio stations in Asia	www.asiawaves.net
Recruitment	Online recruitment	www.jobthai.com www.jobjob.co.th www.jobinthai.com www.jobthaiweb.com
Retirement	Information for retirees in Thailand	www.retiringinthailand.com www.thaivisa.com
Taxation	Revenue Department	www.rd.go.th
Tax Forms	E-filing	http://rdserver.rd.go.th/publish/en/index.htm
Thai Embassies	Thai embassies worldwide	www.th.embassyinformation.com www.embassyworld.com
Thai Language	Thai language books, online Thai lessons	www.paiboonpublishing.com www.thai-language.com www.learningthai.com
Visas	Immigration and Ministry of Foreign Affairs	www.immigration.go.th www.imm.police.go.th www.mfa.go.th/web/12.php
Work Permits	Department of Employment	www.doe.go.th/workpermit/index.html

Chapter 1
How The Laws Affect Foreigners

On May 15, 2006 the Thai government issued directives affecting foreign investment and immigration. The three main areas concerned are foreign ownership of limited companies, foreign ownership of land, and visa regulations. The underlying trend is tighter enforcement of Thailand's laws concerning foreign investment and ownership of land.

Foreign Ownership Of Limited Companies

All Thai limited companies, except those established under the "Amity Treaty," must be majority-owned and controlled by Thais. (See *The Treaty of Amity and Economic Relations.*) Until recently, many foreigners used Thai 'nominee' (or dummy) shareholders. However, the trend seems to be toward increased scrutiny of the underlying legal structure of foreign companies and enforcement of the existing law.

The Ministry of Commerce may check that Thai shareholders have sufficient funds to invest in the company, and that they receive their allotted share of annual profits. Currently, companies with less than 39 percent foreign ownership are subject to less scrutiny, but this may change.

The Ministry of Commerce may investigate the underlying objectives, ownership, and profit appropriation of foreign-owned businesses. The chances of investigation are higher for foreigners owning more than 39 percent of a company.

To circumvent the government review, some business advisors may recommend establishing a 100 percent Thai company and later transferring 39 percent or 49 percent of the issued shares to the foreigner to defer investigation. Penalties for breaking the law include fines, imprisonment, and potential loss of the investment. There are benefits to having genuine Thai shareholders who are committed to the company's success. As with all advice in this book, we recommend complying with all the legal requirements when engaging in any business in Thailand.

For further information about forming a Thai limited company, refer to "What You Need To Know Before You Start."

Foreign Ownership Of Land

Foreigners are not allowed to own land in Thailand, and the Thai government is now tightening the enforcement of these existing laws. The Department of Land will check that all companies owning land are 100 percent Thai-owned.

There are ways of circumventing the law such as forming a 100 per cent Thai-owed company to buy the land, or forming a second 49 percent company to buy a share of the former entity. But these methods are complex, expensive to maintain, and risky.

Most foreign businesspeople agree that buying land in the name of a trustworthy Thai person, and asking that person to issue a renewable thirty-year lease (registered with the Department of Land), is the safest and most practical method of enjoying land rights in Thailand.

For further information about leasing land, refer to "What You Need To Know Before You Start."

Visa Regulations

For most businesspeople and investors the revised, more restrictive, visa regulations represent a storm in a teacup. It is still reasonably easy to obtain a twelve-month Non-Immigrant visa from a Thai consulate in Europe or North America.

For information about visas, refer to "What You Need To Know Before You Start."

Chapter 2
Thailand: Quick Facts

Area: 513,115 square kilometres (land: 510,885 square kilometres; water: 2,230 square kilometres), approximately the same size as France or the US state of Texas.

Calendar: Gregorian and Buddhist (543 years in advance of the Gregorian calendar).

Capital City: Bangkok (estimated population: 10 million).

Climate: Tropical: southwest monsoon (May to September); northeast monsoon (November to mid-March). Generally divided into three seasons: hot (March-May); rainy (May/June-November); and cool, dry (December-February). But usually always hot and humid.

Currency: Baht.

English-Language Media: The *Bangkok Post* and *The Nation* national daily newspapers; numerous other English-language periodicals and radio stations.

Ethnicity: Thai: 80 percent; Chinese: 12 percent; Malay: 4 percent; Others: 4 percent.

Geographical Location: Southeast Asia bordered by Burma (west), Laos (north and east), Cambodia (east), and Malaysia (south). Coasts: Andaman Sea (southwest) and the Gulf of Thailand (south).

Gross Domestic Product: US$559.5 billion.

GDP Per Capita: US$8,542 (2005 estimate).

GDP Growth Rate: 5.4 percent.

Government: Constitutional monarchy, headed by King Bhumibol Adulyadej since 1946.

Industries: Tourism; textiles and garments; agricultural processing; beverages; tobacco; cement; light manufacturing such as jewellery, electric appliances and components, computers and parts, integrated circuits, furniture, and plastics; world's second-largest tungsten producer and third-largest tin producer.

International Organization Participation: APEC, ADB, ASEAN, CCC, CP, ESCAP, FAO, G-77, IAEA, IBRD, ICAO, ICFTU, ICRM, IDA, IFAD, IFC, IFRCS, IHO, ILO, IMF, IMO, Inmarsat, Intelsat, Interpol, IOC, IOM, ISO, ITU, NAM, PCA, UN, UNCTAD, UNESCO, UNHCR, UNIDO, UNIKOM, UNU, UPU, WCL, WFTU, WHO, WIPO, WMO, WTO.

Internet: ASDL; LAN/Wi-fi.

Land (Unit of Measurement): One *rai* = 1,600 square meters = 0.16 hectares = 0.4 acres = 4 *ngan.*

Land Use: Arable land: 34 percent; permanent crops: 6 percent; permanent pastures: 2 percent; forests and woodland: 26 percent; other: 32 percent (1993 estimate).

Languages: Thai (with English widely spoken in urban centres).

Life Expectancy: 71.4 years.

Median Age: 30.5 years.

Literacy: 94 percent.

Local Time: GMT plus seven hours.

Main Expatriate Centres: Bangkok, Chiang Mai, Chiang Rai, Phuket, Pattaya, Koh Samui, Hua Hin, Khon Kaen.

Major Cities (*With Provincial Population Figures*): Bangkok Metropolitan (10 million), Chiang Mai (1.65 million); Chiang Rai (1.2 million); Chonburi (1.2 million); Nakhon Ratchasima (2.6 million); Ubon Ratchathani (1.8 million); Khon Kaen (1.7 million); Udon Thani (1.5 million); Nakhon Si Thammarat (1.5 million).

Minimum Daily Wage: 184 baht (Bangkok).

Mobile Phone Networks: AIS (1, 2 Call), DTAC, True Move.

Money: Extensive networks of ATMs (Visa, Mastercard, Diners Club, Amex, Maestro, Cirrus), travellers' cheques (US dollars, pound sterling, euro).

Natural Resources: Tin, rubber, natural gas, tungsten, tantalum, timber, lead, fisheries, gypsum, lignite, fluorite.

Office Hours (Standard): Monday to Saturday (09.00-17.00 hours)

Population: 66 million (2005); estimate for 2010: 70 million.

Population Below The Poverty Line: 10.4 percent.

Population Growth Rate: 0.91 percent.

Provinces: 76.

Religions: Buddhist: 94 percent, Muslim: 5 percent, Christian: 1 percent.

Telephone: Country code: + 66 (0); Cellphones: + 66 (0)8.

Unemployment: 1.4 percent (2005 estimate).

Workforce: 34.1 million.

Sources: National Statistical Office, the Bank of Thailand,
and the Board of Investment (BOI).

Chapter 3
Business In Thailand:
Same Same, But Different

Introduction

If you think 'business is business' wherever you are, think again. Things are done differently in Thailand, so don't make the mistake of believing that business success outside Thailand guarantees a similar outcome here.

There are seven key foundations for business success in Thailand, and each must be understood and addressed appropriately. The seven foundations are:

- Management
- Capital
- Legal structure
- Thai partner (or representative)
- Premises (if necessary)
- Employees
- Product concept

If there is a weakness in any of these critical areas, the business will experience problems. If such issues are not acted upon appropriately, the business will not succeed.

Management

For the majority of small to medium-sized businesses, "management" means the owner-manager or entrepreneur—the person running the business and making the day-to-day decisions. Sole proprietors are owner-managers who usually invest their own money in the business they both own and manage.

Decide Whether You Want To Be A Business Manager Or Investor

Many foreigners invest in a Thai business, obtain a work permit, then quickly realise they do not want to work. If your Thai spouse is managing the business for you, and there are sufficient Thai employees, you don't need to go to the trouble of obtaining a work permit.

Some people work as a manager (or director) in one business and as an investor-overseer in other businesses. Greg Lange is managing director of Sunbelt Asia, while also overseeing his Subway franchise investments. For the full story, refer to "Business Brokering" in "Profiles Of Successful Businesspeople."

Do not appoint yourself director of a company you invest in if you do not intend to work there. Directors of Thai limited companies require a work permit. A work permit is necessary for each employer (or company) you work for. However, it is possible to register more than one employer on the same work permit.

Another factor to consider is your commitment to the business. Are you really able to commit to the demands of managing a full-time commercial enterprise? Or are you semi-retired, looking for something to occupy a couple of hours each day? If you fall into the second category, tread carefully because the majority of 'hobby businesses' fail in Thailand.

If You Want To Be A Business Manager, You Still Need A Thai Partner Or Representative

Your Thai partner (or representative) will open many doors barred to foreigners. Your partner must be reliable, honest, and absolutely committed to you and your business. A reasonable remuneration scheme (with performance-based incentives) is essential. Not all Thai spouses are suitable for this job.

You need a trusted Thai colleague to liaise with government officials, interact with Thai customers and suppliers, and to manage Thai staff. Unless you can read Thai, you will need assistance with translation of documents. The need for guidance with Thai customs and etiquette cannot be underestimated.

Why Proprietors Of 'Hobby Businesses' Usually Fail

Typically, owners of hobby businesses are looking for a way out of boredom but they lack the necessary commitment to their venture. Sometimes foreigners buy a business for their spouse—'to give them something to do'—without properly discussing the matter. These are negative reasons for starting a business. It's another matter if you are prepared to finance a hobby you are passionate about.

Do You Have What It Takes?

To be successful as a business manager, you need industry knowledge, management skills, and determination. If you lack the knowledge and skills to start your own venture from scratch, you may consider buying a franchise—as long as you have the right personality. (See "Franchising.")

The business manager must satisfy the demands of the front office (where a smile is important) and the back office (where details are important). Do what you do best and make others responsible for the rest.

The best manager is passionate about the product and totally committed to the business. Several of the people interviewed for this book are determined to be the best in their field. (See "Profiles Of Successful Businesspeople.")

Capital

Cash Management Is Key

The majority of businesses fail due to a lack of cash, as a result of either under-trading or over-trading. The business manager must always keep control of the cash. In Thailand, many foreign-owned SMEs cannot borrow money from local banks. Make sure you start your business with adequate funding.

Minimize your capital requirement by asking for cash in advance for your services and by taking advantage of free credit whenever possible. Occasionally it is beneficial for a business to offer credit terms when the profit margin is high enough to absorb the bad debts.

Business Capitalization

Your business must be sufficiently capitalised to finance its operations and settle all liabilities. The capitalization must also comply with the law which requires a minimum registered share capital of two million baht per foreign employee.

The minimum business capitalization is identifiable by preparing a monthly cash flow forecast until after the business breaks even. Your accountant or consultant can advise you on this matter.

Always be conservative in your planning. Think of all possible costs and add a margin for contingencies. Establish your maximum investment in the business and don't spend over this limit. Plan an exit strategy in case the business fails.

When you transfer money from overseas to your Thai company bank account, ask the originating bank to identify the transaction in the name of your limited company. After the transfer, ask the receiving bank for the foreign exchange document—so you can repatriate these funds without withholding tax later.

Bank Finance

Thai banks lend money to Thai businesspeople and limited companies with an established trading record (supported by audited financial statements) and adequate security (usually equipment, land, or property). Most businesses established by foreigners in Thailand are financed by their own savings.

Some foreigners overcome the lack of local finance by borrowing from banks in their home country. If you own property outside of Thailand, some financial consultants can enable you to release equity from the investment.

Legal Structure

The choice of legal structure is critically important, but the laws governing these options are subject to change. The three main options available to foreigners are:

- Registering the business in a Thai person's name
- Forming a Thai limited company
- Establishing a partnership

There are other legal structures which fall outside the scope of this book; they include representative offices and branch offices. Neither of these is appropriate for most foreigners in Thailand. Representative offices are not allowed to sell products or services.

Registering The Business In A Thai Person's Name

Registration of a business in a Thai person's name is simply a process of your trustee completing a business registration form at the Ministry of Commerce. Other than the business licensing (which depends on the nature of your business), administration and taxation is usually minimal. However, your investment is only as secure as your relationship with the trustee.

The majority of the smaller foreign-owned bars and restaurants in Thailand are structured in this way. Many of these high-risk businesses change ownership regularly. Do not risk money in this way if you cannot afford to lose it.

Forming A Thai Limited Company

The process of forming a Thai limited company is covered in "What You Need To Know Before You Start." This option is the most complicated, but it can limit your investment risk considerably.

Establishing A Partnership

A partnership is a business entity in which two or more parties unite for a common purpose, sharing profits and liabilities according to their agreement. Partnerships may be ordinary partnerships or limited partnerships. In either case, foreign partners (together) cannot own a majority in the entity.

Ordinary Partnerships

In ordinary partnerships, each partner has joint and unlimited liability for all the partnership's debts. Therefore, the choice of honest and reliable partners is important. The partnership agreement should be registered with the Ministry of Commerce.

Limited Partnerships

Limited partnerships, which must be registered, offer some protection to the partners. Partners may limit their liability, but at least one partner must have unlimited liability for the partnership's debts.

Thai Partner (Or Representative)

Every legal business in Thailand needs a Thai partner or representative to interact on behalf of the business with Thai officials and Thai employees. The only possible exception would be foreigners who have lived in Thailand for over twenty years, who both speak and behave like Thai people.

Your Thai partner will liaise with Thai government officers, Thai customers, Thai employees, and Thai suppliers. Many of Thailand's social customs are so subtle they are easily misunderstood or overlooked by foreigners.

Finding the right Thai partner may be the most critical step in establishing a business in Thailand. Communication is vital to bridging the gap between cultures. The Thai partner must command respect from other Thais, have polished 'people skills,' be honest and reliable, and be committed to you and your business.

The personal qualities of your Thai partner are much more important than academic qualifications, experience, or management skills, all of which can be more easily acquired or learned. Don't forget that your partner also needs to advise you on matters of Thai culture and customs, while at the same time you may have to impart your own business knowledge in a way that does not appear condescending. Your Thai partner needs to understand the benefits of conveying both bad news and good. Thais often avoid passing on bad news—even to their managers—because they fear an angry response or blame.

There is a dual pricing system in Thailand, though the disparity between what Westerners might be asked to pay for some goods and services (compared to locals) is not as wide as in neighbouring countries. Often Thai businesspeople might lower prices for foreigners who can negotiate in Thai. Your trusted Thai representative will ultimately save you time, money, and possible embarrassment.

Premises

If your business depends upon passing trade, you need premises in a good location. For more information on this, see "Looking For Suitable Premises" in "What You Need To Know Before You Start." If you provide a specialist service (such as IT consulting), you do not need a prime business location.

Establish a budget for remodelling your premises to suit you and your customers. Refurbishment and interior decoration can be completed inexpensively in Thailand. Customers usually avoid businesses which look neglected.

Serviced Office

Consider a serviced office for a short-term rental at start-up. The main advantage of taking a serviced office is the minimal investment in fixtures, fittings, and equipment. Business tenants share office facilities, alleviating the need to employ a receptionist and other support staff. This instant business address enables quicker start-up and easy relocation.

Virtual Office

If your customers are not based locally and your service is mobile, you may consider a virtual office. Invest in a professional website and attractive name-cards, and meet your customers at appropriate hotels, restaurants, or coffee shops. Don't pay rent when it's unnecessary.

Virtual offices suit freelance website designers, Internet traders, property developers, graphic designers, editors, computer programmers, and other professionals who do not need a 'bricks-and-mortar' office.
An increasing number of such professionals work from home and save on the cost of renting an office. They meet clients in suitable cafés, hotels, or restaurants. The keys to their business are their personal associates and contacts, mobile phone, computer notebook, website, e-mail and business card.

Whether you have a real office or a virtual office, all business entities in Thailand must register their address with the Ministry of Commerce.

Employees

Most of the successful foreign businesspeople interviewed for this book believe their employees are their most important business assets.

Most experienced managers have had past success recruiting graduates with good character and personality straight from university. Employees with previous work experience often find the process of re-training very awkward. Senior professional employees may be too inflexible to fit into a different corporate culture. And be wary of employing people from privileged families—unless they bring you business—otherwise you may lose control.

Hiring Thai workers is much easier than firing them. Many businesses develop a family atmosphere among the staff, so any conflict usually affects office morale. In many businesses, inadequate employees survive through the support of their more competent colleagues. Minimum severance payments are listed in the Appendices.

Managers who recruit effectively do not need to fire employees. Most employers make the mistake of not checking references or the suitability of the applicant for the position. Just because salaries are low in Thailand, there is no excuse for lax recruitment procedures.

For case studies about recruitment in Thailand, read the profiles on Anthony McDonald (IT consulting) and Toby Allen (luxury spa services) in "Profiles Of Successful Businesspeople."

Product Concept

Your business is an expression of who you are. Successful businesspeople tend to work hard and play hard. They are able to work harder than most because they are passionate about what they do.

If the first rule is 'Do what you enjoy,' perhaps the second is 'Find a way of standing out from your competitors by adding value to what is already available.' Be clear about your unique selling points (USPs); these are the reasons customers will pass your competitors to find you.

Your product concept must be flexible enough to integrate into Thai culture and comply with the country's laws. Be careful not to offend Thai sensibilities.

In Chiang Mai there are too many bars serving a relatively small customer base. Many of these businesses change owners regularly, bringing business to the local brokers. Two successful bars in Chiang Mai—owned by Bob Tilley and Ron Holley—are based on unique concepts; both businesses are described in "Profiles Of Successful Businesspeople."

Summary

The following list is a summary of key differences, both good and bad, between doing business in Western countries and Thailand. These differences are diminishing over time. Obvious variations, including the lower cost of living in Thailand and the language barrier, are taken for granted:

- Low taxes and fewer regulations enable foreigners to start a business in Thailand relatively easily.

- The prevalence of 'pirate' copying in Thailand. Copyright law does exist in Thailand, though it is not routinely or effectively enforced.

- Business referral fees (or commissions for introducing business) are common practice in Thailand. Many successful foreign-owned businesses in Thailand take advantage of this additional source of income.

- In Thailand it is essential to appear calm and relaxed at all times. The advantage is that your mistakes will be tolerated

- Thai people are exceptionally responsive to positive appearance, tidiness, politeness, and warm behaviour.

- Foreigners starting a business in Thailand have limited access to credit and business finance. A lot of business in Thailand is transacted on a cash basis.

- In Thailand, relationships with customers and employees are often considered as important as profit.

- A trustworthy Thai partner or representative is essential.

- Jealousy is often an issue in Thailand, thus many successful businesspeople choose to maintain a low profile.

- In Thailand there is a large supply of skilled, English-speaking graduates.

Chapter 4
Pre Start-up: Decisions, Decisions

Start-Up: Buy Or Franchise?

If you want to establish a business in Thailand, there are three main options:

- Starting up from scratch
- Buying an existing business
- Buying a franchise

Starting Up From Scratch

This option is usually the riskiest, but it allows the most potential for independence, reward, and personal gratification. The risk can be limited by thorough research, planning, and support by suitable local partners, associates, and employees.

Foreigners who succeed in start-ups are usually knowledgeable and experienced in their chosen field of business. They are aware of their strengths and weaknesses, and they find others to take responsibility for their areas of weakness. They are also resourceful and committed to the success of their business.

One of the benefits of doing business in Thailand is that Thais are likely to be helpful and friendly. Many will offer assistance without the expectation of a monetary reward. So you have no excuse for not carrying out thorough research on your new venture with the help of the welcoming Thai people.

Before starting up a new business you should be familiar with Thai culture and customs, at least on a basic level, and have a local support network. It may take a few months to find a suitable Thai partner and premises. After these fundamentals are in place, and you have a realistic business plan, maybe you are ready to proceed. For more background information on starting up a new business, see "Profiles Of Successful Businesspeople."

Buying An Existing Business

An existing business is usually purchased as a turnkey operation (or going concern). Ideally the buyer will be able to make a living from the date of business transfer. Working capital (or current assets, such as inventory) is usually included in the sale price.

Choose a business that generates sufficient profit to support your desired lifestyle. Whether you buy a business via a broker or direct from the owner, you are responsible for validating the seller's representations, including the financial information.

Whenever possible, obtain an independent, impartial professional evaluation of the business.

Buying A Franchise

A big advantage of buying a franchise is the immediate access to an established, reputable brand, which could otherwise take years to develop. Franchises for 7-Eleven convenience stores are very successful in Thailand because these outlets are consistently well stocked, competitively priced, and efficiently managed. An extensive franchise network also allows for economies of scale (enhanced buying power, enabling quantity discounts) and greater synergy due to inter-branch referral systems.

Although franchising is relatively new to Thailand, this method of business expansion has grown rapidly over the last ten years. Franchise law in Thailand is currently being drafted by the Department of Business Development (at the Ministry of Commerce). The main trade association representing franchisors in Thailand is the Franchise and Thai SMEs Business Association (www.thailandfranchising.com).

Franchising suits team players who feel comfortable following others' established procedures. Franchisees do not need relevant industry knowledge; in fact, franchisors prefer franchisees without direct relevant experience. The pre-requisites for success as a franchisee are adequate capital, ability to follow established systems, and a long-term commitment to the business.

Although franchisees are more likely to be successful in their business than independent entrepreneurs, they usually need more capital investment. After the initial franchise license fee has been paid, there are ongoing royalty fees to be paid periodically to the franchisor.

For more information about franchising, please refer to the "Franchising" section.

Using Business Brokers

Business Brokers

Brokers (or agents) are intermediaries acting on behalf of the business owner (or seller). The broker has a duty of care to the business seller. The seller agrees to pay the broker a commission on completion of transfer of the business.

Business brokers specialize in the sale of trading entities or "going concerns." Businesses listed by brokers usually employ staff and contain fixed assets (including furniture and equipment) and inventory. Typical listings include small- to medium-sized guesthouses, Internet cafés, bars, restaurants, hotels, resorts, and factories.

Prospective buyers are free to register with as many brokers as they please.

Business Listings

Sales turnover of most listings offered by business brokers is under ten million baht per annum. These listings tend to be priced in the range of 300,000 to ten million baht.

Brokers usually offer no guarantee of the quality of any business listed for sale. The business may be fundamentally flawed, and it is the buyer's responsibility to identify the problems. Don't expect the broker to spend extra time doing your research—thus jeopardising his fee.

Business Brokers' Fees

The transfer of business ownership is much more complicated than the transfer of property. Businesses usually involve landlords, employees, fixed assets and inventory, customers, accounts, and financial statements. Business transfer also requires confidentially.

Business brokers charge higher fees than real-estate agents because of the additional work involved. Typically, business brokers charge between seven percent and twelve percent of purchase price, compared to five percent charged by realtors in Thailand. Independent Thai real-estate brokers usually charge only three percent, without VAT.

Although the business seller may contract with the broker to pay the above fees, the buyer ultimately foots this bill. The businesses listed by brokers rarely include genuine bargains. The broker has an incentive to sell for the highest price possible.

Where To Find The Bargains

Real bargains are found by chance, usually by word of mouth. Typically in such cases, a foreign business owner leaves the country quickly due to personal circumstances. Thus, bargains do exist, but don't wait for one to fall into your hands or life may pass you by. Instead do your due diligence and find the best deal for your investment budget. Consider also that some firms of brokers purchase the best bargains for themselves.

Brokering Is Unregulated

In Thailand, business- and property-brokering is unregulated, so anyone is permitted to offer these services. Quality is, therefore, extremely variable. Contact specialist business brokers instead of companies that sell businesses as a sideline. I personally know of a rather interesting handicraft shop that also sells tea, cakes, and real estate.

Checking The Details

It is the buyer's responsibility to check all information provided by the business owner and their broker. Usually, brokers just pass on information provided by the seller to the buyer without checking it. The broker has a responsibility to question the seller's representations only when, in their professional opinion, those representations do not appear to be correct.

Brokers may assume their client is truthful unless their knowledge and experience leads them to another conclusion. **The broker is negligent if he or she knowingly passes on false information to the prospective buyer.**

In-House Legal Services

Most business brokers provide an in-house legal service to assist with the drafting of leases or the processing of work permits and licenses. Some brokers rent serviced or virtual offices.

The downside of using your broker's lawyer would be apparent if your broker negligently sold a business to you or if the lawyer writes your contract to the advantage of the seller. Who would the lawyer support: his employer or one of many customers?

Buyers are best advised to employ a neutral (or impartial) lawyer, so there is no conflict of interests.

Preparation

If you want the best possible service from your business broker, act like a serious buyer. Turn up to the appointment on time and look like you mean business. Have answers to the following questions ready:

- What is your budget (or how much are you willing to spend)?
- How much cash do you have available to spend now?

- What businesses are you interested in?
- Where do you want to base your business?

The budget you give the broker should be a proportion (say 75 percent) of your total investment (which is readily available in cash). Keep to your budget. Allow for all possible additional costs of set-up including pre-paid rent, security deposits, legal fees, remodelling costs, and replacement of equipment.

Some professional brokers screen the buyer to establish whether or not the buyer has funding in place to meet the investment budget. This practice is designed to eliminate 'tire kickers'—dreamers or those just wanting a free tour of the local businesses for sale. Don't forget that land and property can take years to sell, in case you have no liquid funds available.

It is recommended that you review the broker's business listings via their website *before* your initial meeting. Note the references of the businesses you are most interested in. This will enable you and the broker to save time.

The broker will probably ask you to sign a non-disclosure agreement (NDA). Sometimes these documents are referred to as 'confidentiality agreements.'

Confidentiality

If the seller's employees discover that their employer is about to sell the business, they may lose interest and leave the company. If customers find out that their supplier is for sale, they may switch to a new supplier. Both possibilities can lead to diminishing profits, so confidentiality is critically important in business brokerage.

The NDA is your agreement to keep the seller's information confidential. For example, you may be given access to private financial information. By signing this document you agree not to tell anyone about the sale of the broker's listings without the seller's permission.

The NDA will probably contain a clause stating that all negotiations between the buyer and seller must be mediated by the broker. If the buyer colludes with the seller to avoid payment of the broker's fees, the buyer may also be liable to pay the fees. Sadly this clause does not prevent this happening.

If you refuse to sign this agreement, your broker will probably not show you any businesses for sale. Usually there is nothing onerous to the buyer in this agreement.

Business Viewings

It can be advantageous to view the businesses with a Thai colleague. If the broker is a foreigner, he will probably be occupied in conversation with the potential foreign buyer. If the seller is Thai—or has a Thai spouse—there may be an opportunity for your Thai friend to glean much information from them. The key question is: Why is the business for sale?

As you review the business, make a mental note of every possible opportunity for developing it. Perhaps you know of appropriate additional product lines, ways of improving the layout or organization, or new systems to install. If you want your broker to show you more businesses, demonstrate clearly why the businesses you have already viewed are unsuitable. Legitimate reasons include poor location, inadequate budget, high rent, or even a distrust of the seller. Put the onus on the broker to show you *suitable* businesses.

Questions For Your Broker

- What is the period of the lease?
  Your lawyer may be able to negotiate a favourable new lease with the landlord. However, the seller will probably know the landlord's parameters.

- Why is the owner selling?
  Is the business failing, or is there a legitimate reason for the sale (such as personal or partnership problems)?

- How long has the business been on the broker's books?

- Is the agency 'sole and exclusive' or a 'multiple' agency?
  The better business listings tend to be exclusive.

Advantages Of Using A Broker

- The service is free to buyers, with no obligation to buy.
- The broker and lawyer may assist with your research.
- The broker's in-house lawyer may answer your legal questions without charge.
- The broker should save you time by obtaining information from the seller on your behalf.
- You may view many businesses for sale in a short period of time.
- A reputable broker will return your deposit if your offer is rejected or your conditions of offer are not fulfilled.

Disadvantages Of Using A Broker

- The businesses listed are usually optimally priced.
- The broker's fee is factored into the selling price.
- The broker's duty of care is to the seller, so the buyer is responsible for validating the seller's financial statements and representations.
- The businesses come without any guarantee of quality.
- You may hear about the listed business from other sources *after* you sign the NDA with the broker.
- The broker may lock you into using his in-house lawyer (who will probably ask you to sign disclaimers protecting the broker from any liability).

Premises: Rent Or Buy?

If you are a freelance professional and your customers are limited to a certain location, you may consider renting a virtual office rather than paying for a full office set-up.

Property investment is a specialist business that takes up a lot of time and effort. Therefore, most start-up businesspeople are best advised to rent premises initially.

Advantages Of Renting Premises

- In Thailand, rents are low relative to property values.
- Renting frees more available cash for business assets, including inventory and equipment, so you minimise your investment.
- Property in Asia can take a long time to liquidate, sometimes several years.
- The landlord is normally responsible for the building, maintenance, and repairs.
- Foreigners are not allowed to own property in Thailand (other than condominiums), though long-term lease possession—renewable, at the discretion of the Thai owner, every thirty years—is possible.
- Prime land in Thailand is relatively expensive

Registration Of Long-Term Leases

Foreigners are allowed to lease land for up to thirty years. The lease agreement should be registered with the local office of the Department of Land (www.dol.go.th). The government fee (including stamp duty) for land registration is 1.1 percent of the rent payable over the entire lease term. The registration fee for a thirty-year lease at rent of 10,000 baht per month would be 39,600 baht. There is no legal requirement to register your lease, but doing so protects the lessee.

The documents required by the Department of Land for registration of land are:

- Passport or ID card with its signed copy
- Residence certificate (from Immigration or your embassy/consulate)
- Property documents (*chanote*)

The government officer will complete the (*Tor Dor* 1) form on the computer and ask you to sign the printed form. (See "Appendices" for a copy of this.)

Business Location

The location of any retail business is critically important. If your business depends upon passing trade, do not compromise on location. There is intense competition for the most favourable trading locations, so you should allow at least six months to find suitable premises.

If your business does not rely upon passing trade, spare the expense of a prime business location.

For information about finding suitable business premises, refer to "Looking For Suitable Premises" in "What You Need To Know Before You Start."

Business Development

Do you want to develop an existing business that needs improvement? Or would you prefer to pay a higher price for a fully optimised business with minimal scope for improvement? Development demands creativity backed by management ability and application. Do you really have the resourcefulness to transform a fledgling business?

Let's consider three levels of business development: the undeveloped business, the semi-developed business, and the fully optimised business.

The Undeveloped Business

The undeveloped business often has immense potential for improvement. Maybe the owner-manager has neglected the business. Perhaps there is a need for refurbishment and new furniture and equipment. The capital injection will increase profits and boost the value of the going concern. Make a budget for all development costs, and introduce management controls to improve efficiency.

For every additional baht increase in annual profit, you increase the business value by over two baht. A business can be remodelled and turned around within weeks. Later, if you sell the business, you will enjoy a large capital gain on the sale of your enterprise.

The Semi-Developed Business

The semi-developed business provides fewer opportunities for improvement than the undeveloped business. However, you should be mindful of ways to improve business performance. The layout of the premises could be enhanced; old furniture could be replaced. Get the lighting right because it draws attention and interest. Maybe the employees need training to improve the quality of customer service.

The Fully-Optimised Business

This type of business is well oiled and running like clockwork. The current owner-manager has worked hard to perfect efficiency. It is the ultimate turnkey business and you may struggle to maintain its level of performance. Usually these businesses sell for the highest multiple of earnings (three to five times).

Type Of Business

Your optimal choice of business depends upon your knowledge and experience and the resources you can offer (including funds, assets, technology, and contacts).

Most businesses require a cheerful, customer-services-oriented person to develop relationships with clients at the front end of the business, and a more logical-minded person in the back office to take care of the details. You also need a good personnel manager—preferably Thai—to manage your staff.

Many successful businesspeople advise engaging in business activities you enjoy; ideally an extension of your hobby or interest. Most businesses demand a full-time commitment by the manager, particularly in the entertainment industry. Create your business to suit your personality.

Your choice of business is less important if you buy a franchise.

Legal Ownership

You must register your business. Most foreign-owned businesses are registered in a Thai person's name or as a Thai limited company. The decision depends on your relationship with your Thai partner. Consider which type of legal structure is appropriate for your circumstances.

Do You Need A Work Permit?

If you want to work in your business you must obtain a work permit. Your decision on whether you work will be influenced by the following factors:

- Your knowledge and skills
- The market value of your skills in Thailand; unless your skills are highly specialised, you should consider delegating work to local people.
- Business profitability
- The value you attach to quality time

Don't forget that the cost of a work permit (together with tax and administration) will work out at about 5,000 baht per month in addition to the set-up costs. Therefore consider carefully whether you really need a work permit. If you have a competent Thai manager or partner, maybe you only need to provide 'non-executive' guidance (in which case you may not require a work permit).

For information about applying for a work permit, refer to "What You Need To Know Before You Start." The application forms are in "Appendices."

Establishing An Investment Budget

Establish a budget for the 'total investment' of your business. The total investment includes the following costs:

- Legal fees relating to business transfer
- Remodelling the premises
- Rent payable in advance and security deposit
- Replacement of fixtures, fittings, and equipment
- Recruitment
- Visas and work permits
- Additional working capital
- Company incorporation costs

- Marketing
- Business licenses

Usually rent is payable monthly in advance. In addition, the landlord will demand a security deposit of two or three months' rent (to cover possible damage to the property). Lessees usually claim this deposit from the next owner, but sometimes the landlord returns this money to the tenant when the lease is assigned.

Timing: The Best Time To Start

Probably the wisest advice—often repeated by successful businesspeople in Thailand—is not to rush into any business venture without sufficient research and professional advice. One extremely successful businessman from New Zealand said he did not do any business for his first three years in Thailand, but this is an extreme case. Learning the Thai language, culture, and etiquette can take time—but time spent developing good relationships with Thai people builds solid foundations for your business prospects.

You may be ready to start your business when you have the following in place:

- A working knowledge of the Thai language
- A good understanding of Thai culture, customs, and etiquette
- Some Thai friends you really trust and respect
- Knowledge of the legal system in Thailand, and how it affects foreigners doing business
- An understanding of the business market you want to target
- A researched business plan
- Sufficient liquid funds available to turn your plan into reality

The best time for many start-ups in tourism-related businesses is during the low season (between May and October). It's best to be prepared to take full advantage of potential business available during the peak tourist season. If you are planning any property development, consider the impact of the rainy season between May and October.

You cannot plan the timing of opportunities, but you may be able to negotiate a future date of business transfer. Some owners want to sell after the close of the peak season, which is advantageous for them.

Finally, your timing for start-up may be influenced by your personal cash flow situation.

Guidelines

Do not pay money for a business until you have secured a reasonable lease with the landlord. **Register the business when you start trading.** Do not make the common mistake of forming a company while looking for a business to buy. Many foreigners have dormant companies because they formed limited companies and decided later not to buy a business.

Chapter 5
How To Evaluate Businesses

The Key Determinants Of Business Valuation

Definitions

'Business valuation' concerns the process of calculating the value of a business. 'Business evaluation' is a more extensive process and includes an assessment of employees, the seller (and his reason for selling), business control systems, market trends, and non-financial (or qualitative) aspects of the business.

There are numerous factors influencing the business evaluation process. Examples are location, presentation, profitability, lease terms, personality of the owner, and finance terms of sale. We all have different priorities and there is much more to business evaluation than just financial review.

The main factors determining the value of a business are 'total investment,' net profit (after depreciation and taxes), lease terms, and an estimated value of the assets included in the sale.

Total investment is the price paid for a business plus the additional investment necessary to achieve target performance. Total investment includes remodelling costs, legal fees, payments to the landlord, and replacement of assets.

> Total Investment = Price Paid For The Business
> + Remodelling Costs
> + Legal Fees
> + Replacement Of Assets
> + Rent Payable In Advance
> + Security Deposit (if not included in the sale)

Before evaluating any businesses, determine your total investment budget. In Thailand most businesses are transferred upon payment in cash. Occasionally sellers are willing to negotiate credit terms of sale, typically with fifty percent to 75 percent down-payment.

'Net profit' represents the real business earnings. The earnings include any withdrawals or deductions ('drawings' in US terminology) by the owner in the form of salary or personal (non-business) expenses. A good owner-manager will increase the net profits of the business, increasing both earnings and the value of the business simultaneously.

The earnings of the business determine the payback period of the investment. The payback period (in years) is the estimated time required to recover the investment by the business owner.

Payback Period = Total Investment / Net Annual Earnings

Buyers usually demand a payback period of between one and three years; sellers usually want to sell their going concern at an equivalent payback period of between two and four years. After negotiation, the buyer and seller usually settle on a net earnings multiple of between 2.0 and 3.0. The payback period is higher for businesses that are fully developed.

The value of the assets included in the sale is most significant when the business is not trading. Failed businesses are usually sold for the value of the business assets only (without any premium for goodwill). The assets would be valued at the higher of net book value (i.e. after depreciation, as stated in the fixed asset register) and the market value of the equivalent second-hand assets.

The most common determinants considered by business buyers are:

- Lease terms offered by the landlord.
- Relationship—and level of trust and rapport—between buyer and seller.
- Location of the business. (Is the area improving or degenerating?)
- Offer price.
- Business earnings. (How long will it take to recover your investment?)
- Presentation of the business. (Does the business require modest or extensive development?)
- The value, age, and state of repair of all assets included in the sale.
- Atmosphere of the business and morale of the owner, customers, suppliers, and employees.
- Opportunities for developing the business (or is it fully optimised?)

- Extent of training and support package offered by the seller.
- The reputation of the business (ask the local businesspeople).
- Business trends. (Is sales turnover increasing or decreasing? Try to understand the underlying reasons for the trends.)
- Consider also whether the business can be easily copied or relocated.

Total Investment

To reiterate this vital point, total investment is the total amount of money put into the business. The amount you invest should be below your total investment budget. Total investment is identifiable on a cash-flow statement as the maximum cash deficit.

The amount you paid to the business seller may represent say seventy percent of total investment. In addition to the purchase price, there are the following costs:

- Legal fees relating to the business transfer
- Remodelling costs of the business premises
- Business licensing costs
- The cost of obtaining visas and work permit
- Replacement cost of fixtures, fittings, and furniture
- Recruitment fees for the hiring of new staff
- Increase in working capital (including stocks and receivables)
- Any losses incurred after business transfer (if applicable)

Your Total Investment (TI) should include all expenditure necessary for the business to generate your target profits. The TI needs to be sufficient to fully upgrade and equip the business. Ideally, after spending the TI your business will be self-supporting.

Exercise self-discipline with regard to your budgeted total investment. **Decide on your maximum business investment (or TI) before you start spending money**. If the business is not self-supporting after investing your TI, the business has failed or is not working out to plan. Next, consider how to minimise your losses. Avoid throwing more and more money into a bottomless investment.

If your business is successful, you will recover your total investment (with a good return) during the term of your lease. If you sell the business later, you will make a capital gain by selling above the original TI.

Business Valuation Methods

In Thailand most foreign buyers spend between 500,000 baht and five million baht for small businesses such as guesthouses, restaurants, cafés, and bars. Business profitability can change dramatically, either way, after the business transfer.

A resourceful buyer can turn a loss-making business into a profitable concern within weeks. For this reason, valuation methods for small businesses are not sophisticated. The value of a small business is primarily determined by estimating annual profits and the value of the business assets.

A business is only worth what people pay for it. Let the buyers (who vote with their wallets) be the judges. If there are many similar businesses for sale in the same area, market prices fall. A unique business that is difficult to copy will command a higher price.

US industry surveys show that, on average, businesses sell for eighty percent of the seller's asking price. The same is true of Thailand. Many sellers list businesses with brokers at vastly inflated prices. The seller wants the broker to earn his fee by getting higher net proceeds than would otherwise be possible. Also some 'sellers' are not really serious about selling (unless a buyer offers their fantasy price).

If you like a particular business, work out what it's worth to you, and make an appropriate offer. Your broker has a professional duty to pass on all offers supported by a deposit, even if they are relatively low. You have nothing to lose as long as you **protect yourself with appropriate conditions to the offer**.

Some local sellers have extremely creative valuation methods. One businessman included a personal loan from his sister in his calculation of the selling price. The loan had no relevance to the business. Personal financial arrangements fall outside the scope of business valuation. However, if a seller is willing to offer 'buyer finance,' allowing payment by instalments, this can increase the selling price in Thailand.

Tom West's *Complete Guide To Business Brokerage* lists the following ten key factors to consider when valuing a business:

1– Number of years the business has been in existence.

2– Number of years the seller has owned the business.

3– Terms offered by the seller.

4– Competition. (How much is there in the local market?)

5– Risk. (Is the business inherently risky?)

6– Growth or trend of sales and profits.

7– Location and facilities.

8– Desirability. (How popular is the business in the current location?)

9– Industry. (Is the industry growing or declining?)

10– Type of business. (Is it easily duplicated? In Thailand, profitable businesses are copied in no time.)

Other factors to consider are:

- Sensitivity of the business to external factors such as the tourist high and low seasons.
- Is the rent below or above the market rate? A lease offering rent below the market value increases the business value.
- The length of the lease. A longer lease usually adds value to the business.
- The skills and quality of the employees. If there is an employee you do not want, make sure the seller terminates their employment contract (and settles the severance pay) *before* the business transfer.
- Orders received in advance increase the value of the business (goodwill).
- How accurately can you predict future revenues and expenses? If income and expenses are stable and predictable, the lower risk increases business value.
- Does the seller's personality influence the success of the business? Do customers come to the business to see the seller or because they like the product itself? Will you retain the existing customer base?
- How old is the equipment, and when will it need replacing?
- Is the seller willing to offer sufficient training and support during the initial period after the business transfer?

Multiple Of Adjusted Net Profits

Many brokers value businesses using a multiple of three times the adjusted annual net profits. Most businesses actually sell for about two times the seller's adjusted net profits. This means that the business should pay for itself within two years.

'Adjusted net profits' is the earnings, after paying all operational overheads, including depreciation of fixed assets. Any non-business costs must be added back to the seller's profit. For example, if the owner's spouse was paid a monthly salary without actually working for the business, this item should be added back to the net profit figure.

'Depreciation' is a method of accounting for the cost of wear and tear of the fixed assets (such as machinery, vehicles, equipment, computers, fixtures, and fittings). This allowance for wear and tear of fixed assets is usually applied on a 'straight line' basis over the estimated life of the assets.

If a computer is purchased for 30,000 baht and has an estimated product life of three years, the annual depreciation would be 10,000 baht. Deduct 10,000 baht from the seller's net profit to allow for replacement of the asset.

Any drawings from the business—or salary paid to the owner who is not working for the business—should be added back to the net profits. Only legitimate business expenses should be deducted from earnings to arrive at adjusted net profits.

Mini-Marts

Mini-marts are sometimes valued at a multiple of between 1.0 and 1.25 times adjusted net profits *plus* the stock at valuation (SAV) on the date of business transfer. SAV is always the actual amount paid for the stock, though sometimes it is marked down from the selling price by applying the gross profit margin. If you purchase a mini-mart, supervise the inventory count immediately before completion of business transfer.

Multiples Of Gross Sales

Some business brokers use a specific multiple of gross sales to value each type of business. Examples follow:

Travel Agencies:	0.05 to 0.1 x Annual Gross Sales
Advertising Agencies:	0.75 x Annual Gross Sales
Retail Businesses:	0.75 to 1.5 x Annual Net Profit
	+ Inventory
	+ Equipment

Make an estimate of the net book value of the tangible business assets included in the sale. Write off the value of any old assets which need replacing. The assets may include air conditioners (worth 20,000 baht + each) and the security deposit held with the landlord (if the seller has agreed to include this in the sale price).

Adjustment To Net Annual Profits

The following example demonstrates how the net annual profits figure is adjusted to calculate the real earnings of the business:

Income	Baht
Sales	2,500,678
Other Income	567
TOTAL INCOME	2,501,245
COST OF GOODS SOLD	1,408,449
GROSS PROFIT	1,092,796
	(43.7 percent)

Expenses	
Rent	108,000
Salaries	850,000
Outside labour	56,000
Social Insurance	7,500
Electricity	4,507
Water	3,000
Telephone	42,076
Travel	67,642
Legal fees	5,674
Accounting fees	34,000
Interest	356
Bad debts	2,674
Miscellaneous	24,067
TOTAL EXPENSES	1,205,496
NET PROFIT BEFORE TAX	112,700

Adjustments To Profits	
Add Back: Owner's Salary	720,000
Add Back: Legal Fees Relating To Owner's Personal Issues	5,674
Add Back: Interest Received	567
Subtract: Depreciation Of Fixed Assets	-117,095
ADJUSTED NET PROFITS	721,846

Business Valuation

1. Multiple of 2.0 (Recover investment in two years)	1,443,692
2. Multiple of 3.0 (Recover investment in three years)	2,165,538

If you need to recover your investment over two years, you may pay as much as 1.4 million baht for the business. This price includes all the assets necessary to operate the business. So if the owner wants to exclude specific assets from the sale, you may deduct the cost of replacing them.

Discounted Cash Flow

'Discounted net present value' (NPV), or discounted cash flow, is a more sophisticated method of valuation suited to larger business organisations. The annual cash flows (both inflows and outflows) are discounted using the investor's discount factor or 'cost of money.' The discount factor is usually equal to the cost of borrowing (if applicable) or the return on investment required by the investor.

Example: a cash receipt of one million baht in one year's time would have an NPV of 909,090 baht if the business owner's cost of money is 10 percent. The NPV is the cash received divided by $(1 + X)$, where 'X' is the discount factor. However, this valuation method is usually inappropriate if the cash flows cannot be forecast with sufficient accuracy.

Return On Investment

Aim to get a good return on your investment and remunerate yourself for any time spent on your business. Aim to recover your total investment, together with a return (or profit), during the period of your lease. Although you may sell your business at a profit, it's prudent to recover your investment before you sell.

If you work for the business, give yourself a salary at the market rate and claim any business-related expenses. For financial purposes, treat yourself as separate from your business. This means that your investment in the business is like a personal loan to the business. Similarly, your salary from the business is comparable to remuneration from any third-party employer.

Your target return on investment depends upon the risk of your business. A low risk business, like rental property, should return over ten percent per annum. A business with average risk, like a restaurant, may require a return of twenty to thirty percent per annum. A highly risky business may require a return of over 100 percent per annum. Don't forget you need a higher return than the percentage that your bank may offer you for investing your cash in a savings account.

Investment	Yield Range
Cash In Bank Current Account	0 percent
Cash In Bank Savings Account	1-5 percent
Property Investment	3-14 percent
Mutual Funds	8-20 percent
Business Valued At 3x Earnings	33 percent
Business With Two-Year Payback Period	50 percent
Business With Twelve-Month Payback Period	100 percent

Note that low-end condominiums tend to offer a much higher return on investment (ROI) than shophouses. For example, a condominium valued at 700,000 baht may rent for 8,000 baht per month, thereby yielding 13.7 percent. A shophouse valued at 3.2 million baht may rent for 12,000 baht per month, offering a ROI of only 4.5 percent. In this typical example, the low-end condo yields over three times the profit of the shophouse. Sometimes—for example, in a bank auction—it is possible to buy a number of condo units in the same building at a discounted price.

Case Study

Bill invests two million baht in a guesthouse business. He does not work for the guesthouse, so he does not claim a salary. He requires a return on investment of twenty percent over his three-year lease. This means that Bill needs to recover his capital at a rate of 666,667 baht per annum (two/three baht) plus an average return of 200,000 baht per annum (because the average capital outstanding over the term of the lease is one million baht). Bill needs total profits of 2.6 million baht over the three-year period, or 866,667 baht each year on average. Therefore, if the guesthouse generates less than 866,667 baht profit per year, Bill would reject the investment. Any proceeds from the subsequent sale of the guesthouse would increase the return on investment accordingly.

Payback Period

The 'payback period' is the time taken (in years) to recover your investment in the business out of net adjusted profits. A short payback period of between six months and 2.5 years attracts prospective buyers, whereas a longer payback period of over three years is more attractive to potential sellers. Therefore, buyers and sellers negotiate a price in between, usually with a payback period of between two and three years.

Payback Period (years) = Investment / Adjusted Net Annual Profits

The payback period is equal to the price actually paid for the business (after discount) divided by the adjusted net profits. The business broker and seller calculate the payback period using the price offered for the business; but the buyer's real payback period is increased by any additional costs of investment (such as interior decoration and replacement of furniture and equipment).

Case Study

Brett offers 1.5 million baht for a leased guesthouse. He would need to spend a further 400,000 baht on remodelling and replacing furniture. He wants to recover his investment within the three-year lease with a return of fifteen percent. The net annual profits are stated as 500,000 baht before charging depreciation but after the investors' drawings of one million baht. The assets, which cost 700,000 baht, have an average life of four years.

Total Investment = 1.5 million baht + 0.4 million baht
= 1.9 million baht

Total Return Required (over three years, assuming the capital is repaid on a proportional basis) = 1.9 x 0.15 x 3/2 = 427,500 baht

Total Investment Plus Required Return
= 1.9 million + 427,500
= 2,327,500 baht

Annual Depreciation = 700,000 baht/4 = 175,000 baht

Adjusted Net Annual Profits (ANP)
= 500,000 baht – 175,000 baht + 1 million baht
= 1.325 million baht

> Real Payback Period For Buyer
> = Total Investment + Required Return/ANP
> = 2,327,500 baht/1,325,000 = 1.76 years
>
> This real payback period of slightly over one year and nine months is favourable, so Brett would proceed with the purchase.

Lease Terms

Evaluating The Lease

The lease on your premises is one of the key foundations of the business. A good lease provides security of tenure for a reasonable period with inexpensive rent. Engage your Thai partner or lawyer in all negotiations with a Thai landlord.

Rent Level

Usually the landlord increases the rent whenever there is a change of lessee. You can make an offer for a business conditional on a maximum rent level. If the current owner leases the premises for 15,000 baht per month, you may make an offer subject to a maximum rent of 17,000 baht for the following three years, with a reasonable renewal option.

Research the market rents in the local area. Real-estate agents in the neighbourhood should provide the information you need. Don't forget that long leases with low rent potentially increase the value of the business (and vice versa).

Lease Term

Many landlords offer a three-year lease with an option for a further three years at a higher rent. Leases in prime locations are often one-year renewable contacts requiring payment of the year's rent in advance. You may be able to negotiate a commercial lease of nine years or more. Remember that a longer lease adds value to your business.

Under Thai law, leases over three years should be registered with the Land Department. Many business owners do not register their leases with the Land Department in order to avoid payment of government stamp duty.

Registering The Lease In The Name Of Your Company

It can be advantageous to contract with your landlord using a Thai limited company. It may be easier to transfer your business to a third party in the future by selling your company shares to the buyer. This way, the corporate lessee does not change. The buyer takes over the existing lease, so there should be no sudden hike in rent. Instruct your lawyer to check the lease for clauses relating to business transfer. The contract may require the landlord's approval of the new company director (and shareholders).

Security Deposit

The landlord usually requires a security deposit against damage to the property and its furniture and equipment. The deposit amount is usually between one and six months rent (typically two or three months). Many landlords are loath to return deposits, but don't mind them being used to pay the final period of rent. Often the seller includes the security deposit in the selling price of the business, so it is effectively transferred to the new tenant. This matter should be clarified when making an offer for the business.

Remodelling The Premises

If you intend to make any structural changes to the property, you must get the landlord's written permission beforehand. Try to obtain permission in the lease agreement. If the premises are to be developed, any changes are likely to benefit the landlord. The landlord must understand that you want to increase the value of the property.

Rent Review

In most cases the rent remains fixed for the first three years of the lease. The rent may increase by ten percent or more in the second term of three years. Your offer to purchase the business may be conditional upon the landlord not increasing the rent by more than a specified amount during a defined period.

Assignment Of The Lease

Check all clauses in the lease that may potentially prevent you from assigning the lease to a prospective buyer in the future. Landlords usually prepare new leases with higher rent when a business is transferred. This is a common cause of buyers withdrawing their offer to purchase a business. Do consider how you might assign your lease in the future, so you can sell the business for a reasonable price.

Transfer Fees (T Money)

A transfer fee—sometimes known as 'T money'—represents a one-off fee payable to the landlord for preparing a new lease. Sometimes there is no transfer fee to pay, but if there is, it is usually payable by the seller. It is helpful to know about this expense because it is ultimately passed on to the buyer, like a broker's commission. Also, you will have to pay this fee when you sell the business.

Details of the transfer fee may not be included in the lease agreement. If there is no mention of a transfer fee in the lease, check with the seller. There may be no transfer fee to be paid if the shares of a corporate tenant are transferred from seller to buyer. Check this matter with your lawyer.

Location

Most successful retailers *never* compromise on location. Choose a busy location favoured by your target customers.

There are many factors that influence whether clients visit a business; some depend upon location, others on design and layout; the rest is down to marketing and customer service. The main determinants are:

- Premises situated on the corner of road junctions are favourable because they benefit from additional side access.

- Shops that are open to the street (with less wall area) are more inviting to prospective customers.

- Lighter units are more attractive than poorly-lit shops, so optimise your window area and lighting.

- Attract the interest of your target customers by displaying **eye-catching, bold signage** outside your premises.

- Consider wide shop units because they offer additional access to passing trade.

- Optimise every square metre of space to generate maximum business; get redundant areas working for you. Ensure your lease allows you to make the necessary modifications to the premises

It is relatively easy to assess location; one method is to employ someone to count the potential customers passing your proposed location; and the number of customers visiting your nearest competitor. Note the type of customers frequenting the area and, if you are in a tourist related business, the proportion of foreign visitors, their age, and estimated disposable incomes. Some audacious potential buyers even ask the competition's manager to show them the sales book—and often they get what they want.

The Seller

It is important that you trust the seller. Establishing a good rapport with the seller is a great advantage because you will receive more support (or training) during the early stages of trading.

Some sellers misrepresent their financial accounts, overstating gross sales and understating business expenses. It is the buyer's responsibility to validate all representations made by the seller. Obtain written confirmation that the seller will assume his or her liabilities at the date of transfer. For example, the electricity bill for the business should be apportioned between buyer and seller.

If any of the seller's financial representations do not make sense, ask questions and find out why. Ask your business broker (if applicable). You may have legitimate grounds for negotiating a lower price, possibly subject to credit terms.

To help avoid the possibility of the business vendor setting up a similar business opposite your new business and poaching your employees and customers, ask him or her to sign a non-competition clause in the offer document. Sellers usually agree not to compete in a similar business within a two-kilometre radius of your business for at least two years.

Make sure you understand (and believe) the real reason for the sale before you buy the business. Get third-party confirmation and evidence to support the seller's story. You don't want to start your new business feeling you have been duped by the seller.

Morale

The morale in the business is important. This includes the mood of the owner, the customers, suppliers, and employees. Sometimes the owner has already given up on an exhausted business and the employees adopt the same negative attitude. Clearly there would be a lot of work to be done to turn such a business around.

If faced with this situation, try to discover the inherent problems. Are you able to correct the problem issues? Or is there a fundamental problem outside your control, like a troublesome landlord or severe competition taking away customers?

Asset Sale

Some businesses for sale have ceased trading. After the business closes down, the selling price is usually based on the value of the business assets transferable.

Consider the prospective project as a start-up situation. It may take over twelve months before the business breaks even. Sometimes businesspeople are willing to pay a large premium for an empty shop in a good location. Asset sales usually occur in poor locations rather than prime business spots.

Obtain a list of the business assets, including stock, and work out what they are worth to you. Items that need replacing are worth nothing. It is helpful to have the following information for fixed assets: description of asset, date of acquisition, purchase price, estimated life (in years), and the net book value of the asset (after accumulated depreciation).

Case Study

A bar that has recently closed down is available for sale. It is in a good tourist location and the rent is low. The premium for the lease is valued at 100,000 baht. Most of the furniture is dilapidated and will need replacing. The only items of value are three air conditioners that are two years old, and a music system. A buyer offers 50,000 baht—or half the current replacement cost—for the three air conditioners. The business seller agreed to keep the music system for himself. The buyer negotiated a total price of 180,000 baht to take over the lease (100,000 baht), the security deposit (30,000 baht) and the air conditioners (50,000 baht).

Sometimes sellers present their business as a going concern, even when they are not trading any longer. If trade seems slow or there is a generally quiet atmosphere, this should set off alarms in the buyer's mind. Check the business at different times of the day and week. Don't just visit the business at times specified by the seller; maybe the seller has arranged a party with his friends, or has put on a show of bogus customers, to coincide with your meeting.

Lease Premium

The lease premium represents a surcharge for goodwill associated with the location of the premises and the opportunity to access passing trade. If the monthly rent payable is below the market rate, the premium is higher.

Case Study

Nut wanted to sell her Internet café in Hua Hin. The business included ten computers plus fixtures and fittings valued at 300,000 baht. She put the café up for sale for 400,000 baht (including the assets) or 100,000 (without). She charged a premium of 100,000 baht for the transfer of the lease because the rent was below market value.

Note: you can often avoid paying any lease premium by contracting directly with the landlord.

The Reason For Sale

The most important question to ask the business seller is '**Why do you want to sell?**' Nothing else matters until you understand why the seller wants to part with the business. Ask the vital question after you have established a rapport with the seller.

There are five main reasons why a business owner wants out. They are:

- Burnout, health, partnership problems, or a desire for a change in lifestyle (common in the bar and restaurant trade).
- Retirement. But, if it's a good business, why is the seller not keeping it in the family?
- Poor business or problems with the landlord. Be careful here.
- The vendor is not really serious about selling, but will do so for a high price.
- The seller developed a start-up and wants to realize the capital gain, take a holiday, then start all over again. Be careful here not to lose your customers and employees.

Below are detailed responses to the crunch question: 'Why do you want to sell your business?' Some answers are absurd, but the usual replies are as follows:

Partnership Problems

Sometimes the joint investors disagree on key management issues. However, this usually happens when the business is underperforming. If the business is doing well, what is there to ague about?

Health Problems

Some sellers are forced to give up their business due to severe health problems. The shock of a heart attack may be the catalyst for a complete shift in lifestyle.

One man who ran a number of successful service businesses experienced a serious health problem that required surgery. Immediately he placed all of his companies on the market for sale. His businesses were genuinely profitable and the reason for sale was quite easy to validate. Many of the neighbouring businesspeople probably knew about the operation and some may have visited him in the hospital.

Not Enough Time

Two common answers are 'Not enough time' and 'Need to spend time on other businesses.' Both answers are unconvincing. If an owner is selling his business because of preoccupation with other commercial activity, maybe it's because the original business is an under-performing concern. If the seller does not have enough time, find out what he does allow time for. Usually these sellers have given up on the first business and have already started another one.

I Need More Quality Time

Some semi-retired people buy a business to occupy their time and alleviate boredom. They often discover, to their peril, that the business is much more demanding than they had expected. The business may have potential but they don't have the energy to exploit the opportunity. The seller's reason for sale could be genuine, but get confirmation.

Relocation

Many sellers say they want to relocate to another city, another country, or even another continent. A death in the family or severe sickness of a relative may provide a reason for rapid departure. If the reason given is genuine, they would probably want to sell quickly at a low price. Most sellers wanting out of the business *and* the location have some serious problems they may not be willing to discuss.

Due Diligence

Due diligence is the process of substantiating the seller's representations including the financial statements. Due diligence is the buyer's responsibility; business brokers do not have any responsibility to check the information they pass on from seller to buyer.

Many small businesses in Thailand do not keep any records or accounts. Thai businesspeople usually negotiate a tax settlement with a tax officer from the Revenue Department once a year; maybe every three years. Some businesses maintain two sets of accounting records: one set for the authorities, to minimise tax; and an actual record of the transactions for themselves.

One practical way of checking gross sales is to employ a person to count the number of customers visiting the business.

> Daily Sales = Number of Customers
> x Estimated Average Sales Value

Estimate the average gross sales value per customer transaction. The business seller may provide this information, but watch what the customers order and estimate the average transaction value.

Take into account the time of year. If the business is tourism-oriented, consider estimating annual gross sales in the following way:

Annual Sales = (4 x Monthly Sales [in low season])
+ (8 x Monthly Sales [in the high season])

Sales in the high season may be three times higher than in the low season. Estimate this multiple with the help of businesspeople in the neighbourhood. The seller may provide an accurate multiple.

Continue due diligence testing until you are reasonably sure of the actual business performance. However, if the business is underperforming and you intend to develop the business, future results may improve significantly.

In order to avoid any possible conflict of interests, do not use any advisors who are directly connected with your business broker or the seller. For larger businesses, hire an independent consultant, accountant, and lawyer to audit the financials.

Do not complete the business transfer until you have sufficient evidence to verify the seller's financial representations. If you have sufficient evidence that the seller has misrepresented the performance of the business, re-negotiate or withdraw your offer (and reclaim any deposit paid). After the business transfer, it would be very difficult to claim recourse; the seller may be sipping champagne in the jacuzzi by then.

Business Evaluation Checklist

Before you hand over your life savings to the seller, make sure you have evaluated the business thoroughly. Try this checklist:

- ❏ **Business Location:** Is the location suitable for your purposes? Don't forget that being only thirty metres away from a good location may be too far away without a sound marketing strategy.
- ❏ **The Landlord:** Are the lease terms reasonable? Is the remaining term of the lease long enough to recover your investment and make a reasonable return? Is there any evidence that the landlord will maintain the property according to the lease terms? Have you checked the rent level against the market rent for similar properties in the area?

- ❏ **The Seller:** Do you have a good rapport with, and trust, the seller? Why is the owner selling? Is the customer base loyal to the seller, the business, or the product?

- ❏ **Accounts:** Has your due diligence and research supported the seller's representations and financial statements? If there are no proper accounts available, have you prepared your own budgetary forecasts?

- ❏ **Legal Structure Of Acquisition:** Are you buying the assets of the business, or are you buying shares in the seller's company (which owns the business assets)? If you need a work permit there are advantages to taking over the seller's limited company. This avenue will save you government stamp duty, time, and lawyer's fees; also, because the lessee does not change, dealings with the landlord may be more straightforward. It may save you a rent increase and transfer fees, too.

- ❏ **Environment:** Do you like the environment of the business? If you will be working full-time, or even part-time, you must like being there.

Case Study (Asset Sale)

The following case study of a beauty salon is typical of the listings published on the Internet:

A partnership dispute forces the sale of this six-month-old Pattaya beauty salon. The business is offered for sale at asset value. The shop measures forty square metres and is in a shopping mall near the city centre. The partners spent 800,000 baht on fixed assets and 300,000 baht on inventory. The salon has been well promoted and has its own website. There is a growing loyal customer base. The estimated gross sales for the first year are 1.5 million baht. Monthly rent is 24,000 baht and monthly salaries total 24,000 baht for three full-time employees. There is ample parking space for customers. The salon offers a full range of beauty services including massage and reflexology. Asking price: one million baht.

Projected profits for the first twelve months (all figures in baht, unless otherwise stated):

Sales	1,500,000
Rent	288,000
Payroll	288,000

```
Depreciation . . . . . . . . . . . . . . . . . . 266,666
         (800,000 baht of assets over three years)
Cost of consumables . . . . . . . . . . . . 300,000
Services . . . . . . . . . . . . . . . . . . . . . . . 60,000
Accounts and legal. . . . . . . . . . . . . . . 50,000
Total Costs. . . . . . . . . . . . . . . . . . . 1,252,666

ESTIMATED NET PROFIT. . . . . . . . 247,334
```

The net profit is apportioned between two partners. Each partner is expecting to receive 123,667 baht each year, or 10,306 baht per month.

If the partners aim to recover their capital of 1,100,000 baht over a three-year period with a return of twenty percent, they need net profits of 476,667 baht each year (compared to 247,334 baht).

If the business only generates net annual profits of 247,334 baht, they need just under four and a half years to recover their investment without any return. Clearly the partners would have had fewer arguments if they had invested their money somewhere else.

Conclusion: the above business failed. The investors want to cut their losses and get out as quickly as possible. They are open to any offers.

If you or your spouse is knowledgeable of this trade, the location is good and the lease terms are reasonable, consider making a low offer for the business assets. Make a list of the assets you want, estimate their purchase prices, and offer a proportion of the total depending on the condition of the assets. The sellers may eventually give the assets away—or even pay someone to remove them.

Property Prices

If you want to buy land or buildings you must consider property values separate from the value of the business. If the buildings are old, and you need to demolish them, research the market value of the land *less* the cost of demolition and removal of waste.

Land prices vary enormously from province to province, from city centre to rural areas, and even within confined areas. In rural areas, land may cost under 100,000 baht per *rai*. In cities, it may cost over 40 million baht per *rai*.

One method of assessing the value of land is to obtain a valuation by the nearest office administered by the Department of Land (DOL). However, be aware that the DOL's values are usually below market value because property buyers often register lower property prices to reduce land transfer fees.

The Department of Land's website is: www.dol.go.th and the telephone number in Bangkok is + 66 (0)2 448-5448. An alternative website is www.treasury.go.th.

Before the DOL release valuation data, they require the following information: property deed (*chanote*) number, map reference number, and the name of the administrative area.

The average cost of building a property in Thailand during 2006 was estimated as follows:

- 5,000 baht per square metre for a bungalow.
- 10,000 baht per square metre for a standard two-level house using concrete.
- 15,000 baht per square metre for a luxury villa with high-quality fittings.

The cost of buying a condominium varies from as little as 10,000 baht per square metre for an unfurnished unit to over 60,000 baht per square metre for a furnished luxury apartment. The cost per square metre is an effective way of comparing condo prices (by dividing the asking price of the property by the area in square metres).

Caution: it is unlawful for foreigners to buy land in Thailand. However, your lawyer can arrange a long lease of up to thirty years; there may be an option to renew the lease for a further thirty years. Previously, many foreigners purchased land using Thai limited companies with 'nominee' shareholders who neither invested in the company nor participated in the profits. This practice is illegal and the government is cracking down on this method of property acquisition. See "How The Laws Affect Foreigners" for more information

Chapter 6
What You Need To Know Before You Start

The Stages Of Buying A Business

The key stages of buying a business are:

- Defining your objectives
- Research
- Sourcing businesses
- Business evaluation
- Offer to purchase
- Negotiation
- Due diligence
- Completion

Defining Your Objectives

Be clear about what you want to give—and take from—the business. Below is a list of questions to ask:

- What is your maximum total investment in the business?
- What will be your role in the business?
- What is your required payback period and return?
- Which types of business will you consider?
- Which locations will you consider?

Research

During the research stage you should become as familiar as you can with Thai culture and etiquette. Try to acquire a working knowledge of the Thai language. Meet local businesspeople and find out how business is done in Thailand. Look for businesses for sale on the Internet. (See the list of business brokers in "References.")

Sourcing Businesses

If you are good at networking and doing independent research, sourcing businesses for sale is straightforward, with or without a broker. Ask as many businesspeople and expatriates as possible. Many expats and Thais have friends who want to sell a business. The introducer would normally receive a three percent commission from the seller upon transfer of ownership.

In Thailand the majority of businesses are potentially for sale 'at the right price'; but the selling price may not suit you, the buyer. Therefore, don't restrict your search to businesses that are actively marketed for sale.

A good starting point is the online listings of local business brokers. The website addresses of the major brokers are listed in the "References" section. Note down the reference of any listings that interest you and visit them.

Businesses are advertised privately by owners in the *Bangkok Post*, *The Chiang Mai Mail*, *The Pattaya Mail*, and Bahtsold.com. The website addresses are listed in the "References" section. Also consider the business classifieds posted on the following Thai websites: www.hunsa.com; www.pantip.com; and www.sanook.com.

Business Evaluation

Businesses for sale sometimes display a 'for sale' sign outside their premises, but these owners are usually desperate to sell. Also check local public notice boards. If you see potential in any of these businesses for sale, work out what it is worth to you, discount the number, and make an offer. The sight of crisp bank notes can sometimes facilitate a quick (and favourable) decision by the seller.

Be careful if you choose to approach business owners directly. Visit with a polite, presentable Thai colleague so he can deal with the Thai owners. If the owner is Thai, it is usually wiser to ask whether he knows of any businesses for sale in the area. He may even be offended if you ask him directly if his business is for sale.

Direct canvassing of specific businesses in targeted locations can be very effective. If you know what you want, there are few businesses to target. A buyer might approach fifteen guesthouses in the same area on the

Business brokers advertise in The Bangkok Post

same day. Exchange name-cards with each owner and follow up a few days later.

Ask as many Thai businesspeople, including real-estate brokers, if they know of any suitable businesses for sale. The best freelance sales people have adept customer-service skills, commission-induced motivation, initiative, and resourcefulness. They are worth their weight in gold.

Some brokers distribute circular letters 'for the attention of the business owner,' written in both English and Thai. This approach could suit a buyer, too. Write a polite letter to the owner explaining that you are looking for a business in the area, and also have it translated into Thai.

Offer To Purchase And Offer Price

How much is the business worth to you? Try the following formula to estimate an appropriate offer price:

Offer Price = (Payback Period [years]
                x Adjusted Net Profits [real earnings)]
                – Additional Costs)

The payback period (in years) is the maximum period to recover the total investment. Additional costs include property refurbishment, replacement of furniture and equipment, and advances to the landlord.

Example: John wants to recover his investment within a two-year period. The real earnings of the guesthouse are 1.5 million baht per annum. He estimates additional costs, including replacement of furniture, to be 350,000 baht. Using the above formula, his offer price would be 2.65 million baht.

Direct Offers

If you are not using a business broker, do not support your offer with a deposit, unless you are prepared to lose the money. If the seller is unscrupulous, he or she may accept a higher offer the next day, and it may be difficult, in some cases impossible, to recover the deposit.

You need to convince the seller that you are a serious buyer and have the funds. After establishing the terms of the new lease, arrange a meeting between your Thai representative, the seller, and landlord. Exchange your certified bank cheque for a signed lease and specified business assets.

Offers Via Brokers

The offer to purchase marks the beginning of negotiations. The business broker prepares the offer document on behalf of the buyer. The offer is accompanied by the buyer's deposit (of between ten percent and twenty percent of the price offered). Your broker will tell you that an offer without a deposit is not a real offer.

The offer provides the names and addresses of the buyer and seller, the date of offer, and the proposed date of completion. The document also states the price offered for the business, the deposit paid, and balance payable. Assets included in the sale are specified (such as furniture, fittings, equipment, trademarks, goodwill, and inventory). All business liabilities remain the responsibility of the seller unless agreed otherwise.

Most offers stipulate specific conditions. Typical conditions are:

- Landlord's permission to modify the property as required.
- The maximum acceptable rent on the new lease.
- The minimum lease term.
- The landlord's security deposit is included in the selling price
- No competition by the seller in a similar trade within a radius of two kilometres of the premises for two years.
- Training and support for two weeks after transfer of the business.
- The seller is responsible for the payment of all business liabilities as at the date of completion.
- The seller agrees to finance the transaction by accepting sixty percent down-payment with the balance payable in two equal instalments, three months and six months after completion.
- The seller agrees to allow the buyer access to all accounting and financial records between the offer date and completion.
- The seller agrees to terminate the employment of (name of employee) before completion; the buyer will reimburse the legal cost of severance.
- The seller agrees to include a minimum value of inventory in the sale.

Your broker takes your signed offer to the seller. There are three possible outcomes: acceptance, outright rejection, or counter-offer. There are many variables to negotiate, other than price, including exclusion of the security deposit or specified assets, and buyer finance (or credit terms).

Once the offer has been agreed and signed by both parties, it is the seller's responsibility to meet the conditions of the offer. If the seller does not comply with the offer terms, the broker must return the buyer's deposit in full. The buyer has until the agreed completion date to fulfil all due diligence and validation of the seller's representations. If the buyer can show evidence of misrepresentation by the seller, the offer is annulled.

A common obstacle in business transfer is the landlord increasing the rent to a level unacceptable to the buyer. Sometimes the landlord is not prepared to offer long enough lease terms to suit the buyer.

Obtain a detailed list of all assets included in the sale, signed and dated by the seller. Go through this list item by item and estimate the value of each asset before completion.

Completion

Completion proceeds after the conditions of the offer to purchase have been fulfilled and the seller's representations have been validated by the buyer. The date of completion is the cut-off point for due diligence. The key stages of completion (in order) are:

1– Signing of a new lease by the buyer and landlord (the buyer pays rent in advance, plus a security deposit to the landlord).

2– Agreement of the terms of business transfer.

3– The buyer pays the agreed purchase price to the seller by bank cheque or in cash and receives a written receipt.

The business transfer is complete when:

- The new lease has been agreed and signed by the buyer and landlord.
- The business transfer agreements (including asset transfer agreement) have been signed by the buyer and seller.
- The seller has complied with all conditions of the offer.
- The seller has agreed to settle all liabilities of the business as of the date of completion.
- The buyer is satisfied that all fixed assets and inventory included in the sale are on the premises.
- The buyer pays the seller for the business.
- If you use the in-house lawyer of your broker, he will probably insist that you sign legal disclaimers relieving them of legal responsibility.

Attend the completion meeting with a totally reliable Thai representative or lawyer. **Your Thai colleague must check the property registration documents against the landlord's ID card and the lease contract.** Sometimes the 'landlord' is actually a sub-lessee; if he says he 'forgot' to bring the property registration documents to the meeting, do not proceed. Refer to "Pitfalls And How To Avoid Them."

The documents recognised under Thai law are those written in the Thai language. Therefore, accurate translations are important. Consider getting your translation checked by another translator.

Obtain signed copies of the ID cards of both the landlord and seller. Bring your passport to the meeting along with copies for the landlord and seller. If your Thai limited company is to be the lessee, remember to take the company block stamp to the meeting.

The buyer is advised to pay the seller by banker's cheque. Sometimes sellers ask for payment in cash; if necessary, arrange for cash payment on your bank's premises. The seller will probably discourage completion on Sunday or public holidays when the banks are closed, since they want to receive their money and have it in their bank soon after the time of the sale.

How To Deal With Sellers

The main objective of the first meeting with the seller is to establish rapport. Without rapport, the seller will not offer the information and support you need. Leave the detailed financial questions for later.

Observe everything around you while establishing rapport with the seller. Use all your senses (especially taste, if the seller is a restaurateur) and your intuition. What is the mood of the staff and customers?

Ask the seller open questions and let him do most of the talking. Find out why the business is for sale and what are the seller's plans?

Selling a business can be nerve-wracking, especially when providing private information to people who may not be genuine. Be sensitive to the seller's predicament and demonstrate interest in the business. If you enjoy friendly conversation over a drink with the seller, you have achieved the objective of the initial meeting.

Finding A Lawyer And Accountant

If you make only a small investment and register the business in a Thai individual's name, you may decide not to use a lawyer or accountant. Your Thai partner will apply for the necessary business licenses. Tax officers from the Revenue Department are used to negotiating personal income tax settlements with Thai business owner without any accounting records.

If you register a Thai limited company, you need a local lawyer and an accountant. Some foreigners register their companies and obtain work permits with the help of their Thai partners. You may decide to employ a Thai book-keeper or legal assistant to deal with all the statutory returns and periodic reporting requirements.

If you establish a company and obtain a work permit, you may have the following monthly reporting requirements:

- Payment of personal income tax on your minimum salary.
- Payment of Value Added Tax (being the difference between the VAT collected on sales invoices less the VAT paid on purchase invoices).

- Payment of withholding tax on services purchased (usually two percent is deducted from the purchase invoice and paid to the Revenue Department at the end of the month).

Local accountants usually provide a monthly tax accounting service for the above taxes at a starting fee of 2,000 baht per month. You would pay at least an extra 2,000 baht per month for financial accounting (or book-keeping) but clients usually maintain their own records. At the end of the calendar year, your accountant must certify the financial statements, usually at a fee of around 10,000 baht.

Ask local businesspeople if they can recommend a good lawyer or accountant. Meet two or three and select your favourite. Their linguistic ability may be an important factor. **Ask some technical questions during the initial meeting to check their knowledge.** As long as you believe in their professional ability, your decision will be down to trust and rapport.

Forming A Thai Limited Company

Allow up to six weeks to form a Thai limited company, though in some cases it may be completed within two or three weeks. The steps in forming your Thai limited company are:

- Reserve your proposed company name
- File a Memorandum of Association
- Convene a statutory meeting
- Company registration
- Tax registration

Most people are advised to use an independent professional lawyer to establish their Thai limited company. The legal costs of forming a limited company are typically in the range 10,000 to 40,000 baht plus government fees and disbursements. Ask your lawyer for an **all-inclusive quote** covering:

- Advice concerning share structure
- Registration of the company name
- Registration of shareholders (minimum of seven)
- Drafting the minutes of meetings of shareholders and directors
- Obtaining the corporate tax ID number.
- The company block stamp
- The Memorandum of Association
- The Certificate of Incorporation

- Government fees (including the stamp duty payable on the registered share capital)

Company Name Reservation And Registration

Check whether your proposed company name is available at the Commercial Registration Department, which is part of the Ministry of Commerce. The availability of your proposed company name may be checked online at the Department of Business Development: www.dbd.go.th. Every Thai company has the suffix 'Co., Ltd.' (e.g. ABC Co., Ltd.).

The above-mentioned online company name search yields the following information: name of company, date of registration, registration number and registered address.

Once you have chosen your company name, and you know it is available, you may reserve it online. It is necessary to register with the Department of Business Development to obtain a user-name and password. Select 'Business Name Registration' and complete the online form. After the name has been approved, the ministry will confirm your newly registered name by e-mail. Print out the approval certificate and register it at the local registration office. The name will be reserved for thirty days. Therefore, apply to register the company within this temporary name reservation period.

There are several advantages of naming your company as you propose to name your business. For example, if you want to trade under the name 'Sabai Dee,' register your company as 'Sabai Dee Co., Ltd.' All VAT purchase invoices or receipts must bear the name of your limited company, otherwise you cannot claim the VAT back.

The Memorandum Of Association

The Memorandum of Association is a legal document which your lawyer will prepare and file with the Commercial Registration Department. This document includes the following information:

- Company name
- Province of business registration and trading
- Business objectives
- Registered capital (including number of shares and nominal par value)
- Names of seven shareholders (or promoters)

Your stated business objectives should be as broad as possible, in case you decide to diversify your activities in the future. The objectives must not include any prohibited occupations (listed later in this section).

Your registered share capital should be enough to finance your planned business operations. Your cash-flow forecast will identify your capital requirement. **The minimum registered share capital requirement is two million baht per work permit.**

According to the law, 25 percent of the registered share capital should be paid up in cash or in kind within three months of incorporation. The Ministry of Commerce (MOC) could request a copy of the company bank statement to show the cash deposit. In practice, the MOC does not usually check the deposit.

The Department of Labour has the power to revoke a work permit if it has reason to believe the company is under-capitalised or unable to fulfil its financial obligations. The company's audited accounts, which must be filed within five months of the annual accounting period, identifies the capital paid into the company. Therefore, company directors usually have up to twelve months to pay up the remaining share capital.

Payment in kind means transfer of assets—tangible or intangible—from the shareholders to the limited company. Instead of depositing cash into the company bank account, the promoters may transfer equipment, patents, goodwill, or management services in lieu of paid up shares. Any money spent by the company sponsors on behalf of the company increases the paid up share capital.

Here is an example of how two million baht share capital may be paid up:

```
Cash Paid Into Company Bank Account. . . . . . . . . 500,000
Furniture And Equipment
Transferred To The Company . . . . . . . . . . . . . . . . 750,000
Management Services Provided By Sponsors . . . . . .  750,000

Total Paid Up Capital . . . . . . . . . . . . . . . . . . . . .2,000,000
```

Invoices should be issued to the limited company for the fixed assets and the management services provided by owner-directors. The same applies to the transfer of know-how, patents, and copyrights.

The registration fee for the Memorandum of Association is 500 baht per 100,000 baht of registered capital, subject to a minimum fee of 500 baht and a maximum of 25,000 baht. The government duty for registration of a two-million-baht company is therefore 10,000 baht.

The Statutory Meeting

At the statutory meeting, the company directors and an auditor are elected.

Company Registration

The company directors must register the company within three months of the aforementioned statutory meeting.

Company registration forms are available from the Department of Business Development (DBD). These documents are also downloadable from the DBD's website: www.dbd.go.th. The forms must be completed in Thai, so you may choose to obtain a good translation of these.

It is illegal to use nominee (or dummy) shareholders and the government is tightening the law to close this loophole. Some lawyers provide bogus shareholders who do not know what they are being asked to sign.

At the time of writing, Thai shareholders are required to provide a recent bank statement, evidencing sufficient funds to pay up their share capital. For example, if a Thai 'investor' is allocated ten percent of a two-million baht limited company, they must have 200,000 baht in their own bank account at the time of company registration. Later, the company may be required to prove that each of the shareholders really participates in the company's profits.

Tax Registration

Your newly formed company must apply for a corporate tax ID number from the Revenue Department (www.rd.go.th) within sixty days of commencement of trading. The company must also register for VAT if the sales turnover is expected to exceed 1.8 million baht annually.

The Treaty Of Amity And Economic Relations

The Treaty of Amity was introduced on May 29, 1968, allowing Thais and Americans reciprocal benefits in each other's country. This means that Americans enjoy advantages over other foreign businesspeople in Thailand.

By forming a company under this treaty, it is not necessary for Americans to have Thai partners or shareholders. **Although Amity companies allow Americans full control over their business, having a Thai representative is still important**.

This treaty allows Americans to own 100 percent of a Thai limited company, branch office, or representative office in Thailand. However, there are restrictions on the American entity's operations. Under Article IV (2) of the treaty, Americans are prohibited from the following activities: transport; communications; fiduciary functions; banking; exploitation of land and natural resources; domestic trade in agricultural products

An important effect of these restrictions is that **Amity Treaty companies cannot own land.**

The process of establishing a Thai limited company under the Amity Treaty requires authorization by the US Commercial Service in Bangkok. Allow up to three months to form an Amity company. Usually the fees for forming an Amity company are twice as expensive as for standard Thai limited companies.

Business Licenses

Business licenses can be obtained from the Provincial Excise Office. All licenses are issued for a period of twelve months but end on December 31. The fee is not pro-rated for licenses applied for during the calendar year.

When applying for business licenses, take the following documents with you:

- Original ID card or passport together with a signed copy
- Evidence of the registered address, such as a copy of the property registration papers or a copy of the lease agreement.

Administration and enforcement of business licenses varies between districts. Many districts allow a grace period for new businesses in the early stages of start-up; some district officers are particularly helpful.

The business license should be registered in the name of a Thai person, a Thai limited company, or a Thai limited partnership.

Entertainment Licenses

There are four categories of entertainment license:

1– **Dance venues.** including discotheques and *ramwong* (folk/country dancing) venues. The annual fees are: 10,000 baht for venues under 100 square metres; 30,000 baht for venues between 101 and 300 square metres; 50,000 baht for venues over 301 square metres.

2– **Massage parlours.** The annual fees are: 30,000 baht for parlours containing less than 30 massage rooms; 40,000 baht for parlours with 31 to 50 rooms; 50,000 baht for parlours with over 50 rooms.

3– **Entertainment venues.** There are four types of entertainment venue:

a: a place providing a show or other activities for the purpose of entertaining customers, and allowing staff to socialize with patrons;

b: a place providing equipment enabling patrons to sing, and allowing staff to socialize with the patrons;

c: a place that has no dance floor but allows customers to dance on the premises;

d: other places that have light or sound facilities, depending on ministry rulings yet to be made.

The annual fees are: 10,000 baht for an area under 100 square meters; 30,000 baht for an area between 101 and 300 square meters; 50,000 baht for areas over 301 square meters.

4– **Restaurants.** The annual fees are: 10,000 baht for an area under 100 square meters; 30,000 baht for between 101 and 300 square meters; 50,000 baht for over 301 square meters. Restaurants that provide entertainment and close after midnight (primarily venues with cultural shows) must be licensed.

The above licenses should be applied for at the local district police office.

Factory Licenses

Factories are divided into three categories:

1– Factories that do not require licensing (refer to www.boi.go.th).

2– Factories that only require advance notification to government officials prior to operation. Operators may commence as soon as they receive a receipt form from the ministry confirming the application.

3– Factories that require a license prior to operation. Operators may be granted a certificate allowing them to start building the factory prior to licensing, subject to the ministry's discretion.

Licenses are valid until the end of the fifth calendar year from the year in which the business started operations, except when the factory is transferred, leased, or if operations cease. In these cases, the license is regarded as having expired on the date of issuance of a license to the factory's new operators, or on the date of cessation of operations.

Applications for renewal of factory licenses must be submitted prior to the date of expiry, with a fee of 100,000 baht. After submission, renewal is automatic unless otherwise advised. If the application is submitted within sixty days of the expiry date, there is an additional fee of 20,000 baht. Application for renewed licenses should be made within sixty days after expiry of the license.

Factory licenses should be applied for at the Department of Industrial Works at the Ministry of Industry. Tel: + 66 (0)2 202-4000 -14; Fax: + 66 (0)2 354-3390; E-mail: pr@diw.go.th).

Export Licenses

The documents required are:

- A copy of the VAT certificate
- A copy of ID card or passport and work permit
- A copy of the business registration certificate

The fee is 200 baht per annum. Register at the department of Foreign Trade. Tel: + 66 (0)2 547-4837 -39; Fax: + 66 (0)2 547-4757; E-mail: eximdft@dft.moc.go.th.

Hotel And Guesthouse Licenses

The information required for the license is:

- Name of the hotel
- Type of hotel
- The registered office and name of the owners
- The address of the hotel

The fee is 100 baht per room per annum. Register at the local city hall or the provincial hall.

Alcohol Licenses

A license to sell beer, wine, and spirits costs 1,100 baht per annum. Applicants should submit their original ID card or passport (plus a copy), and proof of the restaurant or bar's address (such as a copy of the house registration papers or a copy of the lease agreement). If all supporting documents are in order, the application could take as little as ten minutes to process, but no longer than one day. To obtain any of these licenses, apply at the local district office.

Licenses To Sell Used Goods

Any business selling used products, including second-hand book stores and silver and gold traders must apply for this license. The annual fee is 5,000 baht.

Licenses To Sell Tobacco and Cigarettes

There are three types for license for selling tobacco and cigarettes in Thailand. The annual fee for unlimited sale of cigarettes is 1,000 baht. For limited sale of cigarettes the fee is 500 baht.

Applicants should apply at the nearest city hall with the following documents:

- ID card or passport (with a signed copy)
- Property registration document or shop lease contract
- Personal income tax ID card
- Business registration certificate
  (issued by the Ministry of Commerce)

Trademarks And Patents

The Department of Intellectual Property (DIP) was established in 1992 to administer intellectual property on behalf of the Department of Commercial Registration at the Ministry of Commerce.

Many businesses in Thailand trade under the same name. Sometimes business sellers start a new business using the same name as the business transferred to the seller; registration of the business trademark purchased is one way the buyer can protect the trademark and its associated goodwill.

For information about registration of patents and trademarks, refer to the DIP's website: www.ipthailand.org.

Opening A Bank Account

Personal Bank Account

Foreigners are usually required to possess a work permit before being permitted to open a bank account. Opening a personal bank account is usually straightforward. Bring your work permit, passport (and/or ID card) to the bank with a minimum cash deposit of 500 baht. If you are lucky, you may have a savings account book, ATM card, and a free gift within fifteen minutes of entering the office.

Expect to receive less than one percent interest on a savings account. Most banks provide Internet banking facilities. Your bank may also offer a Visa ATM card enabling withdrawals worldwide.

Company Bank Account

Before you open a company bank account, you need a Certificate of Incorporation and corporate tax ID number. It usually takes at least three weeks to form a limited company in Thailand after the company name has been approved by the Ministry of Commerce.

When you apply for a company bank account, provide the following items:

- Original certificate of company registration
- List of company shareholders/sponsors
- Memorandum of Association
- Company block stamp
- Passport or ID card for each cheque signatory
- Name and address of company directors (with ID)
- Official business licenses
- Lease agreement for property rented
- Cash or cheque deposit

If your company applies for merchant facilities, enabling customers to pay by credit card, allow up to three months for the account to be processed.

Transferring Money To Thailand

The most common way of remitting money to Thailand is by wire transfer using SWIFT or IBAN. The overseas bank will require the account name and number of the payee's bank account, and the name, address, and SWIFT code of the Thai bank. Transfer times vary between three and five days.

Send the funds in foreign currency for exchange in Thailand by your correspondent bank; this way you are likely to get a better rate of exchange. If you are transferring the funds to a Thai limited company, give your bank the name of the company as a reference, such as 'Investment in ABC Co., Ltd.'

Ask the correspondent bank for a foreign exchange form within four weeks of receiving the funds. Keep the foreign exchange form so you can repatriate the funds free of withholding tax in the future.

At the time of writing, withholding tax is levied by the Bank of Thailand (www.bot.or.th) on money transfers to Thailand. The withholding tax may be reclaimed twelve months after the transfer. Currently no deduction is made on transfers valued under 20,000 US dollars.

Looking For Suitable Premises

There is intense competition for prime business locations, so allow at least six months to find suitable premises. Tenants in the best locations are approached by prospective tenants almost daily.

There are two ways to find suitable premises: using a broker or by direct contact with landlords. Business brokers sell businesses rather than act as agents for a commercial property rentals agency. Some real-estate agencies list commercial rentals.

First decide what type of premises you want and the size and location. Talk to as many businesspeople as possible in the target neighbourhood. Conduct your search with a Thai representative. Some people hire opportunistic *tuk-tuk* or taxi drivers to take them on a tour of suitable commercial rental properties. Look out for 'for rent' signs and check the classifieds in local newspapers. Check the market rents in the surrounding area.

Make sure your landlord gives you written permission to modify the property as necessary. Does the landlord meet his or her responsibilities by repairing the property? For example, has water been leaking through the ceiling for years? Are future rent increases limited in the lease agreement (e.g. a ten percent increase after three years)?

Property leases of more than three years (but less than thirty years) may be registered with the Land Department; otherwise, the lessee has no legal recourse. It is necessary to pay stamp duty when you register a lease. For further information about leasing land, refer to "What You Need To Know Before You Start".

Usually businesses for sale require the assignment of an existing lease or the preparation of a new lease. Negotiate a new lease with the landlord (with the support of your Thai representative). Leases registered in a company name simply involve a change of shareholder.

Leasehold Improvements

Any leasehold improvements, and the fixtures and fittings, would usually revert to the ownership of the landlord when the lease expires. Therefore, write off the cost of leasehold improvements over the period of the lease. Any improvements to the property potentially add value to your business by increasing sales and the selling price.

Serviced Offices

Serviced offices are suitable for many professional service businesses such as real-estate brokers or consultancies, where location is less important.

Serviced office providers do not demand 'key money' (a premium payable to the landlord). Usually serviced offices provide photocopying and fax facilities as well as secretarial services. Although rent may be higher, serviced offices minimize the tenant's investment during the initial stages of start-up.

Shopping Malls

In Thailand, many shopping malls operate a voucher system; the customer buys vouchers from a kiosk and they are exchanged for meals at any of the surrounding food counters. Any unused vouchers are refundable at the kiosk.

The shopping malls normally charge 25-35 percent of the licensee's gross receipts. The mall pays the business licensee the net receipts some two months afterwards. Although the licensees can generate good sales, it is necessary to finance two months cost of sales.

Visas

Non-Immigrant Visas

Most foreign investors and owner-managers of businesses in Thailand are advised to apply for a one-year, multiple-entry Non-Immigrant business visa (Type B). It may be possible to obtain a three-year Non-Immigrant visa. Apply for the visa at an appropriate Thai embassy or consulate, ideally in Europe, Australia, or North America. **Save time and money by applying for the visa before visiting Thailand.**

You must have a Non-Immigrant visa (Type B) before applying for a work permit. This type of visa does not necessitate the transfer of funds from your country of origin to Thailand (unlike the retirement visa). Foreigners residing in Thailand for a minimum of three consecutive years on one-year Non-Immigrant B visas are eligible to apply for permanent residence. This allows the dispensation of annual visa renewals, and work permits are renewed annually instead of quarterly.

Even if you restrict your activities to overseeing investment in Thailand, the Non-Immigrant B visa is a good choice. Alternatively, investors over the age of fifty can apply for a retirement visa if they show evidence of funds of 800,000 baht in a Thai bank account (or 400,000 baht if they have a Thai spouse).

Every foreign national must enter Thailand with a valid visa, otherwise they will be issued a transit visa valid for just 28 days.

Warning! Every foreign national in Thailand is required to report to Immigration or leave the country every ninety days no matter what type of visa they have. Foreigners failing to do so must pay a fee of 500 baht for each day over-stayed. The over-stay fee is capped at 20,000 baht. Many foreigners overstay by mistake, thinking that their twelve-month visa excludes them from the ninety-day rule. Do not make this mistake.

In Asia, Thai embassies and consulates usually only issue three-month Non-Immigrant visas; they also have more stringent criteria for granting visas than in Europe, Australia, and North America.

Other Types of Non-Immigrant Visa

The other types of Non-Immigrant visa are:

- Non-Immigrant IM (relating to Thai government)
- Non-Immigrant IB (Board of Investment sponsorship)
- Non-Immigrant EX (skilled expert classification)

The Application Process

The application procedure for obtaining visas is detailed on the website of the relevant Thai embassy or consulate. The application usually requires the following:

- Bank cheque or money order for the visa fee (in local currency of the consulate or embassy)
- A completed application form showing the type of visa required (single- or multiple-entry for three months/one year/ three years)
- Two passport-sized photographs
- A sponsorship letter signed by a Thai company (or other Thai juristic body) accompanied by a copy of the sponsor's Certificate of Incorporation and details of share capital
- Other documents specific to the application

Note: Visa regulations are continually changing, so you are advised to contact the relevant Thai embassy or consulate shortly before travelling to Thailand. Thai consulates regularly change their policies and fees for processing visas.

Refer to "Appendices" for a specimen sponsorship letter for a Non-Immigrant B visa. Note that there is no mention of work or any requirement for a work permit. This visa application is essentially for business research and investment. If you are considering the purchase of a condominium, for example, your real-estate broker may be willing to sponsor your Non-Immigrant visa application.

Work Permits

Work permits are regulated under the Alien's Act BE 2521 (1978). Every foreigner working in Thailand is required to have a work permit, even if they are engaged in voluntary work. However, investors do not need a work permit if they have Thai employees doing all the necessary work.

Criteria For Entitlement To A Work Permit

Foreign workers must satisfy the following conditions to be eligible for a work permit:

- Hold a valid Non-Immigrant visa
- The person must not apply for work in any of the prohibited occupations as listed in Royal Decree BE 2522 (reproduced later in this section)
- Possess suitable knowledge, skills, and qualifications for the employment
- Have sound mental health
- Be free of leprosy, tuberculosis, drug addiction, alcoholism, and elephantiasis
- Have no prior prison sentence for violation of Thai Immigration law within the previous twelve months of the application

Application For A Work Permit With One-Year Extension Of Stay

Your employer is responsible for providing all foreign employees with work permits. If you want to work in your own business, the most practical way is to form a Thai limited company. The procedure is as follows:

1– Register sufficient capital for your limited company. The company must have at least two million baht registered share capital for each work permit. The company must have at least four Thai employees with employment contracts.

2– You must pay yourself a minimum salary (between 25,000 and 60,000 baht per month, depending on your nationality) and pay personal income tax on it. For details, refer to "Personal Income Tax". Your company would normally be expected to be VAT-registered.

3– Complete the application forms. These are downloadable from the Department of Employment's website (see "Essential Website Addresses"). Make three sets of all documents.

Obtain copies of your passport and obtain professional passport photographs. Ensure your passport is valid for a further twelve months and it contains at least five blank pages.

4– If you are already in Thailand and do not have a Non-Immigrant visa (Type B), travel to a neighbouring country's Thai embassy or consulate to apply for a three-month Non-Immigrant visa (Type B). Take with you: signed, stamped copies of your company documents (including Certificate of Incorporation, list of shareholders; tax receipts for VAT and personal income tax; details of the directors and the registered office; and Memorandum of Association and employment contract). In addition, your limited company must provide a sponsorship letter (see specimen letter in "Appendices"). Also provide passport photographs, completed application form (provided by the relevant Thai embassy), and visa fee. Your visa will be valid for up to ninety days.

5– Ensure you have all the necessary documents to take to the Labour Department (Department of Employment). Documents include:

- Completed application form (WP1-WP10)
- Three recent (professional) passport photographs
- Employment contract
- Certificate of Incorporation
- Memorandum of Association
- List of company shareholders
- VAT registration certificate
- Organizational chart (for staff employed)
- Copies of passport and Non-Immigrant visa
- CV/resumé and copies of educational certificates
- Health certificate (provided by a Thai hospital or clinic)
- Map (and ideally a photograph as evidence) of your registered office

Allow up to three weeks for this application.

6– Collect your work permit from the Labour Department (in person) and additional forms for extension of stay.

7– Apply for a one-year extension of stay at Immigration on the day your visa expires. They will initially extend your visa by thirty days only. Extend your work permit at the Labour Department on the same day.

8– Extend your visa at the Immigration Office on the date of expiry. Update the work permit. Continue the process of extending both visa and work permit (every thirty days) until you are granted the work permit for one year. Extend your visa at Immigration every ninety days. If you leave the country, obtain a re-entry permit at Immigration or at the airport beforehand.

9– When you renew your annual work permit and visa, you will need company documents, employment contract, audited financial statements, annual income report, and power of attorney (if you are not applying in person).

BOI Companies

The documents required by employees of BOI Companies are:

1– Application form (WP1) and three photographs (5 x 6 cm) taken not more than six months before the date of application.

2– A passport with one copy of all pages, showing a valid Non-Immigrant (Type B) visa.

3– A copy of the company's Certificate of Incorporation issued within six months of the date of application.

4– A letter approving the applicant's employment from the Board of Investment, the Industrial Estates Authority of Thailand, or the Department of Mineral Resources (as applicable).

5– An official form for notification of commencement of work (WP10) attached to a copy of the power of attorney (signed by the employer or sponsor), with ten baht stamp duty.

Your Right To Appeal

If your application for a work permit is unsuccessful, you are entitled to appeal to the Minister of Labour and Social Welfare within thirty days of rejection. The appeal decision will be issued within sixty days.

Government Fees For Work Permits

Period of Work Permit	Government Fee
Three Months Or Less	750 baht
Three To Six Months	1,500 baht
Six To Twelve Months	3,000 baht

Where To Apply

The following offices process applications for work permits:

- The Foreign Workers' Administration Office
- The One-Stop Service Centre for Visas and Work Permits
- Provincial Employment Offices (Department of Employment)

For contact information, refer to the "References" section.

An Alternative To Extension Of Stay

An alternative way of obtaining a work permit is to obtain a one- (or three-) year Non-Immigrant business visa *before* applying for the work permit. This way, the work permit is attached to the visa, rather than the other way around.

The advantages of this method are: the Immigration criteria are not as stringent as for extension of stay, and if your work permit is cancelled, you are not required to leave the country within seven days.

The main disadvantage of this method is that you are required to leave the country every ninety days, as well as extending your work permit.

Tips

- Always keep your work permit in your office, ready for inspection by Immigration officers, who may visit unannounced at any time.
- Ensure your job description does not potentially include any of the prohibited occupations for foreigners.

- If you apply for a one-year work permit (on extension of stay), remember to apply for a re-entry permit (at Immigration or the airport) before you leave Thailand, otherwise your work permit will be cancelled and you will have to start the application process again. Keep spare passport photographs with you for this purpose.
- Your company would also normally be expected to be registered with the Social Security Fund.
- You may ask the Ministry of Labour to register a second job in your work permit; the government officer may ask you for a letter confirming that there is no conflict of interest between the two jobs. For example, an English teacher set up a trading company, and he was required to obtain a letter from his school confirming that it did not object to his trading activities outside normal school hours.

Labour Law

Under Thailand's Labour Protection Law, employees are entitled to weekly leave and paid sick leave and public holidays. Maximum working hours are eight hours per day and 48 hours per week.

Severance Pay entitlement starts at thirty days' pay for employees terminated after 120 days without a valid reason. For severance after longer periods of employment, refer to "Appendices."

For more details about the rights and duties of employers and employees in Thailand, visit the Ministry of Labour's websites: www.mol.go.th and www.labour.go.th.

Prohibited Occupations

According to Royal Decree BE 2522 (1979), foreigners are prohibited from the following occupations:

1– Manual work
2– Work in agriculture, animal husbandry, forestry or fisheries (excluding specialised work in each particular branch) or farm supervision
3– Bricklaying, carpentry, or other construction work
4– Wood carving
5– Driving mechanically-propelled carriages or driving non-mechanically-propelled vehicles (excluding international aircraft piloting)

6– Shop attendance

7– Auctioneering

8– Supervising, auditing, or giving services in accountancy (excluding internal auditing on occasions)

9– Cutting or polishing jewellery

10– Haircutting, hairdressing, or beauty treatment

11– Cloth weaving by hand

12– Weaving of mats or making products from reeds, rattan, hemp, straw, or bamboo pellicle

13– Making of *sa* paper by hand

14– Lacquer-ware making

15– Making of Thai musical instruments

16– Niello-ware making

17– Making of products from gold, silver, or gold-copper alloy

18– Bronze-ware making

19– Making of Thai dolls

20– Making of mattresses of quilt blankets

21– Alms bowl casting

22– Making of silk products by hand

23– Casting of Buddha images

24– Knife making

25– Making of paper or cloth umbrellas

26– Shoemaking

27– Hat-making

28– Brokerage or agency work (excluding international trade or business)

29– Engineering work in civil engineering concerning designing and calculation, organization, research, planning, testing, construction supervision, or advising (excluding specialised work)

30– Architectural work concerning designing, drawing of plans, estimation, construction directing, or advising

31– Garment making

32– Pottery or ceramic-ware making

33– Cigarette-making by hand

34– Guiding or conducting sightseeing tours

35– Street vending

36– Typesetting of Thai characters by hand

37– Drawing and twisting of silk-thread by hand

38– Office or secretarial work

39– Legal or lawsuit services

The above occupations and professions may only be provided in Thailand by Thai nationals. However, it is permissible for foreigners to invest in Thai limited companies offering such services, provided that only Thai nationals do the work. A copy of the Foreign Business Act BE 2542 (1999) is provided in the "Appendices."

The Board Of Investment (BOI)

The BOI offers two basic kinds of incentive for larger business projects, regardless of location; they are tax incentives and non-tax incentives:

- Tax-based incentives include exemption or reduction of import duties on machinery and raw materials, and corporate tax exemptions.

- Non-tax incentives include permission to bring in foreign workers, own land and take or remit foreign currency abroad.

For more information refer to the website: www.boi.go.th.

The Industrial Estates Authority of Thailand (www.ieat.go.th) specializes in general industrial estates and export processing zones.

Leasing Land

Registration Of Long-Term Leases

Foreigners are allowed to lease land for up to thirty years. The lease agreement should be registered with the local office of the Department of Land (www.dol.go.th). The government fee (including stamp duty) for land registration is 1.1 percent of the rent payable over the entire lease term. The registration fee for a thirty-year lease at rent of 10,000 baht per month would be 39,600 baht. It is more difficult for a landlord to break the terms of an officially registered lease.

The documents required by the Department of Land for registration of land are:

- Passport or ID card with signed copy
- Residence certificate (from Immigration or your embassy/consulate)
- Property documents (e.g. *chanote*)

The government officer will complete the (*Tor Tor* 1) form on computer and ask you to sign the printed form.

Are You Ready To Make An Offer? (A Checklist)

The Offer To Purchase

❑ Have you considered making an offer conditional on the seller offering terms of finance?

❑ Have you decided upon all the other conditions of your offer?

The Seller

❑ Do you trust the business vendor?

❑ Do you believe their reason for selling?

❑ Does the seller have daily accounting records to show you?

Premises

❑ Is the location suitable for your purpose?

❑ Are the proposed lease terms acceptable?

❑ Is the rent reasonable compared to average market value?

❑ Is the guaranteed lease term long enough to recover your investment?

❑ Have you obtained estimates of refurbishment?

❑ Does the landlord allow structural modifications to the premises?

❑ Are there any clauses in the lease relating to the future assignment of the lease to a new tenant?

❏ Will your Thai limited company be the lessee?

❏ Does the selling price include the security deposit held by the landlord?

Investment

❏ Is the estimated total investment (including remodelling costs and replacement of business assets) within your budget?

❏ Will you have the necessary liquid funds available on the date of completion?

Business Assets

❏ Which assets do you need and which are included in the sale price?

❏ Which assets on the premises are owned by the landlord, the seller (personally), or another third party?

❏ Have you obtained estimates of all furniture, fittings, and equipment that need replacing?

Employees

❏ Are there any employees working for the seller who are not suitable for your business?

Chapter 7
Red Tape, Customs And Procedures

Thai Culture And Etiquette

Presentation Is Everything

Thais respect smartly dressed, well-mannered people. Dress suitably and act politely to receive the best possible service from Thais. This is particularly important with Thai customers and in government or professional offices. If you look successful, you will be treated accordingly.

Business Style

Aggressive salesmanship does not work with Thais. Thai businesspeople like to develop relationships slowly and do business only when they feel comfortable. Patience is required to develop a trusting friendship before broaching the subject of business.

Usually Thais do not cooperate with people they dislike or disrespect. Relationships are extremely important in Thailand, so time invested with employees, suppliers, and customers is well spent.

Always be calm and never express anger or aggression in front of a Thai. If you raise your voice, a Thai will 'shut down' and never forgive you. Confrontation is taboo.

If you have an accident or problem, ask your Thai partner or friend to negotiate on your behalf. It is usually wiser to settle such matters on the spot instead of reporting them to the authorities.

Generosity

Thais enjoy giving and receiving presents. Colleagues at work usually relate to each other like family. When you go away on holiday, remember to buy presents for your staff. Celebrate the birthdays of your employees.

Avoid Blame

Avoid blaming or criticising anyone. Always take responsibility for problems in the business and hold meetings about how to correct them.

Respect The King And Buddhism

All Thais are bound together by a deep love and respect for His Royal Highness King Bhumibol. The king is a great spiritual leader who has helped many people and initiated over 2,000 royally sponsored projects for his people. He is committed to a self-sustaining economy. He is the longest reigning monarch in the world (since 1946) and probably the most respected.

Most businesses in Thailand display a photograph of the king and queen in a prominent position. It is also common for Thais to have a spirit house inside or outside the property for 'religious' reasons.

Thai Customs

It is customary to invite monks to your new business premises for a communal ceremony before launching the business. The date of the ritual, which is predetermined by astrology, is on an auspicious day. Your Thai partner will organize such a 'blessing' ceremony. Try to abide by the following general guidelines to avoid cultural taboos:

- Do not touch a Thai on the head.
- Remove your shoes before entering a Thai home (and sometimes an office).
- Avoid pointing your feet towards a Thai.
- Do not hold hands or kiss in public.
- Wear formal (long) clothes when you visit government offices or temples.

The formal way of greeting people in Thailand is known as the *wai*, which involves holding both hands in front of your face in a prayer-like position and looking upwards to the person you are greeting. If the person you are greeting has high social status (by way of ancestry, wealth, or age) it is customary to raise the *wai* higher. Do not initiate a *wai* to a young person, a waiter, or other person of lower status, but always return a *wai* greeting if it is given to you first.

Ronnie McDonald greets his customers with a wai

Status

Thais have a sophisticated social hierarchy. Older people, wealthy individuals, professionally educated people, and government officials are highly respected. It may be easier to manage Thai staff having less social status.

For further information on Thai Customs see *Culture Shock Thailand* listed in the "Recommended Books" section.

Business Etiquette And Customs

Name Cards

Always keep a supply of name-cards available to give away at meetings. The exchange of cards is a fundamental part of every initial business meeting. Not offering your card would be considered unprofessional or impolite. Many businesspeople have their name-cards printed in English on one side and in Thai on the other.

Mobile Phones

Protocol governing the use of mobile phones varies between cities and offices. Sadly the trend is toward an increase in interruptions during business meetings.

Credit: Forget It!

It is not wise to give credit to individuals in Thailand. Businesses usually offer one month's credit to limited companies with proven credit history.

Established Thai limited companies with audited financial statements and a positive record of cash management cannot usually borrow from local banks without mortgaging property or other fixed assets. Foreign businesspeople often find it easier to borrow money from their home country.

Some banks are beginning to offer loan products to foreigners in Thailand, but subject to stringent criteria. One such company is TISCO Finance Public Co., Ltd. TISCO Finance will consider giving housing loans of up to ninety percent of the value of the property to foreign nationals who are domiciled in Thailand. Successful applicants are likely to be permanent residents, or able to prove several years of residence in Thailand on a Non-Immigrant visa, and have proof of a secure monthly income in the form of offshore earnings or a permanent job in Thailand (for which a work permit must be presented). Applicants need to show evidence of a solid banking record in Thailand, and lenders may seek additional evidence of long-term commitment to the country, such as having a Thai spouse or dependent children.

Further details may be found from the following website:
www.tisco.com.

Paying Suppliers

Businesses usually pay suppliers by cash or company cheque. Many companies send their sales representatives to collect cheques from their customers. Banks in Thailand usually require company cheques to be both signed and stamped by the company block stamp; otherwise the cheque will be returned. Payment of utility bills can be made at any 7-Eleven store.

Dual Pricing System

There is an unofficial but widely-practiced dual-pricing system in Thailand, though it is not as pronounced as in neighbouring countries. Foreigners who make the effort to order goods using the Thai language are usually offered a lower price. Many successful foreign businesspeople ask their Thai partners to deal with suppliers and government officers.

Referral Commissions

It is customary for local people to claim a referral fee for any business introductions they initiate. The standard fee is between ten and twenty percent of the selling price, though it can be as high as fifty percent where profit margins are high and repeat business is seldom.

Even if you have no established referral agreement, when you refer a customer to a business, ask them about their scheme for referral commission. Referral of buyers to real-estate agents would usually kick back one percent of the price of the property purchased.

Many *tuk-tuk* and taxi drivers earn more from referral commissions than from fares. The buyer pays extra for being guided to the supplier. If you source suppliers yourself, you should claim the referral commission by way of discount.

Promoting Your Business

Marketing your business is a creative process, so brainstorming with colleagues, employees, associates, family, and friends is worthwhile. Never be complacent with your marketing formula because there is always scope for development.

Your marketing strategy starts with clearly-identified, unique selling points. These are product benefits or features giving your business an advantage over competitors. Examples might include "The biggest sandwich in town" or "The quickest, most efficient service."

Listed below are common methods of marketing in Thailand:

- Display advertising in magazines and newspapers
- Classified advertising in magazines and newspapers and on the Internet
- Business signage (on and off premises)
- TV and/or radio advertising
- Press releases, free advertorials in magazines, or feature articles about your business in the local or specialist press
- Brochure distribution in public displays
- *Tuk-tuk* advertising
- Gift marketing (including calendars, T-shirts. and diaries)
- Corporate website and e-mail marketing
- Presentations and networking at expatriate and business clubs such as the Rotary Club and the chambers of commerce
- Networking at social clubs and trade associations
- Exhibitions, trade fairs, and conferences
- Referral agreements and use of freelance agents
- Listings in authoritative guidebooks such as Lonely Planet

Advertising

If you are thinking about advertising in a periodical, it is necessary to know where the publication is distributed and who reads it. Most publishers in Thailand do not provide demographic marketing data, but it is necessary to obtain the following information:

- Print-run (the total number of copies actually printed for each issue)
- Distribution (the number of copies physically distributed)
- Details of the distribution network
- Circulation and readership information
- Analysis of target readership
- Series discounts for repeat advertisements
- Introductory discounts (if applicable)
- Fee for graphic design of advertisement (if any)
- Free website link-exchange or free classifieds
- Free advertorial or a feature article about your new business

One common complaint by businesspeople is that many free magazines are not distributed properly. Some publishers just distribute their magazines to their advertisers (with a sales invoice attached). Some publishers republish the same content but with an impressive new cover.

Referral Agreements

Tourism-related businesses benefit from referral agreements with guesthouses, travel agencies, and information centres.

Prepare promotional displays with photographs and a list of the unique selling points of your business. Approach the managers of the prospective agencies and ask them to display your board. Agree on a referral fee for each customer introduced to your business. The agent arranges the booking and collects the money on your behalf. Then the agent delivers the completed booking form and net proceeds to you (after deduction of their commission).

Display stand in busy location

Guidebook Listings

If your customers are tourists, ensure that your business is listed in the popular travel guidebooks and online publications. The most popular travel guidebooks for Thailand are published by Lonely Planet and Rough Guides. Listings are included free at the discretion of the publisher.

For popular, online travel guides, refer to "Essential Contacts By Location."

Advertorials And Press Releases

Editorial usually generates more enquiries than advertising. However, publishers do not charge for editorial, whereas advertising is usually expensive.

'Advertorial'—which is a fusion of 'advertising' and 'editorial'—is offered by some periodical publishers for newsworthy events. An example is the launch of a new business, event, or product. If you book a series of advertisements, ask for advertorial or an article to be written about your business.

The launch of your new business may be an ideal opportunity for free publicity in many types of media. Publishers are always looking for newsworthy topics to write about. Your business launch is a once-only opportunity, so don't miss it. Create a story for the publishers and highlight any unique aspects. Communicate your business's unique selling points and any special offers. Invite the publishers—and guest speakers—to the launch party of your new business.

The Launch Party

Plan an official launch date for your new business. Invite prospective customers, suppliers, employees, journalists, and friends. Invite local businesspeople and socialites also. The goal is for everyone to have fun.

Publicise the launch party in local magazines that feature a community events section. Prepare a single-page, A4 press release and fax it to local newspapers and magazines. List the event on local websites, with information services, and in the classifieds.

Press releases generate free publicity. Editorial in newspapers and magazines costs nothing, yet it is more effective than paid advertising.

Record Keeping

The law states that businesses should maintain proper accounting records. A proper record-keeping system lists all sales (cash and credit) and expenses (paid and payable). The system enables your accountant to prepare a balance sheet (listing the assets and liabilities of your business) and a profit-and-loss account at the end of the accounting period.

Many businesses, particularly sole proprietors in the provinces, keep no accounting information. Some businesses only maintain a record of daily gross sales, while others maintain two or three sets of accounting 'books' for different parties—one real account for the owner, another for tax purposes, and a third for potential investors.

Every business potentially benefits by recording accurate financial information. The data can be used to provide management information which, if acted upon, improves efficiency and profitability. Accounting controls help to identify theft or mistakes (such as double-payment of an invoice). Profitable businesses without proper accounting records may be more difficult to sell in the future.

Paying Taxes

In Thailand the following taxes apply:

- Personal income tax
- Corporate tax (on net company profits)
- Withholding tax
- Value Added Tax (VAT)
- Specific Business Tax (SBT)
- Stamp duty
- Customs duty
- Signboard tax
- Land tax (or Structures Usage tax)

Refer to the table of taxes in Thailand in "Red Tape, Customs, And Procedures."

There is no specific taxation on capital gains. However, a property transfer fee (which includes SBT) is payable when land is registered at the Land Department. Property transfer fees are apportioned between buyer and seller by negotiation.

Value Added Tax is seven percent of gross sales. Many small Thai businesses are not registered for VAT because they claim their gross annual sales to be less than 1.8 million baht.

Many limited companies do not pay corporate tax during the first two years of trading, unless they record a profit during the period.

Foreign workers (or their corporate employers) are required to pay personal income tax on a minimum expatriate salary (which varies from 25,000 baht to 60,000 baht per month according to nationality).

For investments of ten million baht and above, the Board of Investment (BOI) (www.boi.go.th) offers tax incentives and other benefits to investors. BOI companies investing over forty million baht are allowed to own one *rai* of land.

Currently there is no inheritance tax (or estate tax) levied on a deceased person's estate in Thailand. This means that family wealth does not usually erode quickly from generation to generation.

There are no official indirect (or stealth) taxes in Thailand.

The Revenue Code is the main source of tax law in Thailand. Personal income tax (PIT), corporate tax and withholding tax are payable to the Revenue Department (www.rd.go.th).

Country Of Citizenship	Minimum Salary (Baht Per Month)
Japan, USA, Canada	60,000
Europe, Australia	50,000
Korea, Hong Kong, Taiwan, Singapore, Malaysia	45,000
India, Middle East, China, Indonesia, Philippines	35,000
Burma, Laos, Vietnam, Cambodia, Africa	25,000

Personal Income Tax

Personal income tax (PIT) is a direct tax levied on an individual's income (including salary). PIT is administered by the Revenue Department. This tax is calculated on income received on a calendar year basis.

Corporate employers are responsible for deducting PIT from employees' salaries and settling the account monthly with the Revenue Department. Self-employed businesspeople (including limited partnerships) usually negotiate a tax settlement with a local officer from the Revenue Department whenever they visit.

Taxable income is assessable income less deductions and allowances. The first 100,000 baht of annual assessable income is exempt from PIT; the next 400,000 baht of annual assessable income is taxed at a rate of ten percent. Typically a foreigner working on a salary of 50,000 baht per month would be liable to PIT in the region of 2,000 baht per month. **PIT is payable on the minimum salary whether the business is profitable or not.**

Personal Income Tax Rates			
Taxable Income	Tax Rate (%)	Tax Amount (Baht)	Accumulated Tax (Baht)
0 - 100,000	Exempt	—	—
100,001 - 500,000	10	40,000	40,000
500,001 - 1,000,000	20	100,000	140,000
1,000,001 - 4,000,000	30	900,000	1,040,000
4,000,001 and over	37		

The taxpayer must file a personal income tax return (Form PIT 90 or 91) and pay the tax at the Area Revenue Branch Office by the end of March in the following tax year. Some taxpayers are also required to file a biannual return (Form PIT 94) and pay tax to the Area Revenue Branch Office before September 30 in the taxable year. Any withholding tax or taxes paid biannually should be credited against the tax liability at the year end.

Note that all taxes are subject to change, so check the latest tax rates on the Revenue Department's website: www.rd.go.th.

Corporate Tax

Large companies pay corporate tax at a rate of thirty percent on taxable (net) profits. Small and medium-sized businesses (SMEs) pay corporate tax on a sliding scale, at a rate of 15% (for the first one million baht), 25% of taxable profits (on the second and third million baht) and 30% (above three million baht). The Revenue Department "expects" limited companies to declare profits in their third year of trading (and pay corporate tax thereon).

Value Added Tax (VAT)

If your business earns more than 1.8 million baht per annum (or 150,000 baht per month), it must be VAT-registered. If your annual turnover is less than 1.8 million baht, you may still elect to register for VAT. Most businesses, especially in Bangkok, exceed this threshold. There are harsh penalties for negligently failing to register with the VAT office.

VAT Transactions

VAT-registered businesses must charge VAT on all sales transactions (other than exempted items such as land). Currently there are two rates of VAT in Thailand: Zero rate (0 percent) and Standard rate. The Standard rate of VAT is seven percent. The following businesses and activities are exempt from VAT:

- Small enterprises with gross sales under 1.8 million baht
- Healthcare services
- Charitable and religious organizations
- Leasing of land and property
- Production of food and agricultural products

VAT-registered entities may reclaim VAT paid on specific categories of purchases. The most common purchases subject to VAT at the standard rate are advertising, professional services; furniture, equipment and consumable products. Exports are chargeable to VAT at Zero rate.

The net VAT payable (or refundable) to (or from) the Revenue Department must be settled monthly. VAT payable is the total VAT collected on sales (known as VAT outputs) less the total VAT paid on purchases (known as VAT inputs) for the period.

VAT Payable = Total VAT Outputs − Total VAT Inputs.

Claiming VAT On Purchases

The original purchase invoice (or receipt) is required to claim the relevant VAT input. The invoice date must be within the relevant VAT accounting period; also, the invoice must clearly print the name of your VAT-registered business (the company name or name of the person registered).

VAT And Pricing

If you sell to local 'passing trade,' the VAT added to your sales cannot be reclaimed by your customers (unless they are VAT-registered), so your product may not be competitively priced. However, if your customers are VAT-registered, they are able to reclaim the VAT.

VAT Accounting

Your accountant should prepare and file the VAT return each month, and settle the outstanding balance. The deadline for delivery of the form and payment to the Revenue Department is the seventh day of the following month.

If you register for VAT, ensure that it is accounted for correctly and that procedures are complied with, enabling the recovery of VAT paid on all relevant purchases. Ensure your staff collect and maintain a file of all VAT invoices (for sales and purchases).

Specific Business Tax (SBT)

SBT is chargeable on the gross sale proceeds of land and property (and other immovable property) at a rate of 3.3 percent. SBT also applies to other transactions including banking and financial services. A person buying a condominium for one million baht would pay SBT at a rate of 3.3 percent to the Land Department. SBT payable on the one-million-baht transaction would be 33,000 baht.

All businesses and individuals must pay SBT on these specific transactions, whether they are registered for VAT or not. VAT is not chargeable on any transactions subject to SBT.

Stamp Duty

The rates of stamp duty are stated in the Stamp Duty Schedule of The Revenue Code. The fee varies according to the type of document or transaction. Stamp duty for the certification of documents is usually charged at a flat rate between one baht and 200 baht according to the following table:

Nature Of Instrument/Transaction	Stamp Duty
1. Lease of land, building, or other construction or floating house. For every 1,000 baht or fraction thereof of the rent or 'key money' or both for the entire lease period.	One baht
2. Transfer of share, debenture, bond, and certificate of indebtedness issued by any company, association, body of persons, or organization For every 1,000 baht or fraction thereof of the paid-up value of shares, or of the nominal value of the instrument, whichever is the greater.	One baht
3. Hire-purchase of property. For every 1,000 baht or fraction thereof of the total value.	One baht
4. Loan of money or agreement for bank overdraft. For every 2,000 baht or fraction thereof of the total amount of loan or the maximum amount of overdraft agreed upon.	One baht
5. (1) Bill of exchange or similar instrument used like bill of exchange. (2) Promissory note or similar instrument used like promissory note. For each instrument.	Three baht
6. Bill of lading. If issued in a set, every one of the set must be stamped at such rate.	Two baht
7. Cheque or any written order used in lieu of cheque. For each instrument.	Three baht
8. Letter of credit. (a) Issued in Thailand For value less than 10,000 baht For value of 10,000 baht or over (b) Issued abroad and payable in Thailand For each payment.	Twenty baht Thirty baht Twenty baht
9. Memorandum of Association of a limited company submitted to the registrar.	200 baht

Source: Revenue Department (www.rd.go.th).

Customs Duty

Customs revenue encompasses import and export taxes, duties, and other fees. The main sources of revenue collected by the Customs Department are:

- Customs duties under Customs law
- Excise tax for the Excise Department
- Value Added Tax for the Revenue Department

Imported goods are subject to both Customs duty and VAT. Exported goods are taxable at zero VAT rate and duty is levied on a few specific goods.

For detailed information, refer to the Customs Department's website: www.customs.go.th.

Signboard Tax

Signboard tax is a tax on commercial shop signs displayed outside the business premises. This tax is calculated on an annual basis as a multiple of the signage area, as follows:

- Three baht per 500 square centimetres of signage for signs written in the Thai language only.
- Twenty baht per 500 square centimetres of signage for signs written in both the Thai language and English (or another foreign language).
- Forty baht per 500 square centimetres of signage for displays primarily written in English (or another foreign language).
- The minimum signboard tax is 200 baht.

Land Tax (Or Structures Usage Tax)

The House and Land Tax Act imposes a land tax (or Structures Usage Tax) on owners of commercial property. This annual property tax is not often mentioned by real estate agents, so owners sometimes find themselves liable to land tax for the previous ten to twenty years.

Land tax is often insignificant; in practice the Revenue Department rarely levies the charge. When the government does collect land tax, usually it is collected after several years, when the amount has accumulated.

Land taxes are chargeable at a rate of 12.5 percent on the lower of the actual rent or the assessed gross rent of the property if the property is not leased to tenants. In practice the assessed rent is well below the commercial market value.

Property Transfer Fees

The following property transfer fees are payable to the Department of Land before the new owner can be registered:

- Stamp duty
- Transfer fees
- Specific Business Tax (SBT)

SBT is payable if the property being sold has been owned for less than five years. The property transfer fees for a small condominium selling for 500,000 baht would be 39,000 baht (or 7.8 percent of the selling price). This bill is apportioned between buyer and seller by negotiation.

Land prices registered at the Land Department are usually lower than market value because property owners want to reduce their property transfer fees. So government 'tax assessment values' of properties are below the real value.

Filing Returns And Accounts

Your accountant should prepare and submit tax returns and pay the tax liabilities on your behalf.

Personal income tax and withholding tax is payable to the Revenue Department by the seventh day of the following month. Your VAT return should also be submitted together with any payment outstanding by the fifteenth day of the month end. Finally, a return should be prepared for the Social Security Fund (SSF) contributions payable. For more information see "Social Security Fund" later in this section.

Monthly Returns

Compile the following documents for your accountant at the beginning of the following month:

- VAT purchase invoices and receipts paid during the month (with company name clearly printed).
- List of sales invoices for the month, together with copies of the invoices. The invoices should be sequentially numbered in date order.
- Summary of salaries paid to employees, enabling calculation of personal income tax. If your company is registered with the Social Security Fund (for health insurance), fifty percent of the fund contributions will be deducted from the employees' salaries and the other fifty percent is paid by the company.

- Documents supporting the deduction of withholding tax (e.g. lease with the landlord and purchase invoices or receipts for advertising, professional services, and consumables).
- Petty cash dockets for the month, plus a copy of the petty cash book (showing the date, payee, amount, and nature of expense).
- Copy of your cash book entries for the month.

Usually, your accountant will require the above documents before the fifth day of the following month to meet the submission deadline of the seventh day of the month. Your accountant will calculate the taxes due and request a company cheque to cover:

- The accountant's monthly fee
- Personal income taxes on staff salaries
- Withholding taxes
- VAT payable

Biannual Returns

Corporate tax is payable twice a year to the Revenue Department. The first completed form and tax payment is due before August 31 for the six months ending June 30. The second form should be filed and any remaining tax paid by May 30 (within 150 days of the calendar-year end)

Annual Returns

Financial statements for your company should be prepared for the year ended (or period ended) December 31. The accounts must be certified by either a tax auditor (TA) or a certified professional auditor (CPA) before filing them with the Department of Business Development (DBD).

The deadline for filing audited financial statements with the DBD is five months (150 days) after the year end (at the end of May).

Personal income tax returns must be filed and the liability settled by the end of March in the following year. These annual PIT returns may be filed in paper or electronic form. The electronic forms may be downloaded from the Revenue Department's Bureau of Electronic Processing Administration: http://rdserver.rd.go.th/publish/en/index.htm.

Social Security Fund

The Social Security Fund (SSF) is regulated by the Social Security Act BE 2533 (1990) and amended by BE 2537 (1994) and BE 2542 (1999). Companies are expected to register with the Office of Social Insurance (part of the Ministry of Labour) and pay contributions towards the social insurance fund on behalf of their employees registered in the scheme.

The purpose of the Social Security Fund is to provide healthcare and income for:

- Sickness benefit
- Maternity benefit
- Invalidity benefit
- Death benefit
- Child allowance
- Old age benefit

The Social Security Office collects contributions from registered employers and pays the benefits to insured persons. The Ministry of Labour supervises the administration of the Social Security Fund.

For registration with the Social Security Fund, complete and return the Employer Registration Form (SSO 1-01) and Insured Person Registration Form (SSO 1-03) to the Social Security Office.

Registered employees contribute five percent of their monthly salary towards their fund. The minimum contribution is 83 baht and the maximum is 750 baht.

The employer contributes five percent of the employees' salary, subject to the aforementioned minimum and maximum.

The SSF contributions must be paid at the Social Security Office, area office, or provincial Social Security Office in cash or cheque within fifteen days of the following month end. As an example, March contributions are payable before April 15.

Further details about the Social Security Fund are available at the Social Security Office website: www.sso.go.th; or via the Ministry of Labour's website: www.mol.go.th.

Overheads

The main business overheads are usually rent (typically in the range 6,000 baht to 50,000 baht per month) and salaries. If you need a work permit, you must pay personal income tax on a minimum salary of between 25,000 baht and 60,000 baht; so expect to pay about 2,000 baht per month for PIT.

Allow for accountant's fees of at least 2,000 baht per month for preparing tax returns. Other overheads to allow for are electricity, telephone, water, repairs and renewals, replacement of equipment (depreciation), legal fees (including annual licenses), and marketing costs.

Recruiting Staff

Check the work references of prospective employees, and only employ committed staff with good character and personality.

Thais often find it difficult to re-learn work practices. It is much easier to train an inexperienced graduate than to re-train an experienced, more senior person. Fresh graduates are more motivated, easier to hire, cheaper to employ, and are able to learn new skills.

Be aware that more senior Thai employees, particularly professional staff, may have developed inappropriate practices with their previous employers. Furthermore, they may be incapable of working in a new way and they will probably think that their established practices are best.

There are a growing number of recruitment websites where you can advertise for employees; the cost is minimal or free. Refer to "Essential Website Addresses" for online recruitment services.

You may also consider placing free classified advertisements with local or national magazine publishers. Popular newspapers for recruitment advertising include the *Bangkok Post* and *The Nation*. Check "Essential Contacts By Location" for details of local periodicals.

There is a growing number of recruitment agencies in Bangkok matching employers' permanent and temporary recruitment needs in all industrial sectors.

Preventing Theft

Retail businesses are most vulnerable to theft by customers and employees. The extent of theft depends upon the management of the business. There are three key ways of preventing theft and fraud. They are:

- Implementation of internal control procedures
- Segregation of duties between different employees
- Office policy agreed and signed by each employee

Internal Controls

Internal controls are procedures adopted to prevent errors, inefficiencies, or losses. Examples of internal controls are:

- Monthly bank reconciliations to identify any differences between transactions recorded in the cashbook and the bank statement.
- Reimbursement of expenses upon receipt of original purchase receipt and purchase requisition (previously budgeted and signed by a manager).

- Directors or owners sign all company cheques once a week and the manager is responsible for the petty cash.
- Publicize the termination of employment of senior employees
- Encourage customers to pay by credit card or cheque instead of cash.
- Written quotations signed by the manager before submitting them to customers.
- Disallow staff to benefit from the incidence of obsolete or damaged goods.
- Regular stock counts to compare gross profit margins each month.
- Reconciliation between purchase ledger and supplier statements.
- Ensure every employee takes a holiday each year.
- Regular banking of cash and use of a secure safe.
- Closed circuit TV deters theft in retail outlets.
- Sequential numbering in date order of all invoices and order forms.
- Keep the company chequebook and block stamp in a locked drawer.
- Never write a cheque without supporting original invoices and evidence of delivery; stamp 'PAID' on the invoice and note the cheque number on it.

Segregation Of Duties

Reduce the opportunity for fraud by segregating duties among staff. Examples follow:

- Keep responsibility for production (or service fulfilment) separate from accounting and sales.
- Keep responsibility for purchasing separate from sales.

Ideally there would be different departments for cash receipts, cash payments, purchasing, sales, and service fulfilment, but this is not possible in most small businesses.

Ideally the business owner is responsible for ordering all goods from established suppliers.

Fast-food restaurants can prevent theft by having a cashier taking payments in advance, then meals are dispensed upon presentation of printed receipts. No receipt, no meal.

Office Policy

The office policy must be discussed at a staff meeting, properly explained and agreed (in writing) by all members of the staff. Ideally your Thai partner will deal with these sensitive matters. Every employee needs to understand the benefits of the office policy. Do not collect signatures until everyone genuinely agrees with it.

In Thailand the biggest issue to contend with concerns 'gifts,' tips, and kickbacks given to members of the staff. Typical clauses in the office policy dealing with this matter are:

- Any freelance work conducted by employees outside of the company must be reported to the manager.
- There must never be a conflict of interest between employment and freelance activity outside the company.
- All tips, kickbacks, and gifts must be reported to, and approved by, the manager; failure to do so results in immediate dismissal.
- All office documents remain in the office at all times.

Some companies pool all gratuities and gifts given to staff and they are shared equally.

Chapter 8
Profiles Of Successful Businesspeople

Each of the businesses profiled in this section is either highly profitable or successful in other ways. Small businesses such as bars, restaurants, and guesthouses are researched, alongside multimillion-dollar BOI ventures. Some foreign businesspeople, however, are fulfilling their dreams without profit as their primary motive.

Ed Rose finances his wife's cattery, which is highly reputable across at least two continents. Such a 'hobby business' would be prohibitively expensive to operate in most countries, but it works well in Thailand.

Christopher Woodman helped his wife train as a traditional health practitioner while caring for his disabled brother. During this period, Christopher and his wife's family developed a traditional health centre with accommodation for up to twenty guests. This incredible project is a family venture operating on a shoestring (without borrowing any money).

Building Project Management (Start-Up)

Philip Bryce, 47, is from Leeds, UK. After graduating from Leeds University in computer science, he developed operating systems, compilers, and games for Philips and AT&T Bell Labs before moving to Silicon Valley, California. In California, he worked for various start-up and established companies, developing multimedia software. At the same time he collected an MBA from San Francisco State University. Following the success of his music software, 2112design.com, he moved to Thailand to enjoy life to the full.

"I love the Thai people and the country," says Philip from his home on Koh Pha Ngan, which he built in 2005. He lives on the idyllic island, near Koh Samui, with his Thai wife.

Before Philip came to Thailand, his only experience of construction was limited to DIY repairs. After spending time getting familiar with the island and the local culture, he acquired land. Then he proceeded to build his own luxury home, which he occasionally rents to holidaymakers.

Philip maintained a detailed daily journal for his property development project. After completing the building, he realised the potential value of his journal. He used his notes, photographs, and computer-aided designs as a basis for a publication entitled *How To Buy Land And Build A House In Thailand*.

Since his book was published, Philip has been providing a building project management service for foreigners wanting to build their own homes. Other than his website, he has not spent one baht on marketing.

Philip's clients are foreigners from all over the world. Currently Philip is working on two projects consecutively. Philip lives by his philosophy: "If you offer a quality service, eventually the word gets around and customers will seek you out."

Initially, Philip spends time with the client, designing the new home (on CAD software) to suit the requirements. Then he gives the computer design to a Thai architect, who provides detailed drawings.

Philip's approach is 'hands on.' He spends between six and eight hours on site with his Thai foreman each day. His other duties include planning and reporting to his clients via e-mail. He ensures he always has enough "client monies" in advance to pay for materials and labour. Typically he is paid in five instalments (up front).

Philip's foreman manages about twenty construction workers, who build the foundations, form work, and the external structure. Sub-contractors are employed to install doors, windows, plumbing, and electrical, and for other specialist jobs. The foreman deals with all personnel issues relating to the workers.

Philip pays the foreman a percentage of the building cost (on a rolling basis). This way, the foreman is motivated to complete the project quickly. But Philip doesn't accept shoddy workmanship or shortcuts, so he penalizes his foreman for any mistakes.

Philip's wife handles the book-keeping and purchasing of materials. She liaises with the government officers (at the Ministry of Commerce, the Revenue Department and the Labour Department). Philip relieves himself of these tasks with relish.

Many of the construction workers are from Isaan, the rural northeastern region of Thailand. Philip pays them weekly, to assist them with their cash flows. Labour rates in the South are expensive compared to Isaan. The female workers are usually paid a daily rate of 250 baht, and the men get 350 to 450 baht, depending on their skills.

Land prices vary from 700,000 baht per *rai* inland to fifteen million baht for prime beach areas. Building prices are typically two or three million baht for a luxury two- or three-bedroom dream house. A three- or four-bedroom house with three bathrooms and a swimming pool costs in the region of 4.5 million baht.

Nowadays it is more difficult for foreigners to use a limited company to purchase land. They have to prove that all seven company shareholders invested in the company and participate in the profits. Instead, foreigners tend to purchase land in their spouse's name and register a renewable thirty-year lease at the Land Department.

Philip's Tips

- Don't flaunt your success, otherwise jealous people will interfere with your business.
- Risk as little of your own money as possible and never spend money on behalf of clients until they have paid you.
- Keep your administration system up-to-date and organised.
- Spend time researching land and property in your preferred locations before you acquire property rights.

Conclusion

There are unlimited opportunities in Thailand awaiting entrepreneurial people with good ideas. Philip is very clever with his time. This is a good example of a successful business, driven by word of mouth (or networking).

Commercial Real-Estate Services (Start-Up)

Graeme Laird, 60, is from Scotland. He trained in hotel management at the University of Strathclyde, Glasgow, and later took an MBA in hotel management from Michigan State University. Graeme arrived in Thailand in 1974. He worked as resident manager for The Oriental in Bangkok and as GM of the Royal Orchid. In 1996 Graeme founded NAI Andrew Park in Bangkok to provide commercial real-estate services worldwide, with a focus on commercial realty and hotel brokerage. Graeme is NAI Andrew Park president and CEO.

Graeme, who speaks Thai well, says many of his clients come to NAI Andrew Park *because* he speaks Thai. He has negotiated contracts in the Thai language, too. He advises foreigners to accept the local customs, including referral agreements, rather than try to change the way business in done.

Now Graeme has eleven employees. He has one other foreigner working at NAI Andrew Park. His company share capital is sufficient to allow up to four work permits (at two million baht capital per work permit). Graeme is cautious of employing foreign brokers because many applicants do not possess the required professional work ethic. He advises employers to always check CVs/resumés by diligent referencing; a procedure often overlooked in Thailand.

Graeme advertises in the *Bangkok Post* classifieds, various publications offered by the chambers of commerce, *Exclusive Homes*, and the *Phuket Gazette*. The most popular professional real-estate publication in the country is the *Thailand Property Report*.

In 2003 Andrew Park was invited to join the NAI Global professional real-estate network (www.naidirect.com). NAI Global currently represents over 400 offices in forty countries. The network generates quality property enquiries from all over the world. NAI Global's member organizations pay royalties on the fees earned.

NAI Andrew Park is a full service provider specializing in hotel brokerage. Many Thai hotel managers are reticent to release financial information, so investment valuation can be challenging. Typically a hotel in Thailand is valued at a multiple of between seven and ten times net operating profits (or adjusted earnings). If the hotel is under-performing, the multiple will be lower.

A key benefit of living in Bangkok is the access to so many business networking and social clubs and associations. Graeme is a member of the British Chamber of Commerce in Thailand; the Thai-Canadian Chamber of Commerce; the SKAL Club; and the Hotel, Catering, and Institutional Management Association of the UK. Graeme was a committee member of the travel industry's SKAL club. Other clubs of interest include the British Club (www.britishclubbangkok.org) and the Young Europeans Club.

Graeme's Tips

- Whenever investing (anywhere), abide by the motto '*caveat emptor*' ('let the buyer beware') and carry out proper due diligence; this means instructing an independent lawyer to check legally-binding contracts and professional surveyors to assess and value property.

- Anyone considering the purchase of a condominium should not commit until they have checked the condominium management accounts. Establish whether there is a sinking fund to pay for major structural renewals. Are the juristic charges paid on time by the condominium owners? How much money is owed to contractors? Are there any large receivables? If the condominium accounts indicate insolvency, do not proceed.

- Watch your cash flow at all times.

Conclusion

NAI Andrew Park's success is enhanced by Graeme's customer-focus, professionalism, and flexibility. Presentation and attention to social etiquette are critically important in Thailand. This business is a mature and highly professional organization.

For more information about NAI Andrew Park, visit the website at: www.nai-andrewpark.com or www.andrewpark.com.

Organic Farm And Cooking School (Start-Up)

Nathalie Upasuk is Belgian. She visited Thailand in 1998 while working as a tour leader for a Belgian tour operator, shortly after graduating from university. During this contract she met her Thai husband, Sawat, a tour guide and cook. They built their own home and cooking school in Chiang Mai province. They started their school in 2001.

Sawat has focus and determination combined with a passion for cooking, farming, and music. He wanted to establish a cooking school at the age of nineteen. He cooked for tour groups while working as a tour guide, and people commented that he should establish his own cookery school, so that's exactly what he did.

They purchased 6.5 *rai* of land in Sansai (outside Chiang Mai) for only 150,000 baht per *rai*. The land was a paddy field, so Sawat dug a large pond and raised the level of the ground before building their home and school. Sawat managed all contracting activities except for the construction of their house.

The cookery school employs seven local Thais (one driver, two cooks, two teachers, and two gardeners) on a full-time basis. Sawat says many casual labourers—particularly those without a family—disappear when they have enough money and do not show up for work until they have spent everything on *sanuk* (fun). So Sawat employs full-time staff members who have families and are committed to their job.

It takes between two and three months to train a new employee. New workers are usually paid fifty percent of their full salary (plus food) during their training period. The kitchen staff and casual labours are paid cash daily. All staff have one day off each week.

Natalie would like to teach cooking herself, but realizes that customers prefer to be taught by a Thai.

The unique selling point of Thai Farm Cooking School is Sawat's knowledge and experience of organic farming. They grow their own herbs, fruits and vegetables. The fee for the day's cooking course includes transport, meals, tuition and a recipe book.

Sawat's motto is: "Everybody makes money from Thai Farm." Thai Farm shares its success with the local community, employees, friends and anyone referring business to them. They pay commission to agents who introduce customers. Approximately 65 percent of their business originates from their agency agreements; the remaining 35 percent originates from their website, locally distributed brochures and direct enquiries at their office or by telephone.

They offer the course even if just one person attends. All the employees are paid to work full-time, so the additional cost of providing a course for one person is the cost of transport, food and a recipe book. However, they are able to teach a maximum of thirty customers each day; they have two separate rooms for teaching.

Other marketing activities include their online booking system (at www.thaifarmcooking.com), brochure distribution and maintaining a sales office near Thapae Gate in Chiang Mai city. Usually they do not advertise in periodicals.

One threat to their business is the increasing price of petrol, vegetables and consumables. But while overheads and fuel costs have increased, Thai Farm has not increased its prices. Thai Farm charges just 100 baht more than city-based cooking schools to cover the extra cost of transport and farming.

Belgian Nathalie and Sawat with their daughters at Thai Farm

A few businesses have tried to copy the Thai Farm concept, albeit unsuccessfully. The business of organic farming requires knowledge, patience and hard work, so it is not a fast-track to riches. One school started cooking classes on a farm but gave up after a few days. The latest copycat employs a former Thai Farm cook.

Sawat And Nathalie's Tips

- Try to minimize your initial investment and keep your overhead to a minimum.
- Do what you enjoy and are most knowledgeable about.
- Stay calm.
- Allow one year for similar building projects.
- Control your own business and don't trust others to do it for you.

Conclusion

The organic farm and cooking school is successful because green-fingered Sawat is passionate about farming and cooking. It's not an easy business to manage, which is why many 'wannabes' have failed. The jewel of their marketing strategy is their referral programme, which spreads out to over 100 guesthouses and travel agencies. Thai Farm has an excellent reputation and many people say it's the best in northern Thailand.

For further information about Natalie and Sawat's cooking school, check out their website: www.thaifarmcooking.com. For information about their educational travel programmes for schools, refer to their website at: www.thaiedutravel.com.

Marketing Consultancy (Start-Up)

Scott Minteer, 33, is from Massachusetts. After studying for his degree, he worked in Colorado for Hewlett Packard's marketing department. He worked as business development manager for Asia providing seminars and training throughout Southeast Asia. He visited Asia four times each year. In December 2003 he moved to Bangkok, where he established his independent marketing consultancy, known as the Brandmade Company.

Scott loves Thailand and he learned to speak, read and write the language over a period of six years. He enjoys living in the diverse multicultural community of Bangkok, which offers an abundant range of activities. He enjoys visiting the beaches of Krabi and rock-climbing.

Scott formed a company under the Treaty of Amity and Economic Relations, so he owns 99.4 percent of the share capital. The remaining six Thai shareholders own 0.1 percent each. Only US citizens are eligible for this special privilege. The cost of forming the Amity company was 65,000 baht including both legal fees and government fees.

For additional information about Treaty of Amity companies, refer to "What You Need To Know Before You Start."

The Brandmade Company designs websites, corporate logos and brochures as well as providing copyrighting services. Most of Scott's clients are SMEs, though he has some multinational clients. His marketing strategy combines extensive networking, a corporate website and referral programmes.

Scott is a seasoned social and business networker. During 2004 he attended four or five social events each week. His favourite clubs are Moby Elite, Bangkok Young Professionals, XL Results Foundation, chamber-sponsored events and Toastmasters. Scott e-mails a comprehensive Bangkok events calendar to his subscribers twice a month. You can subscribe to this by registering online at: www.thebrandmade.com.

Scott is the president of the Capital Club, a branch of Toastmasters (www.toastmasters.org), which is a US-based non-profit organization for professionals keen to hone their communication and networking skills. There are several branches of Toastmasters in Bangkok (and in other parts of Thailand), though the Capital Club has the highest proportion of expat members.

Scott warns advertisers about the lack of demographic information available in Thailand. In the US and Europe, periodical publishers provide their advertisers with media packages containing detailed circulation and readership statistics. In Thailand this data is not usually available, so advertising media can only be tested by trial and error.

Scott's Tips

- Establish referral programmes with complementary service providers.
- Promote your message clearly and succinctly and offer a reason for readers to book an immediate meeting.
- Book a series of advertisements for optimal results, rather than one-off displays.
- Prioritize your marketing messages and consider the need for extra space if you use copy in both Thai and English.
- Ensure you advertise in the appropriate section of each publication.
- Keep positive and motivated at all times.

Conclusion

Scott is extremely positive and energetic. Most of his marketing effort is directed towards networking at professional clubs. However, he has an impressive website and events calendar, which is an effective and inexpensive way of generating enquiries. Scott is working in a competitive market without any significant advantage, other than his marketing skills. He lacks a committed Thai partner or representative with established contacts.

For more information about Scott Minteer's Brandmade consultancy, or about events in Bangkok, visit his website: www.thebrandmade.com.

Business Brokering (Franchise)

Greg Lange, 48, is from Florida. He worked with Sunbelt Business Advisors for over 25 years. He was employed at Sunbelt's corporate headquarters in Charleston, South Carolina, where he was involved with franchise development and business brokering. In 2001 he married his Thai wife, Nui. The following year he invested in Sunbelt Asia and opened an office in Bangkok.

Since 2003 Greg has established six Subway franchises in Bangkok and one Chester's Grill. Sunbelt Asia Business Advisors is the most successful business brokerage in Thailand, with offices in Bangkok, Pattaya, Koh Samui and Chiang Mai. Greg is managing director of Sunbelt Asia, which currently employs 76 people.

Sunbelt Asia earns most of its revenue from business and legal services, providing assistance with visas, work permits, company formation, tax and accounting services. Sunbelt also promotes independent businesses (or going concerns) for sale. It also acts as broker for real estate, from condominiums to luxury resorts. Greg even offers serviced office facilities with executive desks.

Fort Lauderdale, known as the 'Sunbelt' area of America, is where many Americans relocate for retirement. Some operate restaurants for four or five years before fully retiring. There are more restaurants per capita in Fort Lauderdale than in any other part of the USA. This is how Greg acquired specialist knowledge of the restaurant trade.

Greg's wife, Nui, previously vice president of the CP Group, is his reason for being in Thailand. She works full-time for Sunbelt Asia and owns 25 percent of the share capital of the Amity Treaty company. She is the primary contact with government agencies and their Thai employees. She is also involved with staff training at head office and their sub-franchises. Nui has high status in Thai society, and Thais are most obliging and respectful to such people. Nui is therefore Greg's ideal Thai representative because of her social position and also because of her business acumen. In 1998, before she met Greg, she was involved in a 13.7 billion baht business merger between Tesco and Lotus.

Greg owns Sunbelt's master franchise for Southeast Asia. Sunbelt franchises were already in place for Hong Kong and Singapore when Greg started in 2002. His territory also includes Vietnam, Cambodia, Malaysia, the Philippines, Laos, Burma and Indonesia.

Most of Sunbelt's marketing activity is Internet-based because his target market is foreigners. The company's weekly newsletter is sent out to 19,000 subscribers. Sunbelt receives 300 e-mail enquiries daily, 25 percent of which relate to brokerage.

Greg says that most advertising in publications is unprofitable. However, he continues to advertise in *The Big Chilli* because he likes the magazine. He also advertises daily in the *Bangkok Post*. Sunbelt Asia is prominently displayed on the following websites: www.thaivisa.com, www.bahtsold.com, www.stickmanbangkok.com, www.sunbeltnetwork.com and www.businessesforsale.com.

There are many advantages to either buying an existing business or a franchise. Starting a business independently from nothing is a challenge, even in one's home country. Franchisees buy a proven product, a recognised brand name and established management systems. A big advantage is the ability to earn a profit straight away. Usually the business seller will provide training, support and contacts until the new owner has settled in.

Both Sunbelt and Subway are successful franchises. Greg says he usually budgets for a total investment of four million baht for each Subway outlet in Bangkok. These outlets generate an average monthly profit of 100,000 baht (from the day the store opens). The results depend upon the store's location, though the average return on investment is thirty percent.

But not all franchises have been successful in Thailand. TGI Friday and Wendy's restaurant chains both failed in the Land of Smiles. Furthermore, some franchisees fail in Thailand if they do not have sufficient capital or the right personality.

Subway franchises provide a sophisticated inventory management system that highlights any possible theft. Inventory is checked weekly and any variances from budget are investigated. Theft by branch managers is limited by their POS (payment on sale) system and strict control over suppliers used.

Refer to the "Franchising" section for further information on this subject.

Greg's Tips

- If you have passion about what you are doing, everything else will fall into place, so get into a business you will enjoy.
- Be aware of the 80/20 rule; twenty percent of your staff will generate eighty percent of the business.
- Think twice about buying a 'hobby business'—meaning limited commitment—because many half-hearted ventures fail.

- The foreign chambers of commerce based in Bangkok, including the US Commercial Service, provide useful business research data in their members' library.

Conclusion

Greg is passionate about his business and he does it well. But much of the success must be attributed to Nui. Sunbelt deals with a large volume of business at competitive prices. Subway franchises, if managed properly in a good location, offer a reasonable return on investment at relatively low risk.

For further information about Sunbelt Asia and Subway franchises, visit Greg Lange's website: www.sunbeltasia.com.

Traditional Health Centre (Start-Up)

Christopher Woodman, 66, is originally from the US but has lived most of his life in England and France. He now lives with his Thai wife, Homprang, at their traditional health centre. In his own words, Christopher is an overly educated, under-achieving dreamer with degrees from Columbia, Yale and Cambridge universities. His last job was at Chiang Mai University. He has also built several sailing boats and has worked as a sailing journalist and charter skipper. Homprang, 49, is a qualified practitioner and teacher of Thai traditional medicine, herbal pharmacology and massage therapy.

Christopher is a tall, cultured man. He does not regard his health centre as a business but rather as a self-sufficient family project that provides a quality lifestyle for his extended Thai family of thirteen, including five children, none of whom are his. Christopher has a high regard for Thai people, their culture and customs, and he constantly praises Homprang and her family.

Christopher's physically handicapped older brother had lived alone in Thailand in his wheelchair for ten years before Christopher arrived in 1995. Sadly the brother was hit by a drunken pick-up truck driver one night in May 1994 and suffered very serious additional injuries, including brain damage. Christopher came to Thailand as quickly as he could to help his brother in the hospital, and ended up caring for him until his death in September 2006.

Christopher's future wife, Homprang, had studied English with his brother for two years before the accident, and Christopher fell in love with her while they were looking after his brother in the hospital. After they married, they built a house around the brother, and Homprang began to study Thai traditional medicine. She is now a licensed traditional doctor, pharmacologist and midwife. With the help of her family, Christopher and

Homprang have, little by little, developed the beautiful place where they now live.

This is a story of a visionary couple who patiently oversaw the development of a unique, traditional Thai health centre over a ten-year period. This centre provides employment for both the family and the community. The skills taught and practiced by Homprang, her two brothers and their wives, are all rooted in traditional Thai culture.

Christopher Woodman blends into Thai Culture at Baan Hom

Christopher developed three *rai* of land in Saraphi over a period of five years. There are twelve traditional wooden buildings situated in an orchard of *lamyai* trees. Two buildings contain steam baths; five provide guest rooms; three accommodate Christopher and his family; one *sala* is used for teaching and another *sala*, situated above a pool, is used for massage therapy.

Christopher purchased two plots of land adjacent to each other ten years ago. He paid 1.5 million baht for the total of three *rai*. The land, the houses, and the business are all in Homprang's name, and Christopher has no control over any of them.

Christopher purchased the wood and houses from local families who were no longer interested in living in such simple and outdated buildings. Typically he paid between 20,000 baht and 50,000 baht for each house. Christopher's family disassembled each house and transported the pieces, bit by bit, in the family pick-up truck to their own land. Naturally, Homprang and her family helped with the negotiations, not only to get an appropriate price but to respect the sensitivities of the old owners who were, after all, selling their own family homes.

Christopher financed the building project out of his 60,000 baht per month US property income. He spent 3.6 million baht on materials and salaries for his family workers. The total investment of five million baht over ten years, including all family living expenses, were financed by his US income. There were no loans, but there were also no profits.

A very unusual aspect of all this is that Christopher and his brother lived in Thailand for three years without valid visas. The task of transporting his bed-ridden brother to Chiang Mai's Immigration office had become more and more difficult each year, and eventually Christopher simply gave up. Once his brother's visa had been allowed to expire, Christopher didn't dare to renew his own. His main concern was that the authorities would deport his brother, and he ended up living in a very precarious way in order to protect him.

In October 2006, the Thai government introduced new visa regulations, and by a quirk of fate it was just ten days before the law was enforced that Christopher's brother finally died. Christopher finally explained his story to Immigration officers, first in Chiang Mai and then in Mae Sai. He took a letter from his Thai doctor explaining the exceptional circumstances. The Immigration officers were amazed that both foreigners had overstayed their visas by three years without getting caught. Under Thai law the maximum penalty for overstay is 20,000 baht. This fine does not apply to deceased persons. Christopher explained that he rarely left his village and never travelled outside Chiang Mai province for three years, which is why he had never been apprehended.

Christopher paid a fine of 20,000 baht for his three-year overstay, and has now acquired a fully valid Retirement visa. Christopher says the Immigration officers were very helpful and understanding, but he would never recommend anyone try the same stunt. Visas have a very real purpose in any country, and he says he cannot think of any other reason why anyone should do what he did.

Refer to "What You Need To Know Before You Start" for more information about visas.

The health centre's marketing activities include poster and brochure distribution, and referral agreements. Christopher designed the centre's website: www.homprang.com.

Christopher's Tips

- Never overstay your visa.
- Learn how Thai people think and feel, and try your best not only to respect their customs, but to understand them. Dress appropriately all the time, don't shout or point or criticize anyone, and be prepared to realize that many of your own

assumptions are even more ridiculous than the Thai ones you laugh at.

- Develop a trusting relationship with a Thai who is willing to communicate on your behalf, and who can guide you through the labyrinth of Thai customs and etiquette.
- Never forget that for a Thai, family will always come first. If you buy anything from the family of a friend or even spouse, do not assume your friend or spouse will protect you from being cheated by other family members, because they won't. Indeed, try never to put a friend or spouse in that position.

Conclusion

Christopher used his teaching skills and creativity to care for his brother, his wife, her family and the local community. We reap what we sow; I feel certain that Christopher's kindness will be reciprocated during his retirement. Thailand offers many advantages to retirees. Currently there are no estate (or death) taxes. Thais respect and care for old people, particularly those who have paid their dues

Luxury Spa Services (Start-Up)

Toby Allen, 45, is from Florida. He worked for a tour operator in China and Hong Kong for eight years, then as executive director of an American company, setting up control systems for new offices worldwide. After living "the American dream," Toby moved to Southeast Asia to unwind and relax. In 1998 he came to live in Thailand, where he established an orphanage in Fang and a chain of branded luxury spas.

Since 1984 Toby has helped under-privileged children in Romania and China. He came to Thailand to fulfil his dream of establishing an orphanage before staring his spa business. "Thailand is a country which allows many people to realize their dreams instead of shelving the ideas until a day which never arrives," he says.

For Toby, the administrative process of forming a charitable foundation in the mountainous area of northern Thailand was a bureaucratic marathon lasting eighteen months. It was necessary to provide evidence that the project was humanitarian and free of any self-interest, because the legal status of a registered foundation facilitates fund-raising and sponsorship by NGOs and other non-profit organizations.

The orphanage comprises seven buildings, on 25 *rai* of land, that accommodate fifty orphans. Toby lived and worked in Fang for four years.

In 2002 Toby and his Thai partner, Pakin Ploywaen, researched the market for luxurious health spas in Chiang Mai. There were 35 spas in

Chiang Mai in 2002, of which just ten provided a full range of health treatments. Toby and Pakin decided to develop a mid- to upper-class spa, offering several traditional health treatments including Ayurvedic massage, aromatherapy and herbal treatments.

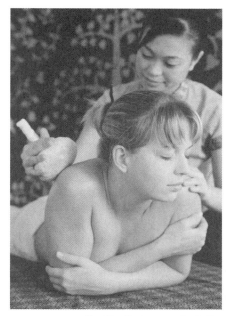

Healthy Business at Oasis Spa

They started the Oasis Spa in 2003. Now there are four Oasis spas in Chiang Mai and one in Bangkok. Their clientele includes members of the royal family, politicians and media stars; in other words, the brand is successful.

Toby and Pakin complement each other perfectly for this business. Toby is responsible for administration, planning, control systems and marketing. Pakin's expertise is in personnel development, training, customer service and aesthetic design.

Toby believes the reason for their success is their policy for staff recruitment and training. It takes up to twelve months to train each employee. They spent two months training staff before opening their first spa. Staff development is a long-term investment in the business's most valuable assets.

Good character and personality are the key qualities Toby and Pakin seek in their recruits. Age, beauty and experience are relatively unimportant. Many of the spa's workers are employed immediately after completing their university education.

Now, Oasis employs 150 people in five locations. Half of the employees are therapists and the rest are support staff (including buyers, accountants, call-centre staff and drivers).

Oasis Spas' most potent marketing medium is referral and repeat business based upon high quality service. Toby promotes his brand in magazines (although he says there is a lack of quality magazines in Thailand reaching the high-end Thai market), at brochure stands, on their websites and with standard referral agreements (at hotels and other appropriate venues).

Each of the Oasis spas is linked by a sophisticated computer network, allowing real-time, multi-location reservations management. This system enables call-centre staff to divert drivers to a different centre if a spa becomes fully booked.

Toby's Tips

- Take special care of your employees and train them to provide a high quality service.
- Offer the highest possible standard of service and pay attention to details.
- Consider the quality of a magazine's distribution when planning your advertising schedule.

Conclusion

The US formula for success is to build an empire, become a politician, and perhaps toss a little excess towards NGOs (in return for publicity). Toby's first mission in Thailand was the establishment of the charitable foundation (with his own money). He made a valuable contribution towards Thai society *before* starting his business. The key theme throughout the development of Oasis is a high standard of quality control, particularly in all relationships with partners, employees and customers.

For additional information about Oasis Spas, visit their website: www. bangkokoasis.com.

Boutique Guesthouse (Start-Up And Building Project)

Laurie Simmons, fifty, is from Sydney, Australia. He worked with both the Australian Federal Police and the Commonwealth Police for over twenty years before establishing a successful vehicle rental business in Sydney with his Thai wife, Orapin. In 2000, Laurie and Orapin relocated to Thailand. Then, in 2006, they built the Mini Cost boutique guesthouse near Thapae Gate, Chiang Mai. The building project lasted one year, and since completion in March 2006, the guesthouse has been fully booked.

Laurie also works as a volunteer for the Thai Tourist Police (www. touristpolice.net) in Chiang Mai. Volunteers are employed to act as intermediaries between the local Tourist Police and foreigners. Duties include interpretation and offering guidance to troubled tourists and expatriates. Laurie says this community work is rewarding and it enables him to meet a lot of people, including dignitaries.

Laurie noticed there were numerous rooms available in Chiang Mai in the price range of 100 to 300 baht per night; and many luxury rooms costing over 3,000 baht per night. So Laurie and Orapin decided to target mid-range customers, at an average daily rate of 800 baht. The research

Orapin with Laurie in his Tourist Police Uniform

paid off and Mini Cost is successful.

What makes a boutique guesthouse? Spacious and tastefully decorated rooms, Internet, and details like using air atomisers to keep rooms fresh. Orapin joined a two-week government course on managing boutique hotels to stay ahead.

Note: any advertisement containing the word 'boutique' generates over three times as many enquiries!

Laurie sourced the land and acquired it for five million baht. **If you want to buy land, ask an official (from the local Land Office) to survey the property and provide a valuation.** There is a fixed fee for this service. Usually the value estimated by the Land Office is slightly lower than market value, because many people selling land report a lower selling price to reduce the property transfer fees (which comprise stamp duty and Specific Business Tax). Refer to "Leasing Land" for more information about acquiring property rights in Thailand.

Laurie formed a limited company to purchase the land. The company borrowed from the bank (using the land as security) to finance the building project. Laurie says the bank was very helpful with monitoring the progress of construction and identifying any defects. This resulted in higher quality workmanship. Refer to "Forming A Limited Company" for further information.

Initially, Laurie employed a firm of builders to demolish the existing buildings and erect the basic structure of the building. Later, he took over as project manager, allocating work to specialist contractors on the basis of their quotations.

Materials and labour cost ten million baht, so the total cost, including land, of this twenty-room luxury guesthouse was fifteen million baht. Within six months of completing the project, Laurie was offered 24 million baht for the property.

Their monthly income, including motorcycle rental, laundry and Internet is over 330,000 baht. The return on investment is over 25 percent.

Laurie says he cannot achieve such a high return on his Australian investments.

Orapin manages their three employees, including her niece. Laurie credits his wife with adept negotiating skills. Laurie "sticks to the knitting" with planning and preparation of contracts.

Most customers are referred to Mini Cost by satisfied customers. The website generates three or four enquiries each day. Laurie uses a professional photographer to enhance both the website and brochure.

Orapin says they receive many enquiries from *The Rough Guide To Thailand* (www.roughguides.com), which categorises Mini Cost in the medium price range and describes it as a "Smart new place located just around the corner from Thapae Gate offering spacious rooms, all tastefully furnished and with staff that are eager to please." Correct!

Laurie's Tips

- Choose your location carefully, especially for a guesthouse.
- Obtain permission from the authorities to demolish buildings.
- Thoroughly research the business and the Thai bureaucratic systems and procedures. Laurie believes there are numerous business opportunities in Thailand for foreigners with business skills and cash if they learn to work with the local systems and procedures.
- Use the best professionals, including lawyers and accountants; if you are not referred to a suitable professional, ask at your embassy.
- Pay your contractors progressively for work done; never pay in advance, or you lose control.
- Source your own contractors and suppliers to save referral fees of at least ten percent.
- **Ask your contractors to sign an agreement containing a penalty clause to prevent them missing the deadline.**

Conclusion

This is a model case study of how to conduct business in Thailand successfully. Working as a volunteer with the local Tourist Police is a sure way of securing status in the community and contributing to society. All the *really* successful foreign businesspeople in Thailand give their time or money to some worthy cause.

For more information about Mini Cost boutique guesthouse, refer to the website: www.minicostcm.com.

Financial Services (Start-Up)

Alan Hall, 48, is from Lancashire, England. He has worked as a financial advisor for over 22 years and is registered with the Financial Services Authority (FSA). Alan married a Thai lady in England before moving to Thailand in 2001. He is a partner in a mortgage brokerage in Burnley, northern England. In Thailand he heads a company called Personal Finance Management (PFM), which offers advice on investments and taxation issues. PFM is based at the ICO law office, near Payap University. Alan has a mutually beneficial business relationship with the local law firm, and he has two foreign financial consultants working for him.

Alan is easy to identify as the 'foreigner who wears a tie' in Chiang Mai. His style is affable and low key, rather than the stereotypical 'hard sell' associated with the financial services industry.

When Alan came to live in Thailand he worked in Pattaya every other three-month period, and he worked for his Burnley firm in between Asian stints. He loathed the unsettled lifestyle, but since reducing his share in the UK firm, thereby relinquishing control, he has been able to stay in Thailand full-time.

Alan offers advice about investments, insurance, mortgage finance and taxation. His firm in the UK arranges re-mortgages for expats owning property in the UK. Occasionally he acts as broker for clients wanting to buy condominiums in Thailand.

Alan's latest product for expats—SOS Chiang Mai—offers real peace of mind. SOS provides bilingual volunteers to work with officials at the local Immigration office, and provides representation in the event of detention by the police or Immigration, or hospitalization or death. The premium is 2,000 baht per annum. Alan has a second work permit for SOS Chiang Mai. The website address of SOS Chiang Mai is: www.soschiangmai.com.

If your home or business is registered in your Thai spouse's name, you and your spouse should write separate wills and get them signed at the local *amphur* office. If the legal document is signed by *amphur* officials, it cannot be contested in the courts of law. Independently prepared wills (or wills prepared by lawyers) can be contested in court.

If your spouse dies intestate (without a valid will) a house and business registered in your spouse's name would normally be transferred to the spouse's family. Therefore your spouse should clarify his or her intentions concerning probate and appropriation of their property. Usually the spouse would write a will bequeathing the house and business to their spouse who originally paid for the property.

Alan Hall offers an inexpensive will preparation service. He arranges the translation into Thai and certification of the document at the local *amphur* office.

Alan is president of the Chiang Mai Expats' Club. The club, whose motto is 'Expats helping expats,' has over 500 members and convenes twice every month. It attracts high profile speakers from all walks of life, including documentary producers and well-known writers. There are interest groups for computing, photography, learning Thai and writing. The club is a great place for networking and support. It has its own newsletter with details of upcoming events. The club's website address is www.chiangmaiexpatsclub.com.

Most of the successful businesspeople profiled in this book have a desire to make some contribution to Thailand. Alan wants to raise public awareness about road safety. Thailand, which has a similar population to the UK, has over fifty times more deaths on the road.

Most of Alan's business originates from referrals. His marketing philosophy is based on professionalism, networking and ethics. Satisfied clients refer Alan to their friends, and he does not usually advertise in periodicals.

Alan explains that he often sacrifices short-term gain for long-term success. It may be in a client's best interest to defer the purchase of an investment or to buy a product which kicks back less commission to the financial advisor.

Conclusion

Alan is an excellent financial advisor, networker, and marketer. Everything necessary for establishing a successful business in Thailand is in place: president of the local expats' club, a low cost local insurance product to generate enquiries, a shared office with a local law firm and a mortgage brokerage in the UK.

For further information on any of the services listed in this profile, Alan may be contacted via Chiang Mai Expats' Club or SOS Chiang Mai.

Book Store (Start-Up)

George Goldberg, fifty, is from San Francisco. He worked as a concierge at hotels in California, and visited Thailand for the first time in 1989; it was his first trip outside North America. Initially, George worked as an English teacher in Thailand, but in May 2000 he borrowed money from a fellow bookworm to start a book store in Chiang Mai. By 2006, George owned four book stores in the city.

George's main qualification for running the bookshop is his appetite for reading books and an appreciation of the needs of his customers. He had no prior business experience.

When George started Gecko Books there was only one other used book store in Chiang Mai, but that shop did not meet George's literary needs. One of George's friends, who also loved reading and travelling, offered him finance to start the business. George says they both wanted a book store with a wider range of books. Gecko Books fulfils their literary needs and provides a good living for George.

Initially George rented a single shophouse and incorporated a Thai limited company to own the business and sponsor his work permit. George now works full-time as business manager.

George's main challenge is to source suitable books. Internet search engines enable him to identify used-book dealers around the world. His preferred supplier of used spiritual books is in Delhi, India. Buying used books in bulk is risky because the selection is broad and some books will not sell, so George travels regularly to source new suppliers.

George's partners are active in the business and add value to the company, which employs over ten staff. All the employees have previous experience working in English book stores. They relate to each other like family. George even allows his staff to select new employees.

Competition: The Two King George's of the Book World

Gecko Books has increasing local competition. Since 2000, the number of used bookshops in Chiang Mai has grown from one to fourteen. George claims that competition encourages him to open new stores. By 2006 he had opened his fourth store.

George's main competitor—also called George—is based next to Gecko's main store. The other George owns Backstreet Books and supplies Hobo Books, which is only fifty metres away from George Goldberg's Thapae Books. It is a real-life game of Monopoly in the world of used bookshops.

Gecko buys back books from customers at fifty percent of the original selling price (if returned within a month). George's target gross profit margin is over 100 percent. Some books remain on the shelves for years and are given away eventually. Although the gross profit margin is relatively high, George needs to allow for many stock write-offs. Gecko's success is due to the diversity of inventory.

Eighty percent of his customers are tourists looking for books recommended by their friends. The remaining twenty percent are residents seeking bargains.

All four of George's shops use prominent signage. George advertises in many magazines, his favourite being *Citylife*. He believes that most advertising pays for itself.

George is planning to open a fifth branch in Chiang Mai. He also found a partner to start a book store in Bangkok. He is developing an inventory tracking system for his estimated 65,000 books and is considering selling holistic products to health spas. He is interested in natural medicine, which is a popular subject for his backpacking customers. Gecko Books has a website at: www.geckobooks.net.

George's Tips

- Do what you enjoy. If you do what you enjoy, you are more likely to survive the hard times.
- Success in the book trade depends on diverse stock of marketable titles, so selection of suppliers is the key to success.

Conclusion

George has excelled since 2000, when he started in business with neither experience nor much money. He is an aggressive marketer and is willing to experiment with new advertising media. His business is vulnerable to tourism fluctuations, particularly the numbers of backpackers visiting northern Thailand, but he would appear to be winning this particular version of Monopoly.

Anthony McDonald's Start-Ups

Anthony McDonald, 41, is from Sydney, where he studied at the University of New South Wales and with the Securities Institute of Australia. He moved to Thailand in 1990 after marrying his Thai wife, whom he met at university in Australia. During 1994 and 1995, Anthony studied for an MSc in marketing at Bangkok's Thammasat University. This two-year, part-time course (which is in English) has an excellent reputation internationally. Anthony, who graduated with first-class honours, was the only Western student on the course, and he made excellent contacts.

Anthony successfully established businesses in vehicle distribution, IT consulting, and property development. Each of these three businesses is profiled below under the following headings:

- Vehicle Distribution
- IT Consulting
- Branded Resort Hotels

Vehicle Distribution (Start-Up)

In 1990 Anthony started the Rover cars Thailand country distributorship in Bangkok. He developed the business from three staff to over 300 within three years; in the fourth year, turnover exceeded eighty million US dollars.

Anthony's wife's family owns a vehicle assembly plant and distributorships in Thailand, so he already had access to the industry knowledge. He carried out feasibility studies for the start-up of an exclusive Rover Group (Rover/Land Rover/MG) distributorship in the country. When the Thai government slashed import duties on Rover cars from 600 percent to 150 percent in 1992, Anthony's Thai Ultimate Car Co., Ltd. really took off.

Anthony established eight wholly owned Rover/Land Rover/MG dealerships in Bangkok. He visited vehicle dealers country-wide to establish new distribution contracts for the Rover Group. Many of these dealerships were family businesses, and often different family members would be responsible for each brand of vehicle.

When the Rover Group in the UK was taken over by BMW, Thai Ultimate Thai Car Co. was downgraded from distributor to dealer. Anthony resigned as GM of the company in 2000, and his wife took over the reins.

For the first eight months, the distribution company had to pay for the vehicles by letter of credit; then, after a positive track record of trading, Anthony was allowed 'open account' credit terms. During the 1997 economic crisis, the banks immediately withdrew the company's credit facility (worth several million dollars), so it was necessary to switch back to the original letter of credit terms.

IT Consulting (Start-Up)

From 2000 to 2005, Anthony established an IT consulting firm called Hyro Consulting. Hyro, a BOI company, specializes in Microsoft technology solutions; their clients include IBM, AIS, the Bank of Thailand, Bangkok Bank, GE Capital and Lehman Brothers. Anthony built up the company from three staff to over 100. In 2005, Hyro made a partnership deal with an Australian IT consulting firm and eventually sold out entirely.

Anthony McDonald's team at Hyro

Hyro is a Board of Investment company, so it was granted an initial six-year tax holiday. Details concerning BOI incentives for foreign investment in Thailand are available on the website: www.boi.go.th. Hyro was formed as a 100 percent foreign-owned company because it is an IT consulting company.

Anthony quips that he has developed highly successful personnel "cloning techniques." Hyro employees look the same, eat the same food, and even wear the same clothes. Most of his trainee consultants were 22-24-year-old Thai-Chinese graduates of King Mongkut's Institute of Technology.

Recruitment and training in consulting firms is critically important. Anthony tests job applicants using psychometrics and in-house technical examinations, and he checks references thoroughly. He recruited a dozen fresh graduates every six months, with starting salaries for these IT wiz-kids at around 12,000 baht per month.

Branded Resort Hotels (Start-Up)

Anthony is now establishing Thailand's first chain of designer resorts (to be branded "X2 Resorts"), which he is starting in Hua Hin and Koh Samui.

Since 1994, he has also been managing an international property company called Astudo. Whenever his family has spare cash, they invest in quality property for long-term growth. Over ten years, the property investment firm has achieved ten percent annual capital growth with an average return on investment of forty percent. Currently, Astudo is investing in beach resorts throughout Thailand.

Anthony's Tips

- Give careful consideration to your selection of a Thai partner or representative, because the wrong choice can be costly.
- Establish a well-defined corporate culture and carefully recruit team players to fit the specification.

- Set the firm's standard of professionalism; communicate the company's expectations of employees to all staff; release staff that fail to meet the defined standards.
- Always adhere to the Thai labour laws.

Conclusion

Anthony's experiences demonstrate that with adept management skills, sound contacts and capital, it's possible to succeed in almost any industry in Thailand. He thoroughly researched each business, conducted feasibility studies, and drafted workable business plans for each venture. University graduates are Anthony's main source of first-class employees. Anthony's management style is sufficiently flexible to cope with the ever-changing political and economic climate of Thailand.

Further information is available at the following websites: www.astudo.com; www.biz-concierge.com; and www.x2resorts.com.

A Cattery

Ed Rose, 74, is from Philadelphia. He worked as a technical researcher and systems engineer, and later as a land reform advisor in Vietnam. He has been living in Thailand since 1975.

In 1981, Ed and his Thai wife, Malee, started up their Chiang Mai Cattery. Ever since, they have won numerous competitions at cat shows in Bangkok. The cattery is well known in the cat world, particularly in America, and their felines have been featured in newspapers; appeared on BBC

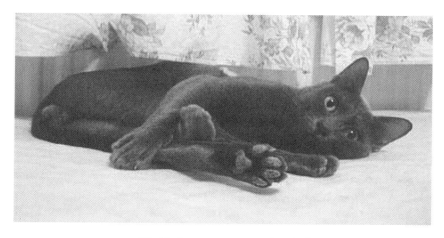

The Thai government recognises the korat as a national treasure

Television; appeared as models on several of Thailand's postage stamps, on a calendar for the electronics giant, Panasonic, and were photographed for the book *Siamese Cats: Legends And Reality* by Martin R. Clutterbuck, published by White Lotus Press.

In their heyday, Ed and Malee kept 108 cats, but these days they only have about thirty. The breeds are mainly Siamese, Korat and Burmese.

Many Thais dump unwanted cats in temples, but Ed and Malee really care about the welfare of cats, and want to educate people about how to care for felines. Ed hopes there will one day be a Cat Fanciers' Association of Thailand.

Ed also works part-time as an English teacher at Chiang Mai University's Faculty of Medicine. He enjoys reading, computing and amateur radio.

Ed does not regard the cattery as a business. "Really it's an expensive and time-consuming hobby," he says—although an extremely successful one.

Ed is chairman of the board of directors and record-keeper. There is one full-time employee who cleans the cattery and feeds the animals twice a day. Malee supervises their employee and organizes the diet and routine healthcare of the cats.

Ed rarely advertises in periodicals, but he and Malee promote their cattery in the following ways:

- Registration with the Cat Fanciers' Association of the USA
- Presentations at local clubs, including the Rotary Club and the Informal Northern Thai Group
- Word-of-mouth and referrals resulting from awards at the Bangkok cat shows

Ed's Tips

- Commit yourself to stay in Thailand for an extended period; don't come here to earn a fast buck.
- Make the effort to learn the Thai language.
- Establish a relationship with a confident, ethical Thai person of good character as partner and manager.
- Respect the Thai culture and customs.
- Work together with Thai people as equals.

Conclusion

Ed and Malee's hobby business is very successful and provides them with a great deal of pleasure. Ed admits that he would not be able to afford such a pastime in America. The Chiang Mai Cattery offers a valuable service and contribution to the local community by raising public awareness about how to care for cats.

For further information about the Chiang Mai Cattery, phone: + 66 (0)53 282-272, or contact the Cat Fanciers' Association of the USA or KCFA (www.koratworld.com/kcfa.html).

The Bar Trade (Start-Up)

The Number 1 place to advertise

Freddy Laureys, 46, is from Belgium where he ran his own food and beverage businesses. He started his life in Thailand in 1999 and describes his first year in the country as a full-time holiday. He started a bar in Phuket, which he ran for four years before selling out to his business partner. Then he opened the Number 1 Bar in Chiang Mai. He enjoys a good living with his Thai wife, Joi.

The Number 1 Bar is clean and friendly, with free Internet and a pool table. Freddy sells Belgian beer as well as local beers. There is a 'chill-out' area with comfortable sofas and armchairs and the staff members are courteous and friendly.

Freddy found the double-unit property himself by driving around the city and "knocking on doors." The premises, which are twenty metres from a main road, were previously used as a massage parlour. Freddy paid no premium or 'key money' to the landlord. The business is now worth over two million baht and there are many potential buyers.

Joi trains the bar's sixteen employees. Freddy offers a one week's trial; if successful, the applicants are offered an employment contract. After six months, they can join the government health insurance scheme; half of these insurance contributions are paid by the employer.

The employees wear 'Number 1'-designed shirts at work, with a different colour for each day of the week. On birthdays and other special occasions they can wear free-style in accordance with the assigned colour of the day.

Joi explains that when a member of staff makes a mistake, she always waits until the following morning to discuss the matter face to face. This approach prevents any potential for loss of face (and loss of staff).

Freddy does not advertise in the local free magazines; instead he draws customers via his website, through *tuk-tuk* advertising and sponsorship of Chiang Mai golfers. The bar also participates in the local pool league.

Joi says that eighty percent of the bar's customers are residents of Chiang Mai. Most customers are from the USA, the UK and various European countries.

Freddy advertises the bar on 100 *tuk-tuks*. Contracts are for a minimum of three months at a rate of 150 baht per *tuk-tuk* per month. Freddy is satisfied with the results.

The customers have developed three websites for the bar, including: www.nr1pub.com and www.number1barthailand.com. The websites receive 60,000 hits each month because they are well-connected and ranked highly by the major search engines. Number 1's website has a page for the bar staff.

Freddy asks his customers to complete feedback forms. The completed questionnaires enable him to refine his marketing plan. So customers get what they want.

Freddy is also a member of the Chiang Mai Expats Club. Refer to the "Financial Services" profile for more information about the club.

Freddy's Tips

- Research your project thoroughly and don't rush into business.
- Train your staff properly and look after them.
- Avoid partnerships (unless necessary).
- Use a Thai limited company to protect your investment.
- If you are in a tourist-related business, develop a local clientele to support your trade during the low season.
- Look after your health and take regular exercise.

Conclusion

Freddy knows the trade well and he runs the bar efficiently. How many bars do you know that use customer feedback forms? Customer service is a high priority. The bar draws expatriate pool players, golfers, and members of the local expats' club.

For more information about the Number 1 Bar, enhance Freddy's website statistics by clicking on: www.nr1pub.com.

Search Engine Optimisation (SEO) (Start-Up)

Andrew Bond, 37, is a UK national who was born in Zimbabwe. He worked as a radio presenter and DJ in South Africa, and as an editorial/content advisor for a dot.com company in UK. His real passion is travelling, and he came to Thailand in 2002.

Andrew came to Thailand with three trump cards: an education in media and marketing, travelling experience and experience of writing content for websites. Initially he taught English in Bangkok while writing website content for a client during his spare time. Then he relocated to Chiang Mai and his business grew rapidly.

In mid-2003, when his website content business really started to take off, he met Lek, his Thai wife, and they established Virtualtravelguides.com as their search engine optimisation (SEO) flagship. Since 2005, Andrew has launched a series of six comprehensive travel-related websites on Thailand.

Developing the proper content to be recognised by Internet search engines for travel websites is a key aspect of Search Engine Optimisation (SEO). Getting ranked at the top of the Google listings is so lucrative to e-commerce that a whole industry engineering sites for SEO has evolved. It involves critical, strategic knowledge and labour-intensive resources to 'beat' Google's complex algorithm to have your client's website listed at the top of the search results, and Andrew became known for his expertise in SEO and providing the necessary resources.

During 2005, Andrew launched his own tourist information site at: www.1stopchiangmai.com. This website receives over 50,000 visits each month, and the number is rising. Based on this success, in 2006, Andrew launched '1stop' websites (using the same format and branding) for Bangkok, Pattaya, Samui, Krabi, and Phuket. His plan is to gradually transfer his business activities from SEO to website publishing.

Andrew says that people visiting websites usually have only five minutes to read a webpage, so the information must be clear and succinct. His websites provide more than a hotel booking service; they cover all aspects of Thai tourism. Most first time visitors find their way to his sites via Google, but getting well placed by the search engines takes hard work, time and expertise. Most of the company's marketing activity is online.

Andrew is interested in the local real-estate market and contributes to *Thailand Property Report* (www.property-report.com).

Within fifteen months of start-up, Andrew employed over twenty people; all of them worked from their virtual offices at home. The Thai employees develop e-mail databases and website links for clients as well as registering the sites on Internet directories.

Andrew contracts with several freelance foreigners (living in various countries) to write online travel guides for his clients. His top earners make more than any English teacher in Thailand and the team produces the equivalent of two Lonely Planet guidebooks each month. Andrew manages website content for the growing online travel service industry.

When Andrew was visited by a Thai Immigration official, the officer could not believe that the company employed Thai staff because they worked at home. Lek, who has a senior position with a local publishing company, assists Andrew with payroll accounting and other administrative duties.

Andrew's clients are mainly from the UK; he usually visits his clients once a year and he contacts them by the online Skype phone every week. He has strong personal relationships with his overseas clients; three of them attended his wedding celebrations in Chiang Mai. Andrew's main challenge is to meet his clients' deadlines using committed professional writers with a sound work ethic.

Andrew's Tips

- Target your writing to your actual readership, not your peers.
- Check your lease and business contracts properly and consult a trustworthy and professional lawyer.
- Be careful, because many people think it's acceptable to cheat in business, so people getting something for nothing are considered smart.
- Expect your business to be copied if it is successful.

Conclusion

This is a good example of how a business can operate virtually with over twenty contractors or employees working from their homes. Andrew works from home with a Thai personal assistant. The fixed overheads of the business are nominal.

For further information about SEO, refer to Andrew's website: www.virtualtravelguides.com.

Re-Manufacturing (Start-Up)

David Frost (also known as Anant Thongkhamtang), 63, is from West Ham in London. He worked for a prestigious firm of printers in London

before travelling to Australia. David came to Thailand in 1967 at the age of 24. He worked for the *Bangkok Post* as production manager and was responsible for 200 staff. He resigned ten years later when he was executive director. In 1979 he invested in TV Rentals (Thailand) Co., Ltd. and was managing director of the company for twelve years. David is currently managing a company which re-manufactures ink cartridges. Annual sales of the company exceed ninety million baht.

Few people born overseas have Thai citizenship, but David is one of the lucky ones and the privilege has afforded him a distinct advantage. The Commercial Section of the British Embassy has referred many British business enquiries to David, and this relationship has originated many partnerships over the past forty years. David has been involved in mining, retailing, and direct selling of watches.

David says it's easy to find a partner in Thailand, but it can be difficult finding a suitable executive partner. He recommends testing a potential Thai partnership by outsourcing a function initially. He also advises networking at Rotary Clubs, the Lions and chambers of commerce. David was vice president of Bangkok Rotary Club (South) for nine years and a member of the Royal Bangkok Sports Club.

Central Office Products Co., Ltd. was established by David and two other partners to buy empty printer cartridges and re-manufacture and resell them. His company introduced tele-sales to Thailand. It now has 100 employees in Bangkok.

David's other company, Copytex, has 22 staff in Chiang Mai. The tele-sales staff work from a script, selling to businesses listed in the Yellow Pages.

The limiting factor of the business is supply of empty ink cartridges, so David offers cash for them and credit for the re-manufactured product. Enough business is generated by tele-marketing to fulfil export orders.

David employs a Thai manager (assistant MD) to supervise the office while he is away. He works two hours each day. "If you are working more than two hours each day, you are not delegating properly," he says.

David's formula for delegation is to employ the person as an assistant for up to one year while they demonstrate their initiative and ability; then he hands over responsibility to them. The assistant MD either sinks or swims.

David's Tips

- Invest in a niche business offering a high profit margin.
- Pick your local partner carefully.
- Foreigners wanting land should consider a thirty-year lease with an option for renewal. Long leases should be registered

with the Land Department for full protection of the investment. Refer to "Leasing Land" for more information about long property leases.

- Delegate whenever possible so you can enjoy a good lifestyle.
- Learn a working knowledge of Thai as quickly as possible.
- Don't get uptight and never shout.

Conclusion

Over a period of forty years in Thailand, David has more business experience and contacts than most. He has perfected the art of delegation and benefited from Her Majesty's British Embassy in Thailand.

For more information about re-manufacturing, visit Copytex Company's website: www.copytexink.com.

Mexican Restaurant (Start-Up)

Michael Mangnanti is from California and has lived in Thailand since 2004. He does not need to work because he has a pension, but he is driven by his passion for cooking the best Mexican food in town. Mike's Mexican restaurant, Miguel's, in which he invested 1.3 million baht, is his sixteenth restaurant.

Mike says his first year in Thailand was holiday time in Phuket. He loves the country for its freedom and relaxed pace of life. He also likes the climate and the beautiful people. He feels safe walking the streets at any time.

In just three years Mike established two popular restaurants and sold one of them at a good profit. He likes to work hard establishing a business; then he might sell it and take time off to travel ... before starting over again.

Mike first founded the popular Mike's Burgers in Chiang Mai. He claims that Mike's Burgers was the top grossing restaurant per square metre in Thailand.

The signs outside his Mexican place, Miguel's, are massive, bright and bold. The restaurant is clean and the staff cheerful. He employs six Thai staff. They are trained well and receive a bonus and social insurance contributions. Mike is 'hands on' so he works with his staff in the kitchen.

Mike recommends allowing up to twelve months to source suitable premises. He canvassed the local area for a good location on his own. He uses business brokers to sell his businesses only. His previous business, Mike's Burgers, has an unbeatable location on the corner of a prominent junction.

"Get a minimum three-year lease contract with an option to renew for a further three years; but aim for a nine-year lease. Register the lease with the Department of Land," advises Mike.

Mike pays 20,000 baht per month to his landlord. He has accommodation above the restaurant and a parking lot for his customers.

Mike does not advertise in magazines or on the Internet. His philosophy is to develop the business through customer satisfaction and referral. The proof is that he has a growing base of loyal customers

Mike's Tips

- In the catering business, try to attract both foreigners and locals (Thais love burgers, pizza and barbecues).
- Aim to be the best in whatever you do.
- Invest only what you can afford to lose.
- Source your suppliers carefully.
- Learn the dynamics of marketing from market leaders such as Subway and McDonalds, because they know the business of food.

Conclusion

Mike knows his trade well and delivers a good product at a reasonable price. His style is intensely individualistic, so 'Mike' is forcefully branded on everything he does. The fact that he doesn't need to work demonstrates that he really loves the food business.

The Bar Trade (Business Transfer)

Ron Holley, 59, is from the United States and his background is in sales and marketing. He spent eight months relaxing in Pattaya before moving to Chiang Mai in 2001. In January 2002, he purchased the Chiang Mai Saloon, which he developed into one of the most successful bars in northern Thailand.

When he came to Thailand, Ron eventually wanted a small business to occupy his time and supplement his investment income. He did not intend to run a bar. Initially he was considering business in real estate.

Ron paid 1.5 million baht for the bar—later to discover the accounting books had been manipulated by the seller—and invested an additional 600,000 baht to improve it. He overhauled the kitchen to Western standards. He replaced the bargirls with family-oriented staff. He refurbished the property and purchased a new pool table and a large screen TV. The new Chiang Mai Saloon grossed 180,000 baht in the first twenty days of trading.

The Saloon offers a relaxed ambience, reasonably priced food and drink and free Internet and pool table. The bar's hybrid menu is influenced by popular international restaurants. Ron's burgers were voted best in Chiang Mai by *Citylife* magazine in 2005.

Ron governs the bar with an iron fist. He does not serve drunks. Men are not allowed to pester women. Single Thai ladies are not allowed to pick up men at the bar or they are banned from the saloon. Ron courteously asks customers to make space for others.

Ron and his wife used to live above the bar before moving into a new home in Mae Rim. Now, Ron's brother-in-law manages the bar.

Ron registered his business as a Thai limited company. After his brother-in-law took over the management of the bar, Ron dissolved the limited company and re-registered the business in his wife's name. This strategy wiped ninety percent off his tax bill.

During 2005, Ron's employees deserted him to work with a foreign competitor who offered them cash incentives to leave him. Ron had to re-hire staff during October and November of 2005. Now he is back on top with gross sales quadruple what they were 5 years ago.

At the beginning of 2006, Ron was offered a fifty percent share in a bar (now known as Chiang Mai Saloon 2) for a nominal investment. The second bar is patronised mainly by backpackers. Ron's Canadian partner purchased this bar using a business broker.

Nobody is likely to pay the standard business broker's price of ten million baht for the Chiang Mai Saloon (based on three years' net profits). Most buyers would not pay more than four million baht for a similar bar. Therefore, Ron chose to secure his investment by acquiring long-term possession of the building; otherwise his short lease would revert to the landlord unless he sold his business for a price he considers unacceptably low.

Ron never advertises in magazines, but he has a website. The Chiang Mai Saloon is listed in the Lonely Planet guide to Thailand (2006 edition) and *Frommer's Guide*. Most people are referred by friends. Many bar owners negotiate agreements with the police so they can stay open later. The alternative is to apply for an entertainment license.

Ron's Tips

- Establish your bar in a good location, ideally surrounded by hotels.
- Develop your own concept bar instead of just copying another bar.

- Plan your bar to maximize revenue per square metre of floor space.
- Attract customers with value-added services.
- Don't put "all your eggs in one basket" and have a back-up plan.
- **If you buy a business, make sure you validate the seller's financials.**

Conclusion

Ron is a perfectionist and many people say the Chiang Mai Saloon is the perfect bar business. Ron has developed a highly successful bar, and now that he has handed it over to his wife's family he has more time to relax with his family and play golf. Ron says he has more "buying power" in Thailand than 100,000 US dollars per annum offers in America. His house in Mae Rim would cost two million dollars in San Diego, where he used to live. Thailand offers more freedom and quality of life.

The Chiang Mai Saloon's website address is: www.chiangmaisaloon.com.

Publishing And Multimedia (Start-Up)

Pim Kemasingki, 33, was born in Thailand to a Thai mother. Her father, John Shaw, a British citizen, was the honorary British consul for Chiang Mai. Pim was educated at a school in Switzerland, studied art in London, and completed a degree in English literature at Aberdeen University in 1996. In 1997 she returned to Chiang Mai to manage her father's newsletter, the *Chiang Mai Newsletter*. Pim developed the newsletter into *Citylife* magazine and established Trisila Co., Ltd. as a full-service multimedia publishing house.

When Pim took over her father's newsletter, she paid herself a salary of 2,500 baht per month. She did everything from writing, editing, and selling advertising to graphic design and distribution. She worked with her husband and father. After the Asian economic crisis of 1997, the business grew organically into Chiang Mai's prominent publishing and multimedia house.

In 1998, Pim started publishing online at: www.chiangmainews.com. This website is ranked number one by Google's search engine and receives over 80,000 hits daily. Pim completely overhauls the structure of her website every three years. Now the company offers a range of search engine optimisation (SEO) services.

Trisila has a unique corporate culture based upon Pim's open-door policy, team orientation, commitment to goals, 'thinking outside the box' and transparency. Every employee is encouraged to contribute ideas at daily team meetings. Pim's company is not hierarchical; her open office is designed to break down barriers between her extended family of "creatives."

Recently, Pim was awarded a training grant by a non-profit organization called Leading Women Entrepreneurs of the World. This association of over 300 career women promotes the benefits of their role in the global economy. The association's website address is www.leadingwomen.org.

The company employs 85 staff including fifty financial researchers who work for their City Web Watch division. Pim's husband, Dean Henderson, is the CEO of the London-based City Web Watch, which provides financial research services to international banks in Europe.

Pim works with five website programmers, five freelance writers, seven editors, seven sales representatives, plus graphic designers and support staff.

Pim recruits university graduates without any work experience. Her employees "must love their work." Experienced recruits find difficulty adjusting to *Citylife's* corporate culture; it is more difficult re-training employees than training them for the first time. Pim invests heavily in personnel development, including training and assessment.

During the company's infancy, it survived on the brink of bankruptcy. Pim's loyal employees offered to waive part of their remuneration to keep Trisila afloat. Pim says the foreign freelance writers were the first people to jump ship. During 2006, the company's gross sales surged by fifty percent.

Pim's Tips

- Always be ethical in business.
- Create your own corporate culture reflecting your personality and values.
- Check the references of all job applicants.
- Develop a strong team with regular staff meetings.
- Use a good lawyer and accountant.

Conclusion

Pim's company is highly dynamic and innovative, and Pim is usually receptive to new ideas. She is blessed with being Thai and having a British diplomat as a father. Most foreigners living in Thailand do not have such advantageous business foundations to start from, so they need to work harder to develop local contacts, knowledge and language skills.

For more information about *Citylife* magazine, visit the website: www.citylife-citylife.com.

Real Estate Agency (Start-Up)

Gary McDonald, 48, is from Australia's Gold Coast. He worked as a chiropractor before his career in project management with a firm of stage management consultants. In 1993 Gary was transferred to Pattaya for a nine-month contract to restructure a client's transvestite show. After the contract he studied for an MBA in Australia.

Gary returned to Thailand and opened a convenience store and two other businesses in Fang with his Thai wife. Later they started a Thai restaurant in Australia, which they ran for four years. In 2005, Gary returned to the Land of Smiles to start up the First National Real Estate agency in Chiang Mai. He had previously attended a course about real estate before starting his business. (First National Real Estate in Australia—www.first-national.com.au—offers training courses that prepare delegates for work in the real-estate sector.)

Gary's total investment in First National is estimated at 1.8 million baht. The purchase and maintenance of vehicles is a major cost to the business.

Gary has the ideal temperament for doing business in Thailand; he is always relaxed, patient and personable. During 2006, he worked with a

Property Listings at First National Real Estate

business partner who offended many people with his aggressive behaviour. The partnership was dissolved after only a few weeks.

The initial challenge of every new real estate (or business) broker is to establish a sizeable stock of quality property (or business) listings to show clients. Many realty agents open their doors to clients when they have at least twenty marketable property listings.

Stock of inventory can be developed by canvassing suitable properties and employing Thai listing agents. Listing agents do not have to speak English but sales negotiators must speak some English.

First National has many quality listings displayed in front of the office. Gary favours the business of real estate agency because the inventory has an indefinite shelf life, unlike food and other perishable goods. Also, a real estate agency is not as vulnerable to seasonal trade fluctuations as other businesses.

Gary sells many low-end condominiums; these properties make good investments with a return of around twelve percent. It is possible to establish a monthly income of 50,000 baht by investing five million baht in low-end condos. Shophouses are less attractive because they usually yield around six percent, unless they are in a prime location.

Thais are increasingly using real estate agencies. Gary has to monitor prospective buyers and sellers carefully to avoid losing any commissions earned. On one occasion, Gary was asked by a Thai lady for a 500,000 baht "commission" after her husband sold his property.

Gary employs four listing agents and one receptionist. Two of the listing agents are able to negotiate sales. The listing agents are paid salary, commission and expenses. Thirty percent of the fees charged by the company are allocated to the listing agents (fifteen percent to the person who listed the property and fifteen percent to the sales negotiator).

In Chiang Mai it is difficult to attract professional English-speaking sales negotiators. Part of the issue concerns the Thai culture, which discourages direct, overbearing behaviour.

Gary's Tips

- Always check that your instructions have been acted upon.
- Choose your business partners carefully.
- Stick to what you do best and enjoy most, and delegate the rest.

Conclusion

Gary has a good variety of quality properties on his books, plus friendly staff to take clients to view them. His Chiang Mai office is in an excellent location for this type of business.

For more information about First National Real Estate visit Gary's website: www.firstnationalthailand.com.

Concept Bar (Start-Up)

Robert Tilley, known as Bob, is sixty-something and comes from Somerset in England. He is a journalist by profession and has worked with numerous media companies over forty years, including The *Sunday Telegraph*. In 2000, Bob came to live in Thailand. Three years later, he and his Thai wife, Tong, started the Writers' Club in the heart of Chiang Mai. This club is *the* meeting place for writers and other media professionals.

Bob says the concept of his bar was influenced by a bar he visited in Belgrade, which used the same name. The idea is to offer a congenial atmosphere for conversation, like a press club or foreign correspondents' Club. There is no similar bar in Chiang Mai attracting authors and journalists.

Tong and Bob were told by a neighbour about a shophouse on the busy "Sunday Market Walking Street." They liked the property and location; however, it was a "dirty shell" when they acquired the lease. They refurbished the property throughout. No premium was payable to the landlord.

Bob is the club's investor and chief networker. Tong, who had previously worked in the restaurant trade, manages the bar and restaurant. Bob has a retirement visa because he has no need for a work permit. Tong's two sons help at the bar during their holidays and weekends. The unconditional support from family and friends is a major benefit of having a family business in Thailand.

Bob and Tong have never been asked for money by the local police. The business is registered in Tong's name, so she is visited once a year by a Revenue officer to negotiate and settle a modest tax liability. They used to record daily receipts but not expenses; now they pay a bookkeeper 1,000 baht each month to record all the club's transactions so they can prepare financial accounts.

The bar has excellent cash flow, and all sales are settled in cash each day. A similarly successful bar business would sell for around 2.5 million baht.

Bob's Tips

- Develop the business upon a specific concept.
- Invest enough money in the business to create a desirable ambience, then minimize the overheads.
- If you want to sell your business, keep proper accounting records.
- Develop the bar to suit your own style.
- Do not run a bar on a part-time (hobby) basis.

Conclusion

The Writers' Club attracts Chiang Mai's growing number of writers and media professionals. Friday evenings are best for meeting Chiang Mai's well-known writers, including Joe Cummings (Lonely Planet) and Bertil Lintner (who writes about Burma and Asia). There are an estimated 100 writers living in Chiang Mai. The bar has a unique, warm and relaxed atmosphere. Sometimes publishing contracts result from meetings at the Writers' Club. For more information, visit the website at: http://writers-club.chiangmai-news.com

Chapter 9
Franchising

Are You A Suitable Franchisee?

Be realistic about your suitability as a franchisee. To be a successful franchisee, you need to be a committed team player with sufficient funding for the business.

Individuality

Do you always insist upon doing things your own way, or are you comfortable following someone else's procedures? Successful franchisees are usually more team-oriented than individual. Franchisees are obligated to conform to the franchisor's established systems and procedures (as stated in their operations manuals). Adherence to the systems ensures uniformity throughout the franchise network. If you prefer to devise your own systems and product lines, you may not be an appropriate franchisee; if so, maybe you should consider starting your own business or buying an independent going concern.

Total Investment

Adequate funding is essential for a franchised outlet. The franchisor will provide the business know-how, systems, training and use of the trademark, but the franchisee funds the operation of the outlet. The total investment includes not only the franchise license fee, but also any leasehold improvements, lease security deposit, capital expenditure and working capital requirements. For example, the total investment of a 7-Eleven franchise may be three million baht, half of which is accounted for by the franchise license fee. The franchisor usually discourages the franchisee from getting a loan to finance the investment because the loan interest increases the possibility of failure.

Objectives

What are your objectives in becoming a franchisee? If it is simply to get a good return on your investment, then a franchise may not be the right investment tool for you. A franchise is an active investment that requires the franchisee's participation in management. There are other less demanding investment vehicles than a franchise. Get involved in a franchise if you want to get a good return in the process of running an ongoing business.

Franchise Evaluation Checklist

Concept

When looking into a company for possible franchising, first of all, look into the product or service. Before you look into the details of their franchise programme, understand the total concept first. What is unique about their concept? How is it different from the rest?

Before you become a franchisee, you should first become a customer. Do you like the product? Are they marketing an innovative product or service? Even if there are similar products in the market, what makes this company different? What makes them special? Is it the product quality? The price? The service quality?

Only after you have understood the concept and have become a satisfied customer should you begin to examine their franchise offering. If you are not sold on the concept, you will be hard-pressed to sell it to your future customers.

Investment

Find out what the initial investment amount quoted by the franchisor covers. It typically includes franchise fee, initial inventory, equipment and renovation. Franchisees often need to allow additional capital. Other initial investment costs include training expenses, rent deposits, business permits and licenses, grand opening expenses and working capital. With these additional investment costs, will the investment payback be significantly longer than the figure quoted by the franchisor in his franchise literature?

Training And Support

What type of support will the franchisor give? The franchisor can assist you in all stages of operating the business—site selection, lease negotiation, training, construction, procurement, grand opening planning, personnel recruitment, etcetera. After your outlet has opened, how often will the franchisor visit you for support? How often do you need to attend training programs after opening?

Franchise Agreement

The franchise agreement is the contract between the franchisor and the franchisee. It enumerates the rights and obligations of both parties in the relationship. It covers the beginning, the length of the term, the renewal provisions and the end of the contract.

Important provisions that should be examined in detail are the territory granted, fees and payment schedule and conditions resulting in breach or eventual termination of the agreement. In most reasonable franchise relationships, the franchise agreement, once signed, is put away and the parties manage the relationship through mutually beneficial business practices.

Other Considerations

Below is a checklist of questions for researching each franchise business:

- ❏ How long has the franchisor been in this type of business, and when did they start franchising?
- ❏ How many franchises do they operate and where?
- ❏ How many of their outlets are owned by the original franchisor?
- ❏ Is it possible to buy an existing store instead of starting a new business?
- ❏ Can the franchise guarantee uniform quality throughout its franchise network?
- ❏ Does the franchise have an operational procedures manual to facilitate quality control and consistency throughout the franchise network?
- ❏ What is the franchisor's fee for the franchise license, and what does the fee include?
- ❏ Is the franchise brand-name registered with the Department of Trade and Industry?
- ❏ Is it possible to meet existing franchisees to discuss their business?
- ❏ Is the franchise registered with the International Franchise Association (IFA)?
- ❏ Does the franchise agreement allow the transfer of the franchise license, and if so, what is the transfer fee? Are there any other penalties for termination of the franchise license?

- ❏ Is the franchise ISO (International Standards Organization) registered?
- ❏ What control procedures does the franchise have?
- ❏ What promotional support is offered by the franchisor upon and after opening the new business?
- ❏ Does the franchisor offer exclusive territorial rights?
- ❏ Which territories are available and which ones have been assigned?
- ❏ Is it permissible to spend a few days observing the operations of an existing franchise?
- ❏ What are the estimated costs of remodelling the premises, inventory and other working capital requirements?
- ❏ How does the purchasing and stock control system operate?
- ❏ Is the franchisee bound to procure all inventories from the franchisor?
- ❏ What royalties are payable to the franchisor, and when are they payable?
- ❏ What joint national marketing is organised by the franchisor and how is it charged to the franchisees?
- ❏ What are the operating sales and profits, and is it possible to obtain financial statements?
- ❏ Have any of the company's franchisees failed, and if so, for what reasons?
- ❏ Does the franchisor offer any flexibility regarding the products and services offered for sale?
- ❏ What is the term of the franchise agreement, and what is the fee for renewal?
- ❏ Are discounts available to franchisees who buy additional franchises?
- ❏ Are referral fees offered to franchisees who introduce the business to other prospective franchisees?
- ❏ What support does the franchisor offer in identifying suitable premises and remodelling the store?

Ask for a copy of the franchise agreement and the operations manual. Ask your lawyer to review the franchise agreement. Don't forget that the agreement must be equitable to both parties at all times, otherwise the franchise will not be successful.

Consider, also, the level of saturation in your targeted market. For example, in Thailand, at the time of writing, there were around 10,000 convenience stores. Of these stores, 7-Eleven had 3,750 outlets, Family Mart had 650, V-Shop had 800, and Freshmart had 300. The deputy managing director of CP 7-Eleven, a subsidiary of the Charoen Pokphand Group, claims that the market will be saturated when there are 20,000 convenience stores in the country, and that 7-Eleven will limit its outlets in Thailand to 5,000.

Buying A Franchise: The Pros And Cons

The Advantages Of Buying A Franchise

If you want to go into business, but you lack the experience of business management or the type of business you want to venture into, why not consider buying a franchise?

A good franchise offers a complete business package including training, marketing, start-up, and operational procedures. Most franchisors do not require their franchisees to have previous experience of the business. Many successful franchisees have no business experience whatsoever. Franchisors are looking for motivated people with good communication skills from all backgrounds.

Business knowledge is an essential component of every successful business, and every good franchise has access to sound business knowledge and experience. The franchisee accesses this business knowledge via training and ongoing support offered by the franchisor.

Many franchises offer strong national branding, which leads to familiarity of the franchise across the marketplace. The consumer is likely to trust the products offered by a franchise that has a strong brand name. This means that a new store within the franchise network can achieve much higher sales from the outset, compared with a business operated by a sole proprietor. It can take many years to build a strong brand nationally or internationally.

The key benefit to the potential franchisee is reduced risk of business failure. Statistics demonstrate that franchisees are much more likely to succeed in business than individual sole proprietors offering a similar service.

A good franchise is operating a proven business model. Any franchisee with sufficient motivation and reasonable communication skills should make a success of the franchise, unless they are particularly unlucky. The franchised business is controlled and monitored by the franchisor because the franchisor also has a vested interest in the success of all the franchisees.

Good franchisors will assist their franchisees in the following areas:

- Assistance with identifying a suitable location for the new store
- Support for fitting and remodelling the new store.
- Well-known company name, logo and slogans
- Access to a successful product range
- Systematic and efficient procurement systems and stock control
- Training for new franchisees and their staff
- Operations manuals and business forms
- Accounting control systems
- Quality control procedures
- Promotional support at launch of the new store
- Joint advertising (and other marketing) at a national level
- Leads and referrals from the head office (or franchisor)

In addition to the above benefits, the franchise agreement may allow the franchisee to sell the business for a large profit in the future. Alternatively, the management or ownership may be taken over by the franchisee's sibling or other relation.

The Disadvantages Of Buying A Franchise

Two key reasons for not buying a franchise might be unsuitability of personality of the franchisee and the additional investment involved.

The cost of starting in business as a franchisee is likely to be higher than starting in business independently. But it may be worth the additional cost for the reduction in risk and the access to a turnkey operation.

Some people are not suitable franchisees, particularly those who insist upon making all the decisions. Franchises are controlled according to the operations manual and the franchise agreement. For example, the franchisor is unlikely to allow the sale of products outside the product line established by the franchise. Therefore it is necessary to conform to the standard procedures of the franchisor.

Occasionally, franchisees are resentful at having to pay large royalty fees to their franchisor once they have achieved success. They may feel that they (the franchisees) are doing all the work, and the franchisor is receiving a large share of their profits. However, the franchisee may never have achieved such success without the support of the franchisor in the first place.

The business relationship with the franchisor may turn sour. Therefore, it is essential to have an 'exit strategy' that may involve selling the franchise back to the franchisor or to an outside party. Check the franchise agreement carefully, particularly with regard to any transfer fees payable to the franchisor upon sale of the business. Usually, franchisors insist that all franchise owners are qualified and vetted by the franchisor, so any transferee would need approval by the franchisor.

Some franchisors may be difficult to work with; usually the same people take more from their franchisees than they are willing to offer by way of support. One disgruntled franchise licensee of a prominent business brokerage publicly bragged about how he cheated his franchisor out of numerous royalty commissions. After selling his franchise license, a prospective buyer of the license reported the fraud to the franchisor. So check out your prospective franchisors and their associates carefully because the relationship is very important.

Franchise Categories

Products

- Art Supplies and Frames
- Automobile: Truck Rental and Purchase
- Bath and Closet
- Beauty Salons, Supplies, Cosmetics and Modelling
- Books and Publications
- Clothing and Shoes
- Construction, Remodelling and Home Improvements
- Drug Stores
- Dry Cleaning and Laundry
- Equipment Rentals
- Fire Protection
- Floor-Related
- Florists and Plants
- Food: Bakery, Bread and Doughnuts
- Food: Chicken Wings
- Food: Coffee and Tea
- Food: Grocery and Speciality Stores

- Food: Ice-Cream, Yoghurt, 'Smoothies', Candy, Popcorn and Beverages
- Food: Mexican
- Food: Pizza
- Food: Restaurant, Drive-in, Carryout and Delivery
- Food: Sandwiches, Subs and Salads
- Food: Sports Theme Restaurants
- Food: Steaks
- Furniture-Related
- General Merchandising Stores
- Gift Items
- Greeting Cards and Stationery
- Home-based Businesses
- Home Energy
- Home Furnishings and Decorating
- Home Furnishings: Windows and Treatments
- Houseware and Kitchen Items
- Jewellery
- Lawn and Garden Supplies and Services
- Martial Arts Related
- Hotels and Motels
- Optical Centres
- Party and Paper Goods
- Pet Centres and Pet-Related
- Photography
- Real Estate
- Retail (General)
- Security Systems
- Shipping, Packaging and Mail Centres
- Shoe Repair and Care
- Sports Equipment and Accessories
- Tools and Hardware-Related
- Vending
- Video and Audio Products
- Vitamins and Supplements
- Water Conditioning and Treatment

Services

- Advertising and Direct Mail
- Accounting and Tax Services
- Auto Products and Services
- Business Aids and Services
- Children's Products, Education and Services
- Computer Sales and Service
- Concrete Services
- Consumer Buying Services
- Dating Services
- Educational Products and Services
- Employment and Personnel Services
- Environmental Products and Services
- Financial Services
- Franchise Attorneys
- Franchise Consultants
- Franchise Services
- Health Aids, Fitness Centres and Services
- Home Inspection Services
- Internet-Related
- Insurance
- Maid and Home Cleaning Services
- Maintenance and Cleaning
- Personalised Products and Services
- Printing and Copying Services
- Recreation and Entertainment
- Recycling Services
- Sign Products and Services
- Telecommunications Products and Services
- Travel Services
- Weight Control Centres

Draft Franchise Agreement

Below is a specimen franchise agreement.

1. THIS AGREEMENT is made on .... day of .... between
.... having its registered office at......................... (hereinafter called "the Franchisor") of the first part and ....
having its office at .... (hereinafter called "the Franchisee") of the second part.

WHEREAS: The Franchisor has spent time, money and effort in developing knowledge of and expertise ("the Know-How") in ....
(hereinafter called "the Services").

The Franchisor wishes to expand the provisions of Services and is willing to grant to the Franchisee the rights set out herein.
The Franchisee desires the right, during the continuance of this agreement,
to provide the Services from the premises specified in Schedule 1.

2. NOW IT IS AGREED AS FOLLOWS:
Rights granted:
The Franchisor grants to the Franchisee the right to carry on the business
in accordance with this agreement from the premises, to utilize the Know-
How and to use the Trademarks.
Term:
Subject as herein appears, this agreement shall be for a period of ....
years, commencing from the .... day of ....

3. FRANCHISOR'S OBLIGATIONS
The Franchisor shall:
Assist the Franchisee to establish and efficiently operate the business.
Train the Franchisee and his staff in the correct operation of the business.
Give the Franchisee such reasonable continuing assistance and advice, as
the Franchisor considers necessary.

4. FRANCHISEE'S OBLIGATIONS
The Franchisor authorizes the Franchisee to use the Trademark solely for
the purpose of promoting the business.
The Franchisee undertakes not to do anything to prejudice or damage the
goodwill in the Trademarks or the reputation of the Franchisor.
The Franchisee agrees, in order to protect the Franchisor's intellectual
property rights and maintain the common identity and reputation of the
network, to comply with the quality specifications laid down by the equipment.

The Franchisee agrees to carry on the business under the Trademarks and no other name.

The Franchisee undertakes to use his best endeavours and the highest standards in all matters connected with the business diligently and in a manner to the reasonable satisfaction of the Franchisor.

The Franchisee agrees to insure with a major reputable insurance company in an adequate sum against all normal and reasonably foreseeable risks relating to the conduct of the business including product liability.

The Franchisee undertakes to indicate on all correspondence and notice board outside the premises the fact that it is an independent Franchisee of the Franchisor and is in no other way connected with it.

To indemnify and keep indemnified the Franchisor from and against all damage or liability suffered by it as a result of the Franchisee's acts or omissions.

5. FINANCIAL OBLIGATIONS

The Franchisee shall pay to the Franchisor, immediately upon signing this agreement, a franchise fee of .... Further, a monthly management fee, equivalent to .... percent of the previous month's turnover will be paid to the Franchisor.

6. PROMOTION AND ADVERTISING

The Franchisee shall, upon receiving written notice from the Franchisor, pay on a monthly basis, a sum equivalent to .... per cent of the previous month's gross turnover into the Franchisor's promotion and advertising fund. Such fund shall be used solely for the national and regional advertising of the services.

7. FRANCHISEE'S ACCOUNTS AND AUDIT

The Franchisee shall maintain proper books of accounts relating to the business and shall supply the same to the Franchisor within thirty days after the end of each financial year with an audited certificate.

The Franchisor, or its auditor, shall be entitled to inspect and audit the books of accounts and all supporting documentation of the Franchisee relating to the franchised business.

8. THE SALE OF THE BUSINESS

The Franchisee may not assign or delegate his franchise or any other right or obligation under this agreement, but may sell the business with the prior written consent of the Franchisor.

9. TERMINATION

The Franchisor may terminate this agreement by a notice in writing to the Franchisee if it has committed any material breach of his obligations specified under this agreement, or if any sum, required to be paid under the terms, has not been paid, at the latest, within 21 days following its due date.

10. FORCE MAJEURE

This agreement shall be suspended during the period and to the extent of such period that the Franchisor reasonably believes any party to this agreement is prevented or hindered from complying with its obligations under any part of it, by any cause beyond its reasonable control including, but not restricted to, strikes, war, civil disorder, and natural disasters.

11. ARBITRATION

In the event a dispute or deadlock arises in connection with the validity, interpretation, implementation or breach of this agreement, the parties shall attempt, in the first instance, to resolve such dispute through negotiations within thirty days or within such longer period as may be agreed between the parties in writing. In the event that the dispute is not resolved through negotiations, or such negotiations do not begin within the reasonable time period set out in the notice calling for the same, either party may refer the dispute to arbitration, with each party nominating one arbitrator, and the two arbitrators, so appointed, shall nominate a third arbitrator to constitute a three-member arbitral tribunal. The arbitration proceedings shall be conducted in accordance with the rules on arbitration framed by the International Chambers of Commerce or such other state bodies entitled to do the same.

12. MISCELLANEOUS

Language: This contract and all data and documentation, reports and other written materials, and all communications between the parties pursuant to performances of this contract, shall be in the English language.

Amendments: No modification, amendment or waiver of the terms and conditions of this agreement shall be valid or binding unless made in writing and duly executed by both parties.

Headings: The headings used in this agreement are for convenience only and are not to be used in construction or interpretation.

Contents Of The Operations Manual

The operations manual is the business blueprint which typically documents in detail the following aspects of the franchise:

- Shop layout
- Staff schedules
- Staff uniforms, appearance and etiquette
- Staffing requirements of outlets
- Job descriptions of staff
- Contracts of employment
- Disciplinary procedures
- Grievance procedures
- Training requirements
- Service standards
- Pricing policies
- Purchasing policies and standard form contracts
- Storage requirements
- Opening hours
- Stock rotation
- Accounting procedures
- Point of sale requirement
- Advertising and marketing practices
- Maintenance of equipment requirements
- Technical information about equipment used
- Cleaning routines
- Internal directory of franchisor's organization
- Menus, recipes and variations
- Explanation of relevant laws
- Customer complaints procedures
- Guarantees and warranties
- Approved suppliers list

Franchise Finder

Name and Category)	Contact Details	Other Information
7-Eleven (Convenience Stores)	7-Eleven Co., Ltd. CP Tower (25th floor), 313 Silom Road, Bangrak, Bangkok, 10500. Tel: + 66 (0)2 711-7800 E-mail: nutkamoltho@7eleven.co.th Internet: www.7eleven.co.th	Franchise Fee: 1,500,000 baht Branches in Thailand: 3,500
API-NET (Internet Cafés)	API Net Co., Ltd. 2220 Paholyothin Road, Bangkok, 10900. Tel: + 66 (0)2 940-2121 Fax: + 66 (0)2 940-1119 E-mail: apinet@apinet-new.net Internet: www.api-net.net	Branches in Thailand: 30
A.R FOR YOU (Book Stores)	Advance Co., Ltd. Tel: + 66 (0)2 642-3400 Fax: + 66 (0)2 642-2395 -6 Internet: www.ar.co.th, www.ar4u.com	Franchise Fee: 1,000,000 baht
AROMAVERA SPA (Health and Beauty Products)	Aromavera Co., Ltd. 41/75 Aromavera Building, 64 Patanakan Road, Bangkok, 10250. Tel: + 66 (0)2 322-9707 -9 Fax: + 66 (0)2 322-9737 E-mail: peter@aroma-vera.com Internet: www.aroma-vera.com	Year established: 1997
BLACK CANYON (Coffee Shops)	Black Canyon (Thailand) Co., Ltd. Tel: + 66 (0)2 376-0014 -8 Fax: + 66 (0)2 376-0019 Internet: http://blackcanyoncoffee.com	Franchise Fee: 600,000 baht Branches in Thailand: 90
BORNTRAS SPA PRODUCTS (Health and Beauty Products)	Borntras (Thailand) Co., Ltd. 142 Moo 6, Chiangraknoi Bangpa-in, Ayuthaya, 13180. Tel: + 66 (0)2 908-5711 -14 Fax: + 66 (0)2 908-5710 E-mail: cr@thaiherbalgoods.com Internet: www.thaiherbalgoods.com	

BUD'S ICE-CREAM (Ice-Cream Shop)	American Food Co., Ltd. Tel: + 66 (0)2 377-3281 -2 Fax: + 66 (0)2 377-3281 -2 E-mail: pinnacle@ksc.th.com Internet: www.afcthailand.com	Franchise Fee: 800,000 baht
CAFÉ D'ORO (Coffee Shops)	729-728 Soi Rachada, Rachadapisek Road, Bukkalo, Thonburi, Bangkok, 10600. Tel: + 66 (0)2 876-0291 -5 Fax: + 66 (0)2 876-0350 E-mail: info@vppcoffee.com Internet: www.vppcoffee.com	Franchise Fee: Variable Branches in Thailand: 65
CAR-LACK 68 (Car-Care Services)	Car-Lack (Thai-German) Co., Ltd. 77/6 Moo 9, Soi Klongnongyai, Sukhapiban 1 Road, Bangkok, 10160. Tel: + 66 (0)2 454-2876 -80 Fax: + 66 (0)2 454-2743 E-mail: carlack_68@yahoo.com Internet: www.carlack68.co.th	
CATHERINE BEAUTY HOUSE AND SPA (Spa and Beauty Salons)	Ever Glory (Thailand) Co., Ltd. 1200/156 Soi 103, Sukhumvit Road, Bang Na, Bangkok, 10260. Tel: + 66 (0)2 748-9124 -5 Fax: + 66 (0)2 729-7595 E-mail: info@catherinespa.com Internet: www.catherinespa.com	Franchise Fee: 250,000 baht Branches in Thailand: 17
CHESTER'S GRILL (Restaurants)	Chester Food Co., Ltd. Tel: + 66 (0)81 555-7679 Fax: + 66 (0)2 651-2228 E-mail: natthipa@globalkitchen.co.th Internet: www.chestergrill.co.th	Franchise Fee: 7,000,000 baht Branches in Thailand: 113
CHOKDEE DIMSUM (Restaurants)	Chokdee Interfood Co., Ltd. 48/4 Soi Chula, 7 Bantadthong Road, Wangmai, Patumwan, Bangkok, 10330. Tel: + 66 (0)2 611-5745 Fax: + 66 (0)2 611-5747 E-mail: no.1@chokdeedimsum.com Internet: www.chokdeedimsum.com	Franchise Fee: 50,000 US dollars Royalty Fee: Five percent of sales Marketing Fee: Five percent of sales

COCA SUKI (Restaurants)	CMIC Tower B (22nd Floor), 209/1 Sukhumvit Road Soi 21 (Asoke), Klongtoey Nua, Wattana, Bangkok, 10110. Tel: + 66 (0)2 261-6890 -1 Internet: www.coca.com/index/ www.exquisinethai.com/	Franchise Fee: Varies Branches in Thailand: 33
COFFEE WORLD (Coffee Shops)	E-mail: franchising@gfacorp.com Internet: www.coffeeworld.com/ franchise.asp	Franchise Fee: 600,000 baht Total Investment: 2,000,000 baht Cost of Sales: 23 percent
DOUBLE A STATIONERY (Stationery Retail)	Advance Agro Co., Ltd. Rungrueng Peuchpon Building 122, North Sathorn Road, Bangrak, Bangkok, 10500. Tel: Hotline 1759 Fax: + 66 (0)2 267-1848 / 7157 Internet: www.doubleapaper.com E-mail: double_a@advanceagro.com	Franchise Fee: 50,000 baht Branches in Thailand: 150
DREAM CONES (Ice-Cream Shops)	Dream Cones Co., Ltd. 25/26 Phetkasem Road, Hua Hin, Prachuab Khiri Khan, 77110. Tel: + 66 (0)6 979-1928 Fax: + 66 (0)2 616-9953 E-mail: info@dreamcones.com Internet: www.dreamcones.com	Franchise Fee: 350,000 baht Branches in Thailand: 12
EF ENGLISH FIRST (English-Language Schools)	EF International Language Service Co., Ltd. 287 Liberty Square Tower (8th Floor), Bangrak, Bangkok, 10500. Tel: + 66 (0)2 631-1920 Fax: + 66 (0)2 631-1919 E-mail: charoenporn@englishfirst.com Internet: www.englishfirstthailand.com, www. efpinklao.com/index.html	Franchise Fee: 1,000,000 baht Branches in Thailand: 12

EPSON DIGITAL PHOTO (Digital Imaging)	C. Image Digital Co., Ltd. 1201/22 Soi Lard Phrao, 94 Town In Town 14 Road, Wungthonglang, Bangkok, 10310. Tel: + 66 (0)2 530-8225 -7 Fax: + 66 (0)2 530-2120 E-mail: webmaster@cimage.co.th Internet: www.cimage.co.th	Franchise Fee: 30,000 baht Branches in Thailand: Over 100
GAFAE TUK-TUK (Coffee Shops)	Gafae Tuk-Tuk Co., Ltd. 301/4 Moo 6, Paholyothin Road, Anusawaree, Bangkhen, Bangkok, 10220. Tel: + 66 (0)2 972-9427 -9 Fax: + 66 (0)2 972-9430 E-mail: info@gafaetuktuk.com Internet: www.gafaetuktuk.com	Franchise Fee: 500,000 baht
HAAGEN-DAZS (Ice-Cream Shops)	Haagen-Dazs Franchise Ltd. Franchise Office: Hong Kong Tel: + 852 2629-6188 Fax: + 852 2824-2804 Internet: www.haagen-dazs.com	
HANAKO (Beauty Salons)	Hanako Cosmetics (Thailand) Co., Ltd. CP Tower (25th Floor), 313 Silom Road, Bangrak, Bangkok, 10500. Tel: + 66 (0)2 231-0880 Fax: + 66 (0)2 631-0745 E-mail: office@hanakocosmetics.com Internet: www.hanakocosmetics.com:	Branches in Thailand: 5
MA-ED (Chinese-Language Schools)	Mandarin Education Group Co., Ltd. Tel: + 66 (0)2 718-5146 -7 Fax: + 66 (0)2 718-5748 E-mail: info@ma-ed.com, ma_ed@ samarts.com Internet: www.ma-ed.com	Franchise Fee: 300,000 baht Branches in Thailand: 10
MATHNASIUM (Maths Teaching Centres)	Math Gym Co., Ltd. Tel: + 66 (0)2 513-0913 Fax: + 66 (0)2 513-0628 E-mail: info@mathnasium-thailand. com Internet: www.mathnasium-thailand. com	Franchise Fee: 450,000 baht Branches in Thailand: 3

MINIPUMP (Gasoline Machines)	VTS Mini Pump Co., Ltd. 165/2-3 Moo 1, Bang Preng Road, Samut Prakan, 10560. Tel: + 66 (0)1 570-6813, + 66 (0)1 840-9574, + 66 (0)2 338-1254 Fax: + 66 (0)2 338-1598 Internet: www.minipump.co.th E-mail: vasinee@minipump.co.th, sakolsachdev@yahoo.com	Franchise Fee: 190,000 baht Branches in Thailand: 3
MISTER DONUT (Bakery Retailer)	Central Restaurant Group Co., Ltd. Silom Tower (5th Floor), Bangrak, Bangkok, 10500. Tel: + 66 (0)2 635-7930 Fax: + 66 (0)2 635-7940 E-mail: restaurant@crg.co.th Internet: www.crg.co.th	Franchise Fee: 1,000,000 baht Branches in Thailand: 169
M MOBILE (Telecoms Shops)	M Mobile Co., Ltd. Tel: + 66 (0)2 741-5400 Fax: + 66 (0)2 741-5400 E-mail: webmaster@m-shop.co.th Internet: www.m-shop.co.th	Franchise Fee: 60,000 baht Branches in Thailand: 3
NAI IN BOOK STORE (Book Stores)	Amarin Book Centre Co., Ltd. 65/60 -62 Moo 4, Chaiyapruk Road, Taling Chan, Bangkok, 10170. Tel: + 66 (0)2 882-2000 ext. 3213 Fax: + 66 (0)2 882-2000 ext. 3602 Internet: www.naiin.com	Franchise Fee: Varies Branches in Thailand: 55
NEO SUKI RESTAURANTS (Restaurants)	Neo Suki Thai Restaurants 3678/2 Soi Rajauthit, 1 Pradu Road, Bangkok, 10120. Tel: + 66 (0)2 683-5400 Fax: + 66 (0)2 683-7314 E-mail: info@neosuki.com Internet: www.neosuki.com	Year Established: 1999
OISHI BUFFET (Restaurants)	Oishi Group Co., Ltd. 9 UM Tower (20th Floor), Ramkhamhaeng, Suan Luang, Bangkok, 10250. Tel: + 66 (0)2 717-2244 Fax: + 66 (0)2 717-3920 E-mail: oishi@oishigroup.com Internet: www.oishigroup.com	Franchise Fee: 2,000,000 baht Branches in Thailand: 7

PAK VAN (Book Stores)	Pak Van Franchise Co., Ltd. Tel: + 66 (0)2 930-4840 -1 Fax: + 66 (0)2 930-4842 Internet: www.pakvanfranchise.com	Franchise Fee: 150,000 baht Branches in Thailand: 10
PATA JEWEL-CLONING (Gemstones)	Pata Jewelcloning Co., Ltd. 113/12 Surawong Centre, Surawong Road, Bangrak, Bangkok, 10500. Tel: + 66 (0)2 634-0426 Fax: + 66 (0)2 634-0427 E-mail: contact@jewelcloning.com Internet: www.jewelcloning.com	
POST AND SERVICE I DO (Office Services)	1/33 Tanin Village, Vipawadee-Rangsit Road, Don Muang, Bangkok, 10210. Tel: + 66 (0)2 533-4611 Fax: + 66 (0)2 998-0537 Internet: www.ptminfo.com E-mail: marketing@ptminfo.com, ptm_info@yahoo.com	Franchise Fee: 180,000 baht Branches in Thailand: 60
REALITY WORLD ALLIANCE (Real-Estate Brokers)	Realty World Alliance Co., Ltd. Tel: + 66 (0)2 818-0022 ext. 510 E-mail: webmaster@realtyworld.co.th, franchise@realtyworld.co.th Internet: www.realtyworld.co.th	Franchise Fee: 600,000 baht Branches in Thailand: 17
SIRIUM BEAUTY CARE (Beauty Salons)	Siranon Co., Ltd. 59/8 Phayathai Road, Rachathewi, Bangkok, 10400. Tel: + 66 (0)2 251-5590 -1 Fax: + 66 (0)2 251-5592 E-mail: info@siriumbeauty.com Internet: www.siriumbeauty.com	Franchise Fee: 500,000 baht Branches in Thailand: 15
SMART ENGLISH (English-Language Schools)	Smart English Co., Ltd. 479/4-5 Hualamphong Office Building (1st Floor), Soi Salukhin, Patumwan, Bangkok, 10330. Tel: + 66 (0)2 613-9139 Fax: + 66 (0)2 613-9140 -5 E-mail: info@smartenglish.in.th Internet: www.smartenglish.in.th	Franchise Fee: 350,000 baht Branches in Thailand: 73

SPA OF SIAM (Health and Beauty Products)	Spa of Siam (Beauty & Spa) Co., Ltd. 50/565 Moo 1, Kukod Lumlukha, Patum Thani, 12130. Tel: + 66 (0)2 987-4672 Fax: + 66 (0)2 987-4671 E-mail: info@spasiam.com Internet: www.spasiam.com	
SPICCHIO PIZZA (Restaurants)	Gianni Enterprise Co., Ltd. Tel: + 66 (0)2 650-9601 -3 Fax: + 66 (0)2 650-9605 E-mail: kankorn@spicchiopizza.com Internet: www.spicchiopizza.com/ franchise/	Franchise Fee: 25,000 US dollars
SUBWAY (Sandwich Bars)	Website: www.subway.com E-mail: franchise@subway.com	Franchise Fee: 100,000 US dollars
SUNBELT ASIA (Business and Real-Estate Brokerages)	Sunbelt Asia Co., Ltd. Fortune Town Tower (26th Floor), Rachadapisek Road, Bangkok. Tel: + 66 (0)2 642-0213 -18 Fax: + 66 (0)2 641-1995 Contact: Greg Lange E-mail: info@sunbeltasia.com Internet: www.sunbeltasia.com	Franchise Fee: 50,000 US dollars Branches in Thailand: 5
SWENSEN'S ICE-CREAM (Ice-Cream Parlours)	Minor International Public Co., Ltd. Berli Jucker House (16th Floor), 99 Soi Rubia, Sukhumvit Soi 42, Bangkok, 10110. Tel: + 66 (0)2 381-5151 Fax: + 66 (0)2 381-5777 -8 Internet: www.minorfoodgroup.com	Franchise Fee: Variable Branches in Thailand: 136
THE PIZZA COMPANY (Restaurants)	Minor International Public Co., Ltd. Berli Jucker House (16th Floor), 99 Soi Rubia, Sukhumvit Soi 42, Bangkok, 10110. Tel: + 66 (0)2 381-5151 Fax: + 66 (0)2 381-5777 -8 E-mail: kullavat_vi@minornet.com Internet: www.minorfoodgroup.com	Franchise Fee: Variable Minimum Total Investment: 250,000 US dollars Branches in Thailand: 176
TIPTOP THAILAND (Cleaning Services)	Tiptop Thailand Co., Ltd. Tel: + 66 (0)2 730-6488 -9 E-mail: hongkong@tiptophk.com Internet: www.tiptopthailand.com	Franchise Fee: 29,000 euros

TSUTAYA COMPANY (Video and DVD Rentals)	Tsutaya Co., Ltd. 1032/1-5, 14-16 (3rd Floor), Rama 3 Road, Sathorn, Bangkok, 10120. Tel: + 66 (0)2 679-9709 -24 Fax: + 66 (0)2 679-9726 -8 E-mail: info@tsutaya.co.th Internet: www.tsutaya.co.th	Franchise Fee: 170,000 baht Branches in Thailand: 130
VDO EZY (Video Rentals)	Vdo Ezy Thailand Co., Ltd. Tel: + 66 (0)2 693-2206 ext. 111 E-mail: webmaster@videoezy.co.th Internet: www.videoezy.co.th	Franchise Fee: 300,000 baht Branches in Thailand: 143
V SHOP (Convenience Stores)	Minimart Express Co., Ltd. 158/1 Moo 6, Ngan Wongwan, Tongsonghong, Laksee, Bangkok, 10210. Tel: + 66 (0)2 953-4881 -7 E-mail: v_shop@mweb.com, admin@ vshopexpress.com Internet: www.vshopexpress.com	Franchise Fee: 690,000 baht Branches in Thailand: 792
WONGPANIT RECYCLING MANAGEMENT (Waste Management)	Wong Panit Co., Ltd. 19 Moo 3, Phitsanulok-Bangkrathum Road, Phitsanulok, 65000. Tel: + 66 (0)5 528-4494 Fax: + 66 (0)5 230-1734 E-mail: wongpani@loxinfo.co.th Internet: www.wongpanit.com	

Other Useful Contacts

Asiawide Franchise
420 North Bridge Road,
04-08 North Bridge Centre,
Singapore, 188727.
Tel: + 65 (0) 6743-2282;
+ 65 (0) 9815-9104
Fax: + 65 (0) 6743-1139
E-mail: asiafran@singnet.com.sg
Internet: www.asiawidefranchise.com
Franchise consultants

Queen Sirikit National Convention Centre, Bangkok.
Office of Small and Medium Enterprise Promotion (OSMEP),
Ministry of Industry.
Tel: + 66 (0)2 278-8800
E-mail: wittawat@sme.go.th
Internet: www.sme.go.th
Franchise exhibitions and conference organizer.

Franchise License Asia
E-mail: info@franchiselicenseasia.com
Internet: www.franchiselicenseasia.com
Services: Franchise exhibitions and consulting

Horwath Franchise Services (Thailand) Ltd.
Thai CC Tower (4th Floor),
889 South Sathorn Road, Yannawa,
Bangkok, 10120.
Tel: + 66 (0)2 719-3515 -16
Fax: + 66 (0)2 719-3886
Internet: www.horwathap.com

Thailand Franchise Association
20/25 Seri Village,
Soi Onnut, Sukhumvit 77,
Bangkok, 10250.
Tel: + 66 (0)2 321-5129
Fax: + 66 (0)2 721-2795
E-mail: focus@bangkok.com

The International Franchise Association (IFA)
Website: www.franchise.org

Useful Websites

http://franchise.sme.go.th/index.jsp

www.kiasia.org

www.thaifranchisecenter.com/links/index.php#marketing

www.franchise108.com

Chapter 10
Pitfalls And How To Avoid Them

The objective of this section is to enable you learn from other peoples' mistakes. When you are equipped with sound information, you will be able to avoid the common mistakes made by foreigners in Thailand.

Some of the names in the following case studies have been changed to maintain anonymity.

Check Your Bank Notes

Ron paid 5,000 US dollars (in dollar bank notes) for ten computers. His first mistake was to pay for them in advance without any security. After ten days he had still not received the computers as promised, so he asked for a full refund. Ron received his money back and happily marched to his bank to deposit the money in his account.

The bank teller took one glance at the notes and immediately telephoned the police. The police arrested Ron for using counterfeit notes. The case was investigated and the person who paid Ron was sent to prison. It took Ron six weeks to be cleared of any involvement in the crime.

If you receive a large number of bank notes—for whatever reason—check them to ensure they are not counterfeit. If you have any doubts, go to your bank with the payer. **It is usually more secure to receive payment by bank draft (a cheque drawn, signed, and stamped by a reputable bank on the bank's own cheque).**

Validate The Seller's 'Financials'

Brian, 68, from New Zealand purchased a café in Chiang Mai to supplement his retirement income. He was lured into the deal by the offer of low rent and expected earnings of 35,000 baht per month. According to the seller's financial representations he would recover his investment within two years.

Brian relied upon the seller's representations, which were supported by his business broker. The broker acted as the seller's intermediary without questioning the financial information. Brian did not seek independent advice, despite his Thai girlfriend's warnings about it being "bad business"; neither did he conduct any due diligence.

Within one week of the business transfer, Brian realised he had made a big mistake and decided to sell out as quickly as possible. He calculated that he needed to sell twelve cups of coffee per hour to achieve his target profit; he was only selling two cups per day (during peak season).

It took Brian over ten months to sell the loss-making business at a fraction of the price he bought it for. He had established a limited company to obtain a work permit he did not need because his girlfriend managed the café. Brian could have saved himself over 15,000 US dollars if he had properly researched the business.

Caution: Many sellers have no financial information about their business to offer buyers; others maintain three sets of records (one real account for themselves plus manipulated accounts for the Revenue Department and another for business investors).

Pay Brokerage Fees

When Brian's broker promoted his business for sale, Brian encountered four interested buyers, one of whom purchased his café. Three out of the four prospective buyers asked Brian to sell without declaring the deal to his broker. Brian's response was 'thanks, but no thanks.' Starting a business in a foreign country on the wrong side of the law is a poor start.

Most successful businesspeople use brokers to *sell* their businesses but *not* to buy them because brokers maximize the sale value of businesses listed; but they always pay their dues—because reputation always catches up with them eventually.

Check Your Legal Contracts Thoroughly

When Brian purchased the café, he did not realize he was buying a franchise that obliged him to buy coffee from his franchisor and landlord. He thought he was buying the entire business (without any restrictions).

Brian recommends using a professional lawyer who is absolutely impartial. Brian used his broker's in-house legal advisor. "It's like using your ex-wife's lawyer in a divorce case," says Brian. If the broker is negligent, their in-house lawyer will support their employer before their client.

The legal 'base' document is always written in Thai. The translation is for comprehension purposes only, so **use a reliable translator**.

Do Not Advance Money Before The Lease Has Been Checked By A Lawyer And The Transfer Of Ownership Is Acceptable To The Landlord

Chris, from Cardiff, was offered the opportunity to buy his favourite bar and restaurant. The sale price of 400,000 baht included a premium for goodwill, a music system, pool table, bar, furniture, and inventory. He accepted the offer.

Chris did not have a Thai partner so he agreed with the seller, David, to take over the existing lease, leaving it registered in David's wife's name. Neither Chris nor David mentioned the transfer of ownership to the landlord. Chris willingly paid David the asking price for the bar.

Within ten days of transfer of ownership, Chris was approached by the Thai landlord, who wanted to know who he was and why he was running the bar on his premises. When the landlord realised that his real lessee had transferred ownership of the business without his permission, he cancelled the lease on the spot. The next day the landlord instructed contractors to demolish the building.

Chris lost over 400,000 baht within three weeks of buying the bar because he did not negotiate a valid lease with the landlord or get legal advice. Chris and David were wrong and the landlord was understandably angry. Of course, the landlord is eventually likely to hear about any change of business ownership because people talk.

Research Market Rents In The Surrounding Area

Fiona signed a lease to rent land to enable her to start a new business in the entertainment sector. She did not conduct any research into the market value of property rentals in the local area; neither did she research the feasibility of her project.

After six months, Fiona realised she was paying rent at over three times market value. It was impossible for the business to make a profit. Eventually she asked the landlord to reduce the rent. The landlord refused to discount the rent, knowing that she could not move her business to other premises without considerable difficulty. The landlord tauntingly said that Fiona should have done some research before agreeing the lease terms.

The property was poorly situated for the particular type of entertainment business, so it was difficult to attract customers. Unfortunately the bulky, fixed assets of the business were difficult to transfer to another location. Eventually Fiona abandoned the project and left the fixtures and fittings behind.

If you pay rent above market value, the value of your business is marked down accordingly (and vice versa). If your business cannot make a profit, it is worth the value of its second-hand assets. In this case the assets were worthless and the investor lost millions of baht.

Check Your Franchisor Before Buying A Franchise

Tom paid 1.5 million baht for a real estate property franchise covering northern Thailand. He met the (foreign) franchisors, who were extremely friendly to him. However, after paying the franchise fee to the franchisors, they refused to visit his new office in Chiang Mai. Later, they would not return Tom's phone calls. Shortly after furnishing and equipping his new office, Tom broke his leg and then he decided to "throw in the towel."

Tom discovered that the franchisors were actually rogues—after paying them for a brand which had accumulated "more bad-will than goodwill." They had made false claims about their credentials and business history. They owed money to numerous people in Thailand and overseas.

Research your franchisors thoroughly. Meet other franchisees and ask them how their franchise is performing and how much support they receive from the franchisor. It is positive if the franchisees respect their franchisor; conversely, if franchisees are resentful of their franchisor, do not proceed with the purchase.

For more ideas about how to validate franchises, refer to the "Franchising" section.

Check The History Of The Business

Some businesses are fundamentally flawed (as determined by the seven business foundations in "Business In Thailand: Same Same, But Different. The usual reasons are poor location, intense competition, and onerous lease terms.

These same businesses tend to change ownership two or three times each year. It's no coincidence that none of the previous ten owners managed to make a success of such businesses.

Basic research would highlight these bad businesses. Ask the seller how long they have owned the business and why they are selling. Ask the neighbouring businesspeople whether they can offer any information about its trading history. Ask in the local bars and cafés; it's surprising how much information can be gleaned in a period of minutes.

It is irresponsible to invest thousands of dollars in any business without asking any pertinent questions.

Check The Validity And Identity Of The Landlord

Steve agreed a lease for premises to operate a restaurant. Steve is cautious by nature, so he took both a Thai lawyer and his Thai representative to agree the lease.

After the lease was signed by both parties, he asked his lawyer whether he had checked that the landlord owned the property. The lawyer said that he had done so in front of his Thai representative.

Two weeks later, Steve discovered that the landlord was actually a lessee and not the owner of the property. The lawyer had accepted the lessee's verbal statement that he had "forgotten to bring the property registration documents to the meeting." Without agreement by the real landlord, Steve had no security of tenure over the lease term.

Do not sign a lease until you have evidence in writing that the person purporting to be the landlord actually owns the property. Check the landlord's personal ID card. Ensure that the landlord's name on the lease is exactly the same as that on the ID card and property registration document.

Check That The Business Really Is A Going Concern

Sometimes sellers attempt to present their business as a going concern after they have ceased trading. They manipulate the truth in order to justify asking for a premium for goodwill. Businesses which have ceased trading are usually sold for the nominal value of the second-hand assets.

Typically the seller would plan some activity to coincide with the prospective buyer's meeting. Bar or restaurant owners may ask their friends and family around to a party with a promise of free drinks.

Make 'surprise' visits to the seller's business to see how many customers there are at different times of the day, week, month or year. Do not only judge the business according to visits pre-arranged by the seller.

Make Sure You Both Prepare A Will (If You Or Your Spouse Or Partner Have Valuable Assets In Thailand)

Klaus, 62, is from Germany. He purchased a ten-million-baht luxury home in Pattaya and registered it in his Thai girlfriend's name. Two years later, his girlfriend died in a motorcycle accident.

Neither Klaus nor his girlfriend had prepared a will, so Klaus's girlfriend died intestate. This meant that her estate passed to her parents and sisters. Klaus had to move out of the home he paid for. However, Klaus's lawyer managed to negotiate a settlement of 500,000 baht from the estate, even though the family had no legal obligation to pay him anything.

If Klaus's late girlfriend had prepared a will specifying her intention to bequeath the house to Klaus in the event of her death, her request would have been honoured. Klaus did not have enough money to buy another home, so he had to rent a condominium. Klaus's late girlfriend wished him to keep possession of the home, but there was no way he could prove it to her family or to the Thai officials.

Klaus could also have registered a loan of ten million baht to his girlfriend (on the reverse of the *chanote*) at the Land Department. The Land Department will not allow transfer of ownership of a property until the loan has been repaid.

If you have any assets in Thailand that you want to be transferred to someone upon your demise, ensure that you and your partner or spouse prepare separate wills and get them signed at the local *amphur* office.

Summary

Often 'bad' businesses have multiple problems: typically, poor product concept, high rent, poor location, partnership problems, theft, and low staff morale. Successful businesses excel under each of the seven key foundations. Refer to "Business In Thailand: Same Same, But Different" (page 11.)

Most of the business pitfalls concern property leases and issues relating to partnerships and Thai customs and etiquette. If you act in the following ways, you will give yourself the best possible start:

- Establish a favourable lease in a suitable location with a good landlord and get it validated by a professional lawyer.
- Work with a reliable Thai partner or representative who can manage Thai staff and negotiate with government officials and suppliers.

The Top Ten Do's And Don'ts

Do

- Protect your investment using appropriate legal structures or a trustworthy Thai partner or representative, and write a will.
- Learn the Thai language and respect Thai customs and etiquette.
- Research your business properly before investing any money.
- Choose a suitable location for your business.
- Negotiate an agreeable solution to settle any conflicts and avoid involvement with the police or judicial system if at all possible.
- Attempt to provide employment for your spouse's family.
- Keep proper accounting records and comply with all laws.
- Develop a business concept in a niche market.
- Remember that in Thailand relationships are often more valuable than extra profit.
- Commit yourself to your business to make it successful.

Don't

- Overstay your visa.
- Lose your temper in front of Thai people.
- Reprimand a Thai in the presence of other people.
- Buy a 'hobby business' with money you cannot afford to lose.
- Rely on the business seller's (or broker's) financial representations without validating the information.
- Sign an onerous lease (with a short term, high rent, or poor location).
- Try to change the system—because you will never win.
- Pay anyone in advance—otherwise you will lose control of the money.
- Offer credit terms (or unsecured loans) unless you have a high profit margin to absorb the cost of bad debts.
- Underestimate the importance of relationships and *sanuk* (fun), both inside and outside the workplace.

Chapter 11
Essential Contacts By Location

The places listed in this section are the main centres for foreign businesspeople in Thailand. The key advantages and disadvantages of doing business in each of these locations precede the local contact information.

The locations covered are: Bangkok, Chiang Mai, Hua Hin, Khon Kaen, Pattaya, Phuket, and Koh Samui. Further information about living and working in these places, including interviews with retired expats, is available in *Retiring In Thailand* (see "Recommended Books", page 253).

The population sizes quoted in this section (from wikipedia.org) refer to the urban areas. For the provincial population of each of the major cities, refer to "Thailand: Quick Facts" (page 7).

Publications that are not listed in this section can be found at: www.thaiadvertising.com

Bangkok

Advantages Of Doing Business In Bangkok

Thailand's capital city of at least ten million residents is called Krung Thep in Thai. Most international companies, embassies, and chambers of commerce are based in Bangkok. This business metropolis and international aviation hub is surely the best location to meet and impress overseas investors.

Bangkok offers unlimited choices in entertainment, culture, and socializing. There are many foreign business clubs and social networks to join. If you are a socialite, there are parties and functions for you around the clock.

Bangkok is a shopper's paradise. The city's Panthip Plaza and Fortune Town mall provide computers, software, and accessories at the most competitive prices (if you are willing to bargain). The Siam Square area is home to several massive shopping plazas, including the new Siam Paragon (www.siamparagon.co.th).

A key advantage of doing business in Bangkok is access to an abundant supply of skilled, English-speaking university graduates. Nearly all the high flying graduates are based in Bangkok. The choice of the kingdom's office and professional staff is in Bangkok.

Disadvantages Of Doing Business In Bangkok

Probably the biggest disadvantages of living and conducting business in Bangkok are the traffic congestion, noise and air pollution, and intense heat and humidity.

This crowded city is fast, challenging, and potentially alienating. Be prepared for long queues and higher business overheads. Also be prepared to invest more in a business based in Bangkok. As a general rule of thumb, business overheads in Bangkok are twice that of Chiang Mai. Of course, the higher initial investment is compensated for by a much larger and more affluent market of potential buyers.

Clubs And Associations For Bangkok

American Women's Club of Thailand
Internet: www.awcthailand.com

Bangkok Toastmasters Club
Tel: + 66 (0)2 519-387 -8
Internet: www.bangkok-toastmasters.com,
www.toastmasters.org
Develop your public speaking skills.

Bangkok Expats' Association
E-mail: Bangkokexpatsassociation@thai.com

Bangkok Expats' Club and Bangkok Expats' Business Club
Internet: www.bangkok-expats-club.com
E-mail: Bangkok-expats-club@linuxmail.org

Bangkok Young Professionals
E-mail: callum@mobyelite.com
Internet: www.mobyelite.com/byp
Business seminars and networking events.

The British Club
Internet: www.britishclubbangkok.org

The British Council
24 Soi 64, Phayathai Road, Siam Square, Bangkok.
Tel: + 66 (0)2 252-6136
Internet: www.britishcouncil.org/thailand.htm

European Young Professionals
E-mail: alex@liquid-branding.com
Internet: www.europeanyoungprofessionals.org

The Foreign Correspondents' Club of Thailand
Maneeya Centre (Penthouse),
518/5 Ploenchit Road,
Bangkok, 10330. (BTS skytrain: Chidlom Station)
Tel: + 66 (0)2 652-0580 -1
E-mail: fccthai@loxinfo.co.th
Internet: www.fccthai.com

Rotary Club of Bangkok
Internet: www.rotaryclubofbangkok.org
Info: www.rotaryinthailand.org

XL Results Foundation
WVision Co., Ltd.
10c Unico House Building,
29/1 Soi Langsuan, Ploenchit Road,
Lumpini, Patumwan,
Bangkok, 10330.
E-mail: callum@mobyelite.com
Internet: www.resultsfoundation.com
Coaching and networking.

Golf Clubs: www.golf-bangkok.com

Government Offices For Bangkok

Department of Business Development
44/100 Nonthaburi 1 Road,
Amphur Muang,
Nonthaburi, 11000.
Tel: + 66 (0)2 547-5050
Fax: + 66 (0)2 547-4459
Hotline: 1570
E-mail: webmaster@thairegistration.com
Internet: www.dbd.go.th
Business registration.

Customs Department
Suthornkosa Road, Klong Toey,
Bangkok, 10110.
Tel: + 66 (0)2 249-0431 -40

Department of Employment
Mitmaitree Road, Din Daeng,
Bangkok, 10400.
Hotline: 1694
Internet: www.doe.go.th
Work permits.

Department of Export Promotion
22/77 Rachadapisek Road,
Lad Yao, Chatuchak,
Bangkok, 10900.
Tel: + 66 (0)2 511-5066 -77

Department of Land
Prapipit Road, Phanakorn,
Bangkok, 10200.
Tel: + 66 (0)2 225-5758; Fax: + 66 (0)2 224-0187
E-mail: bangkok@dol.go.th
Internet: www.dol.go.th/eng_version/menu.php
Registration and valuation of land.

Department of Land Transport
1032 Paholyothin Road,
Chatuchak,
Bangkok, 10900.
Tel: + 66 (0)2 272-5322
Fax: + 66 (0)2 272-5416
E-mail: pr.sub@dlt.go.th
Internet: www.dlt.go.th
Vehicle registration.

Immigration Bureau Head Office
507 Soi Suan Plu,
South Sathorn Tai Road,
Bangkok, 10120.
Tel: + 66 (0)2 287-3101 -10
Fax: + 66 (0)2 287-1310
Internet: www.imm.police.go.th
Visa administration.

Ministry of Foreign Affairs
Sri Ayuthya Road,
Bangkok, 10400.
Tel: + 66 (0)2 643-5000

Revenue Department
90 Soi Paholyothin 7, Paholyothin Road,
Bangkok, 10400.
Tel: + 66 (0)2 272-8000
Internet: www.rd.go.th
Administration of taxes.

Tourism Authority of Thailand (TAT)
1600 New Phetchaburi Road,
Makkasan, Rachathewi,
Bangkok, 10400.
Tel: + 66 (0)2 250-5500 Internet: www.tat.or.th

Thai Longstay Management (TLM) Co., Ltd.
TP & T Building (11th Floor),
1 Vipawadee-Rangsit Road (Soi 19),
Chatuchak,
Bangkok, 10900.
Tel: + 66 (0)2 936-1644
Fax: + 66 (0)2 936-1646
E-mail: info@thailongstay.co.th
Internet: www.thailongstay.co.th
Assistance with retirement visas. TLM is partly owned by the TAT

Excise Office.
Tel: + 66 (0)2 668-6601
Internet: www.excise.go.th

Publications For Bangkok

Bangkok Post
Tel: + 66 (0)2 240-3700
Fax: + 66 (0)2 240-3664
E-mail: business@bangkokpost.co.th
Internet: www.bangkokpost.net
National daily newspaper in English.

The Big Chilli magazine
The Big Chilli Co., Ltd.
1/7 Convent Road, Bangrak,
Bangkok, 10500.
Tel: + 66 (0)2 233-1774 -6
Fax: + 66 (0)2 235-0174
E-mail: colin@thebigchillicompany.com
Internet: www.thebigchillicompany.com

Business Day
Internet: www.biz-day.com

Maplus magazine
Bangkokstation Network Co., Ltd.
128 Wall Street Tower (25th Floor),
33/125 Surawong Road, Bangrak,
Bangkok, 10500.
Tel: + 66 (0)2 267-6178
Fax: + 66 (0)2 267-5539
Magazine in English and Japanese.

The Nation
44 Moo 10, Bang Na-Trat Highway KM 4.5,
Bang Na, Bangkok, 10260.
Tel: + 66 (0)2 325-5555
Fax: + 66 (0)2 751-4446
E-mail: ptymail@loxinfo.co.th
Internet: www.nationmultimedia.com
National daily newspaper in English.

The Nation Property Guide
Tel: + 66 (0)2 325-0206 (advertising)
+ 66 (0)2 316-5950 (distribution)
Quarterly real-estate journal in English.

Newspapers Direct
Internet: www.newspapersdirect.com
E-mail: info@newspapersdirect.com
www.clickthailand.com
Newspapers Direct distributes overseas newspapers.

Property Report Thailand
Ensign Media Co., Ltd.
Tel: + 66 (0)2 655-6070
Fax: + 66 (0)2 655-3492
E-mail: info@ensign-media.com
Internet: www.property-report.com;
www.ensign-media.com

Thailand Tatler
Tel: + 66 (0)2 250-0250
Fax: + 66 (0)2 250-0259
Internet: www.thailandtatler.com

Useful Websites For Bangkok

www.1stopbangkok.com

www.bangkok.nu

www.bangkokbob.net

www.bangkokguideonline.com

www.bangkoktourist.com

www.khaosanroad.com

www.stickmanbangkok.com

Chiang Mai

Advantages Of Doing Business In Chiang Mai

Chiang Mai, with a population of 150,000, is the largest city in the north of Thailand. This relaxed city of friendly people is a favourite holiday destination for Bangkok professionals. Chiang Mai is home to myriad spas, resorts, golf courses, cooking schools, massage schools, and tour operators. The city relies heavily on tourism.

The majority of factories in northern Thailand are based in the nearby towns of Lamphun and Lampang. The picturesque town of Pai, 130 kilometres away, is undergoing extensive development, including the construction of a new airport.

Northern Thailand is much less expensive to live in than Bangkok. There are over 30,000 expats in the Chiang Mai area, including many writers, software engineers, website developers, and students of the healing arts.

Disadvantages Of Doing Business In Chiang Mai

The city's major problem is air pollution due to uncontrolled vehicular emissions and seasonal burn-off of vegetation. Increasingly, expatriates are avoiding Chiang Mai for health reasons.

Due to the oversupply of bars, Internet cafés, and restaurants, there is a brisk turnover in ownership of these businesses. Many tourists and residents of Chiang Mai are accustomed to living on a low budget, so prices are competitive. Many foreign businesses are artificially supported by pensions.

It is difficult to attract employees with a professional work ethic in Chiang Mai. Most of the bright and motivated graduates head to Bangkok or overseas.

There are few clubs and interest groups in Chiang Mai, although there is a growing expats club. There is only one chamber of commerce in the city and far fewer business networking opportunities than in Bangkok or Pattaya.

Business operations are less sophisticated in northern Thailand. Many businesspeople seem wary of the internet.

Clubs And Associations For Chiang Mai

British Council
198 Bamrungrat Road, Thanon Watket,
Amphur Muang,
Chiang Mai, 50000.
Tel: + 66 (0)53 242-103
Fax: + 66 (0)53 244-781
E-mail: ukconsul@loxinfo.co.th

Chiang Mai Chamber of Commerce
50-50/4 (3rd Floor), Hill Side Plaza 4,
Huay Keaw Road, Amphur Muang,
Chiang Mai, 50300.
Tel: + 66 (0)53 223-256 -8
Fax: + 66 (0)53 222-482
E-mail: chamber@chmai.loxinfo.co.th

Chiang Mai Expats' Club
www.chiangmaiexpatsclub.com
E-mail: info@chiangmaiexpatsclub.com
Meets on the second and fourth Saturday of the month;

Chiang Mai Gymkhana Club
Old Lampun Road (near Sheraton Hotel)
Tel: + 66 (0)53 241-035
Fax: + 66 (0)53 247-354
Internet: www.chiangmaisixes.com
The club was founded in 1898 by teak loggers and British expatriates to encourage sport in northern Thailand.

First Northern Thailand Toastmasters Club
Tel: + 66 (0)53 311-255
Internet: www.toastmasters.org

Informal Northern Thailand Group
Tel: + 66 (0)53 247-263
E-mail: brihubb@loxinfo.co.th
Internet: www.intgcm.thehostserver.com
Meets on the second Tuesday of the month at the Alliance Francaise.

SOS Chiang Mai
Tel: + 66 (0)53 126-013
E-mail: info@soschiangmai.com
Internet: www.soschiangmai.com
SOS is a non-profit organization whose aim is to help foreigners in the event of an emergency. The annual premium is 2,000 baht. The service covers assistance during the event of detention by Immigration or the police, and hospitalization.

Rotary Clubs of Chiang Mai
Tel: + 66 (0)53 279-892
Fax: + 66 (0)53 279-447
Internet: www.rotarychiangmai.org
There are five Rotary Clubs in Chiang Mai.

Government Offices For Chiang Mai

Commercial Affairs Office
Provincial Hall, Chotana Road,
Amphur Muang,
Chiang Mai, 50300.
Tel: + 66 (0)53 112-668 -9
Fax: + 66 (0)53 112-670
E-mail: cm4@moc.go.th
Internet: www.moc.go.th/chain/chiangmai
Business registration.

Department of Land
Chiang Mai Provincial Hall,
Chotana Road, Amphur Muang,
Chiang Mai, 50000.
Tel: + 66 (0)53 890-484 -7
Fax: + 66 (0)53 890-487
E-mail: chiangmai@dol.go.th
Land registration and valuation.

Employment Office
Chiang Mai Provincial Hall,
Chotana Road, Amphur Muang,
Chiang Mai, 50000.
Tel: + 66 (0)53 112-742 -6
Fax: + 66 (0)53 112 743
E-mail: cmi@doe.go.th
Internet: www.doe.go.th/chiangmai
Administration of work permits.

Export Promotion Centre
29/19 Singharat Road,
Amphur Muang,
Chiang Mai, 50200.
Tel: + 66 (0)53 221-376
Fax: + 66 (0)53 215-307.

Immigration Office
71 Airport Road,
Amphur Muang,
Chiang Mai, 50200.
Tel: + 66 (0)53 277-510,
Fax: + 66 (0)53 277-510.
E-mail: imm3@police.go.th
Internet: www.chiangmai-immigration.com
Visa administration.

Land Transportation Authority
Tel: + 66 (0)53 278-570
Fax: + 66 (0)53 278-265
E-mail: chiangmai@dlt.go.th
Internet: www.dlt.go.th/chiangmai
Vehicle licensing office.

Municipal Office
1 Wangsingkam Road,
Amphur Muang,
Chiang Mai, 50300.
Tel: + 66 (0)53 259-000
Fax: + 66 (0)53 233-952.

Provincial Excise Office
Tel: + 66 (0)53 112-736
Internet: www.excise.go.th

Revenue Office
Airport Business Park 900,
Amphur Muang,
Chiang Mai, 50000.
Tel: + 66 (0)53 220-626 -34
Fax: + 66 (0)53 220-435 -6
Administration of taxes.

Tourism Authority of Thailand (TAT)
105/1 Chiang Mai-Lamphun Road,
Amphur Muang,
Chiang Mai, 50300.
Tel: + 66 (0)53 248-604
Fax: + 66 (0)53 248-605.

Publications For Chiang Mai

Art And Culture Lanna
19 Soi 7, Nimmanhaemin Road,
Amphur Muang,
Chiang Mai, 50200.
Tel: + 66 (0) 53 894-910
Fax: + 66 (0) 53 894-911
E-mail: cm@artandcultureasia.com
Internet: www.artandcultureasia.com

Chang Puak magazine
Mah Kao Ltd.,
200/37 Moo 9, Chiang Mai-Maejo Road,
Sanpisua, Chiang Mai.
Tel: + 66 (0)81 671-4037
Fax: + 66 (0)53 357-350
E-mail: mahkao@rocketmail.com
Free magazine in English and French.

The Chiang Mai Mail
Chiang Mai Mail Publishing Co., Ltd.
333/12 Moo 2, Jea Jea Sports Club,
Chiang Mai-Maejo Road,
Amphur Sansai,
Chiang Mai, 50210.
Tel: + 66 (0)53 230-119 -20
Fax: + 66 (0)53 230-120
E-mail: cnxmail@chiangmai-mail.com
Internet: www.chiangmai-mail.com
Weekly newspaper with free classifieds section.

Citylife magazine
Trisila Co., Ltd.
3 Chom Doi Road,
Chiang Mai, 50200.
Tel: + 66 (0)53 225-201
Fax: + 66 (0)53 357-491
E-mail: info@chiangmaicitylife.com
Internet: www.chiangmainews.com
Free monthly magazine in English with free classifieds.

Guidelines magazine
SP Publishing Group Co., Ltd.
11/1 Soi 3, Bamrungburi Road,
Amphur Muang,
Chiang Mai, 50200.
Tel: + 66 (0)53 814-455 -6
Fax: + 66 (0)53 814-457
E-mail: guidelinecm@hotmail.com
Internet: www.chiangmai-guideline.com
Free monthly magazine in English.

Passport to Suvannaphum
Internet: www.svpmagazine.com
Free monthly magazine for tourists.

Welcome to Chiang Mai and Chiang Rai
6 Nah Wat Gate Road, Soi 1
PO Box 100, Chiang Mai, 50000.
Tel: + 66 (0)53 260-705
Fax: + 66 (0)53 248-033
E-mail: Margaret@loxinfo.co.th
Internet: www.chiangmai-chiangrai.com
Free monthly magazine in English.

Lanna Explorer
Yumeya Graphic & Media Co., Ltd.
Tel/Fax: + 66 (0)53 818-228
Internet: www.lannaexplorer.com
Free monthly magazine in Japanese.

Useful Websites For Chiang Mai

www.1stopchiangmai.com

www.chiangmaiinfo.com

www.chiangmai-mail.com

www.chiangmainews.com

www.chiangmai-news.com

Hua Hin

Advantages Of Doing Business In Hua Hin

Hua Hin, in Prachuab Khiri Khan province, is about 200 kilometres south of Bangkok. The journey takes three and a half hours by car. This fashionable town, with a population of 42,000, offers over five kilometres of beaches and some of the best golf courses in the country. Hua Hin has its own old-world charm and provides a relaxed atmosphere in a clean, mostly unspoilt environment. Perhaps due to the residence of the royal family nearby, there is a low rate of crime in Hua Hin. A popular international Jazz Festival is hosted here every year.

The expat community in Hua Hin is growing rapidly, causing a property boom. Foreign businesspeople own restaurants, bars, hotels, and guesthouses, while others are involved in property development, real-estate agency, and property management.

Disadvantages Of Doing Business In Hua Hin

Property prices are escalating because the town is becoming so popular. Flights to Bangkok are expensive (for details, refer to www.huahinairport.com). This town is most suited to semi- or fully- retired people with a healthy bank balance and a set of golf clubs.

Hua Hin is too far from Bangkok to drive there and back in one day for business meetings. Therefore, trips to Bangkok usually require an overnight stay, unless the journey is taken by air.

Hua Hin is one of the more expensive locations to set up a business. The town is also vulnerable to seasonal trade fluctuations.

Clubs And Associations For Hua Hin

Hua Hin Hash Hound Harriers
Internet: www.huahin-hhh.com

Hua Hin Sports
Internet: www.huahinsport.com

Rotary Club of Hua Hin
Tel: + 66 (0)1 916-6637

Royal Hua Hin Golf Club
Internet: www.golfhuahin.com/royalhuahin.htm

Golf Clubs: www.golf-huahin.info

Government Offices For Hua Hin

City Hall
Tel: + 66 (0)32 512-267

Commercial Affairs Office
61 Sukjai Road, Amphur Muang,
Prachuab Khiri Khan,
Tel: + 66 (0)32 611-380
Fax: + 66 (0)32 611-972
E-mail: pk_ops@moc.go.th
Internet: www.moc.go.th/opscenter/pk
Business registration.

Department of Land
Prachuab Khiri Khan Road,
Amphur Muang, Prachuab Khiri Khan, 77000.
Tel: + 66 (0)32 611-211
Fax: + 66 (0)32 602-038
E-mail: prachuapkhirikhan@dol.go.th
Registration and valuation of land.

Employment Office
133/1, Sukjai Road, Amphur Muang,
Prachuab Khiri Khan, 77000.
Tel: + 66 (0)32 602-270 -1
Fax: + 66 (0)32 603-824
E-mail: pkn@doe.go.th
Internet: www.doe.go.th/prachuap
Administration of work permits.

Immigration Office
Tel: + 66 (0)32 619-038

Land Transportation Authority
199 Moo 4, Phetkasem Road,
Amphur Muang,
Prachuab Khiri Khan, 77210.
Tel: + 66 (0)32 602-034
Fax: + 66 (0) 32 601-900
E-mail: prachuap@dlt.go.th
Internet: www.dlt.go.th/prachuab
Vehicle registration and licensing.

Revenue Office
63/2 Sukjai Road, Amphur Muang,
Prachuab Khiri Khan, 77000.
Tel: + 66 (0)32 611-952 -4
Fax: + 66 (0)32 611-976
E-mail: emailprachuap@rd.go.th
Internet: www.rd.go.th/prachuapkhirikhan
Administration of taxes.

Publications For Hua Hin

Hua Hin Business Directory
Internet: http://hhbd.net

Hua Hin Today
E-mail: info@huahintoday.com
Internet: www.huahintoday.net
English-language newspaper.

Hua Hin Observer
Internet: www.observergroup.net
English-language newspaper.

Useful Websites For Hua Hin

www.hellohuahin.com

www.huahinafterdark.com

www.thailand-huahin.com

Khon Kaen

Advantages Of Doing Business In Khon Kaen

Khon Kaen is the industrial centre and main university city of Isaan, the rural northeastern region of Thailand. It is 445 kilometres from Bangkok and has a population of about 121,000. The city is home to the northeastern silk industry and is recognisved as the main trading and export centre to Indochina. Khon Kaen is experiencing strong growth, especially in construction.

The city provides modern banking facilities and a large pool of university graduates available for work. There are potential business opportunities serving the large population of students.

The cost of living in northeastern Thailand is lower than in central and southern Thailand. Many tourists and 'visa runners' use Isaan as a gateway to Laos and Vietnam, both of which have located their consulates in Khon Kaen to facilitate visa applications.

Disadvantages Of Doing Business In Khon Kaen

Khon Kaen offers few business networking opportunities for foreigners compared to Bangkok, Pattaya, or even Chiang Mai. It is the least developed location profiled here, and most of the foreigners living in this province enjoy a relatively quiet and simple life.

Not much English is spoken by the residents of Khon Kaen. Unless you are a quiet family person, this city may not provide enough services to satisfy you.

Clubs And Associations For Khon Kaen

Khon Kaen Chamber of Commerce
177/54 Moo 7, Mitapraph Road,
Amphur Muang,
Khon Kaen, 40000.
Tel: + 66 (0)4 332-4990 -1
Fax: + 66 (0)4 332-4990
E-mail: kanlayanee49@yahoo.co.th
Internet: www.kkchamber.com

Government Offices For Khon Kaen

Commercial Affairs Office

4/1 Front Civil Road,
Amphur Muang,
Khon Kaen, 40000.
Tel: + 66 (0)4 323-6571
Fax: + 66 (0)4 333-2347
E-mail: kk_ops@moc.go.th
Internet: www.moc.go.th/opscenter/kk/kk4.htm
Business registration.

Department of Land

4 Moo 13, Front Civil Road,
Amphur Muang,
Khon Kaen, 40000.
Tel: + 66 (0)4 323-6528
Fax: + 66 (0)4 323-8106
E-mail: khonkaen@dol.go.th
Internet: www.khonkaenpoc.com/kkdol
Registration and valuation of land.

Employment Office

Provincial Hall, Front Civil Road,
Amphur Muang,
Khon Kaen, 40000.
Tel: + 66 (0)4 323-9010
Fax: + 66 (0)4 333-0749
E-mail: kkn@doe.go.th
Internet: www.doe.go.th/khonkaen
Administration of work permits.

Land Transportation Authority

E-mail: khonkaen@dlt.go.th
Internet: www.dlt.go.th/khonkaen
Vehicle registration and licensing.

Municipality of Khon Kaen

3/3 Pracharajsamran Road,
Amphur Muang,
Khon Kaen, 40000.
Tel: + 66 (0)4 322-1202
Fax: + 66 (0)4 322-4033
E-mail: kkmuni@kkmuni.go.th
Internet: www.kkmuni.go.th

Provincial Administrative Organization

Na-Muang Road,
Amphur Muang,
Khon Kaen, 40000.
Tel: + 66 (0)4 324-3290
E-mail: kkpao.org@gmail.com
Internet: www.kkpao.org

Provincial Industrial Office

Front Civil Road,
Amphur Muang,
Khon Kaen, 40000.
Tel: + 66 (0)4 333-1155 -6
Fax: + 66 (0)4 324-1810
E-mail: khonkaen@m-industry.go.th
Internet: www.m-industry.go.th

Revenue Office

Provincial Hall, Front Civil Road,
Amphur Muang,
Khon Kaen, 40000.
Tel: + 66 (0)4 324-6760
Fax: + 66 (0)4 324-6761
E-mail: khonkaen@rd.go.th
Internet: www.rd.go.th/khonkaen
Administration of taxes.

Tourism Authority of Thailand (TAT)

Northeastern Office: Region 3,
15/5 Prachasamosorn Road,
Amphur Muang,
Khon Kaen, 40000.
Tel: + 66 (0)4 324-4498 -9
Fax: + 66 (0)4 324-4497
E-mail: tatknkn@tat.or.th
Internet: www.tat.or.th/northeast3

Useful Websites For Khon Kaen

www.khonkaen.com

www.kku.ac.th (Khon Kaen University)

www.udonthani.com

Koh Samui

Advantages Of Doing Business On Koh Samui

The islands of Koh Samui (population: 50,000) and Koh Pha Ngan, (population: 10,000) in Surat Thani province, offer some of Thailand's best beaches and resorts. Popular foreign businesses on these islands can be found in entertainment, tourism, property development, real estate, and computer programming.

Disadvantages Of Doing Business On Koh Samui

By land and sea routes, both of these islands can be considered a little remote. Ferries run from the mainland at Surat Thani. Bangkok Airways has a monopoly on flights to Koh Samui, so fares are inflated. The additional time and expense of travelling to these islands increases the cost of all products. Some goods are in limited supply.

Residents of Samui and Pha Ngan can expect seasonal flooding in low-lying areas, occasional water shortages, and power cuts. Internet connections can also be unreliable. Healthcare services on the islands are basic.

Clubs And Associations For Koh Samui

Samui Expats' Club
Internet: www.samuiexpats.com
E-mail: sec@samuiexpats.com

Samui Rotary Club
Internet: www.rotarysamui.org

Government Offices For Koh Samui

Department of Land
Talad Road, Amphur Muang,
Surat Thani, 84000.
Tel: + 66 (0)77 272-178,
+ 66 (0)77 423-252
Fax: + 66 (0)77 272-178
E-mail: suratthani@dol.go.th
Registration and valuation of land.

Employment Office
Civil Office Building,
Amphur Muang,
Surat Thani, 84000.
Tel: + 66 (0)77 355-422 -3
Fax: + 66 (0)77 355-426
E-mail: contact@seso.go.th
Internet: www.seso.go.th
Administration of work permits.

Immigration Office
Tel: + 66 (0)77 421-069
E-mail: s_samui@immigration.go.th
Internet: www.imm.police.go.th/samui
Visa administration.

Land Transportation Authority
Kanchanavitee Road,
Amphur Muang,
Surat Thani, 84000.
Tel: + 66 (0)77 287-988 ext. 13
Fax: + 66 (0)77 283-383
E-mail: suratthani@dlt.go.th
Internet: www.dlt.go.th/suratthani
Vehicle registration and licensing.

Revenue Office
100/1 Donnok Road,
Amphur Muang,
Surat Thani, 84000.
Tel: + 66 (0)77 288-639
Fax: + 66 (0)77 281-111
Administration of taxes.

Publications For Koh Samui

Samui Property Map
Internet: www.samuipropertymap.com

Samui magazine
ArtAsia Press Co., Ltd.
Tel: + 66 (0)77 413-514
Fax: + 66 (0)77 422-658
E-mail: aapress@samuinet.com
Internet: www.samuiguide.com
Annual publication.

Useful Websites For Koh Samui

www.kohphangan.net

www.kohphanganisland.com

http://samui.sawadee.com

www.kohsamui-info.com

www.kohsamui.com

www.kohsamui.org

www.on-samui.com

www.samui.org

www.samuicommunity.com

Pattaya

Advantages Of Doing Business In Pattaya

The resort city of Pattaya, in Chonburi province, is 150 kilometres south-east of Bangkok and has a population of 100,000. It takes about two hours to get there by road from the capital, and slightly less from Suvarnabhumi International Airport (www.bangkokairportonline.com). Pattaya's three beaches and intense entertainment industry draws many retirees and over a million tourists each year from around the globe.

The city boasts two expats' clubs, several local newspapers for foreigners, abundant and reasonably priced accommodation, five Rotary Clubs, two reputable yacht clubs, and over twenty golf courses. *The Pattaya Mail* newspaper has an excellent classified advertising section for business opportunities (www.pattayamail.com/mailmarket/).

Many foreigners own bars, restaurants, hotels, and guesthouses. Other than tourism-oriented businesses, foreigners are engaged in exports, real estate, and business brokering.

Disadvantages Of Doing Business In Pattaya

Pattaya has a reputation for red-light tourism and crime. During the peak season for tourism, the city can get overcrowded and noisy. Pollution and traffic congestion is also on the rise. There is intense competition in real estate and business brokering.

Clubs And Associations For Pattaya

Pattaya Biz Club
E-mail: info@pattayabizclub.com
Internet: www.pattayabizclub.com

Pattaya Bridge Club
Internet: www.pattayabridge.com

Pattaya Expats' Club
Internet: www.pattayaexpats.com
www.pattayaexpatsclub.com
E-mail: info@pattayaexpatsclub.com

Pattaya City Expats' Club
Internet: www.pattayacityexpatsclub.com

Pattaya International Ladies' Club (PILC)
PO Box 262, Pattaya Post,
Chonburi, 20260.
E-mail: pilc262@yahoo.com

Pattaya Rotary Club
Internet: www.rotary-pattaya.com

Rotary Club of Pattaya
Internet: www.rotary-pattaya.org

Golf Clubs: www.golf-pattaya.info

Government Offices For Pattaya

Commercial Affairs Office
43/16 Old Hospital Road,
Amphur Muang, Chonburi, 20000.
Tel: + 66 (0)38 277-217, Fax: + 66 (0) 38 274-279
E-mail: cb_ops@moc.go.th
Internet: www.moc.go.th/opscenter/cb/t_main.htm
Business registration.

Department of Land

46 Wachiraprakarn Road,
Amphur Muang,
Chonburi, 20000.
Tel: + 66 (0)38 285-445 -6
Fax: + 66 (0)38 285-447
E-mail: chonburi@dol.go.th
Land registration and valuation.

Employment Office

199 Moo 3, Montasevee Road,
Amphur Muang,
Chonburi, 20000.
Tel: + 66 (0)38 398-051 -2, Fax: + 66 (0)38 398-053
Internet: www.doe.go.th/chonburi
Administration of work permits.

Immigration Office

Tel: + 66 (0)38 429-409
Fax: + 66 (0)38 410-240
E-mail: c_pattaya@immigration.go.th
Internet: www.pattaya-immigration.com
Visa administration.

Land Transportation Authority

147 Moo 1, Sukhumvit Road,
Amphur Muang,
Chonburi, 20000
Tel: + 66 (0)38 275-200
E-mail: chonburi@dlt.go.th
Internet: www.dlt.go.th/chonburi
Vehicle registration and licensing.

City Hall
North Pattaya Road,
Pattaya.
Tel: + 66 (0)38 429-403 -5
Internet: www.pattayacityhall.go.th

Publications For Pattaya

Pattaya Blatt
Internet: www.pattayablatt.com
German newspaper.

Pattaya Info
Telephone: + 66 (0)38 713-493
Internet: www.pattayainfo.com
Newspaper in English, French, German, and Dutch.

Pattaya Mail
Pattaya Mail Publishing Co., Ltd.
370/7-8 Pattaya 2 Road,
Pattaya City, Chonburi, 20260.
Tel: + 66 (0)38 411-240 -1, Fax: + 66 (0)38 427-596
E-mail: ptymail@loxinfo.co.th
Internet: www.pattayamail.com
Weekly newspaper in English.

Pattaya People
Internet: www.pattayapeople.com
Weekly newspaper in English and Thai.

Pattaya Today
Tel: + 66 (0)38 410-077
E-mail: info@pattayatoday.net
Internet: www.pattayatoday.net
Fortnightly newspaper in English.

Hallo Das Magazin
Internet: www.hallo-das-magazin.de
Pattaya news in German.

Inside Pattaya
Internet: www.insidepattaya.com

Pattaya Lap
Internet: www.pattaya.lap.hu
Pattaya information for Hungarians.

Viking newspaper
Internet: www.scan-siam.com
Pattaya news for Scandinavians.

Pattaya Trader Online
6/28 Moo 9, Sukhumvit Road,
Nongprue, Banglamung,
Chonburi, 20260.
Tel: + 66 (0)38 716-390
E-mail: phil@pattayatrader.com
Internet: www.pattayatrader.com
Free monthly magazine.

Pattaya Pagina NL
Internet: http://pattaya.startpagina.nl
Pattaya news in Dutch.

Useful Websites For Pattaya

www.1stoppattaya.com

www.pattaya.com

www.gopattaya.com

www.pattayahouses.com

www.pattayatrader.com

www.pattayacity.com

www.pattayanet.com

www.pattayarentaroom.com

Phuket

Advantages Of Doing Business In Phuket

Phuket is Thailand's largest and most 'connected' island, with its own international airport and a direct road link to the mainland. The causeway allows direct truck access, which keeps production prices lower than on other islands.

Phuket, a province in its own right, has a population of around 75,000, and there are sufficient foreign businesspeople living on the island to offer numerous business clubs (including F&B Managers' Club, SKAL Club for hoteliers, the Lions Club, Phuket Tourist Association, Toastmasters, the Round Table, and the Alliance Francaise).

The majority of foreign business is involved in property development, real-estate agency, hotels and guesthouses, bars and restaurants.

Disadvantages Of Doing Business In Phuket

During the peak of the tourist season, congestion and pollution are problems. Being an island with limited space, the cost of accommodation is expensive compared to other areas of Thailand.

Clubs And Associations For Phuket

British Business Association Phuket
E-mail: honsec@bbap.org
Internet: www.bbap.org

Phuket Chamber of Commerce
1/1 Montri Road, Amphur Muang,
Phuket, 83000.
Tel: + 66 (0)76 217-567 -8
E-mail: chamber@phuket.ksc.co.th

International Business Association of Phuket
Tel: + 66 (0)81 892-4676
E-mail: info@ibap-phuket.org
Internet: http://ibap-phuket.org

Rotary Club of Phuket
Tel: + 66 (0)76 211-044
E-mail: internationalservice@rotaryphuket.com
Internet: www.rotaryphuket.com
There are seven Rotary Clubs on Phuket.

Phuket Expats' Golf Society
E-mail: expatgolf@expatgolf.com

Golf Clubs: www.golf-phuket.com

Government Offices For Phuket

Department of Land
36 Damrong Road,
Amphur Muang,
Phuket, 83000.
Tel: + 66 (0)76 212-103
Fax: + 66 (0)76 212-103 ext. 12
E-mail: phuket@dol.go.th
Registration and valuation of land.

Employment Office
38/27 Rattanakosin Road,
Amphur Muang,
Phuket, 83000.
Tel: + 66 (0)76 219-660 -1
Fax: + 66 (0)76 354-036
E-mail: info@phuketlabour.th.org
Internet: www.phuketlabour.th.org
Administration of work permits.

Immigration Office
Phuket Road,
Amphur Muang,
Phuket, 83000.
Tel: + 66 (0)76 212-108 -10
Fax: + 66 (0)76 212-108
E-mail: s_phuket@immigration.go.th
Internet: www.phuketimmigration.com
Visa administration.

Land Transportation Authority
42/4 Rattanakosin Road,
Amphur Muang,
Phuket, 83000.
Tel: + 66 (0)76 220-791
E-mail: info@phuketlandtransport.org
Internet: www.phuketlandtransport.th.org
Vehicle registration and licensing.

Revenue Office
Provincial Hall,
Amphur Muang,
Phuket, 83000.
Tel: + 66 (0)76 211-280
Fax: + 66 (0) 76 216-674
Administration of taxes.

Tourism Authority of Thailand (TAT)
Southern Office: Region 4,
73-75 Phuket Road,
Amphur Muang,
Phuket, 83000.
Tel: + 66 (0)76 212-213
E-mail: tatphket@tat.or.th.

Publications For Phuket

Art And Culture South
16 Soi Romanee,
Amphur Muang,
Phuket, 83000.
Tel: + 66 (0)76 288-856 Fax: + 66 (0)76 289-093
E-mail: info@artandcultureasia.com
Internet: www.artandcultureasia.com

Phuket Gazette
The Phuket Gazette Co., Ltd.
367/2 Yaowarat Road,
Amphur Muang,
Phuket, 83000.
Tel: + 66 (0)76 236-555
Fax: + 66 (0)76 213-971
Internet: www.phuketgazette.com
Weekly newspaper with online classifieds;
also publishes Gazette Guide (business directory).

Phuket Guide
ArtAsia Press Co., Ltd.
Tel: + 66 (0)76 264-433
Fax: + 66 (0)76 264-255
E-mail: info-phuket@aapress.net
Internet: www.aapress.net
Monthly tourist guide.

Phuket magazine
ArtAsia Press Co., Ltd.
Tel: + 66 (0)76 264-433
Fax: + 66 (0)76 264-255
E-mail: info-phuket@aapress.net
Internet: www.aapress.net
Published nine times each year.

Phuket Property Map
Internet: www.phuketpropertymap.com

Useful Websites for Phuket

www.1stopphuket.com

www.phuket.com

www.phuket.net

www.gotophuket.com

www.phuketindex.com

www.phukettourism.org

www.phuket-info.com

www.phuketmagazine.com

www.phukettoday.com

http://image-asia.com

Chapter 12
References

This section provides primary contacts for people wanting to do business in Thailand. Wherever possible, each organisation's website is included to enable access to their latest information. All the foreign chambers of commerce listed here are based in Bangkok; some regional chambers are listed in "Essential Contacts By Location" (page 171). The four main private firms of business brokers in Thailand are also listed.

Associations And Government Offices

Association of Securities Companies
Internet: www.asco.or.th

Bank of Thailand
273 Samsen Road, Bangkhunphrom
Bangkok, 10200.
Tel: + 66 (0)2 283-5353
Fax: + 66 (0)2 280-0449
Internet: www.bot.or.th

Board of Investment (BOI)
555 Vipawadee-Rangsit Road,
Chatuchak,
Bangkok, 10900.
Tel: + 66 (0)2 537-8111
Fax: + 66 (0)2 537-8177
E-mail: head@boi.go.th
Internet: www.boi.go.th
Business promotion and tax incentives for foreign investors. Economic and commercial overviews including investment support policies for each province. Further information is available at: www.investmentthailand. com.

Board of Trade of Thailand
150 Rajbopit Road,
Bangkok, 10200.
Tel: + 66 (0)2 622-1860 -76
Fax: + 66 (0)2 225-3372
Internet: www.tcc.or.th

Customs Department
Tel: 1332
E-mail: ctc@customs.go.th
Internet: www.customs.go.th

Department of Business Development (DBD)
Ministry of Commerce
Internet: www.dbd.go.th
This website publishes laws relating to business registration.

Department of Employment
Ministry of Labour
Mit-Maitree Road, Din Daeng,
Bangkok, 10400.
Tel: + 66 (0)2 245-2745
Fax: + 66 (0)2 354-1762
Internet: www.doe.go.th/workpermit/index.html
Work permit applications.

Department of Export Promotion
Ministry of Commerce
Tel: + 66 (0)2 513-1909
Fax: + 66 (0)2 512-1079
E-mail: itict@depthai.go.th
Internet: www.thaitrade.com
Refer to "Regional Export Promotion Centres" (page 211).

Department of Foreign Trade
Tel: + 66 (0)2 547-4771
Fax: + 66 (0)2 547-4791 -2
E-mail: dftwebmaster@moc.go.th
Internet: www.dft.moc.go.th

Department of Industrial Promotion
Tel: + 66 (0)2 202-4414 -18
Fax: + 66 (0)2 246-0031
Internet: www.dip.go.th

Department of Intellectual Property
Internet: www.ipthailand.org
Copyrights, patents, and trademarks.

Department of Internal Trade
Tel: + 66 (0)2 507-6111
Fax: + 66 (0)2 547-5361
Internet: www.dit.go.th

Department of Land
Tel: + 66 (0)2 622-2380
Internet: www.dol.go.th
Registration and valuation of land.

Department of Land Transport
1032 Paholyothin Road,
Bangkok, 10900.
Tel: + 66 (0)2 272-5322
Fax: + 66 (0)2 272-5416
E-mail: pr.sub@dlt.go.th
Internet: www.dlt.go.th
Vehicle registration and licensing.

Department of Mineral Resources
Tel: + 66 (0)2 202-3769
Internet: www.dmr.go.th

Department of Skills Development
Internet: www.dsd.go.th

Excise Department
1488 Nakhonchaisri Road, Dusit,
Bangkok, 10300.
Tel: + 66 (0)2 241-5600 -19
Fax: + 66 (0)2 668-6398
E-mail: webmaster@excise.go.th
Internet: www.excise.go.th/eng-index.html

Export-Import Bank
EXIM Building,
1193 Paholyothin Road,
Bangkok, 10400,
Tel: + 66 (0)2 271-3700
Fax: + 66 (0)2 271-3204
Internet: www.exim.go.th

Federation of Thai Industries
Queen Sirikit National Convention Centre,
60 New Rachadapisek Road,
Bangkok, 10110.
Tel: + 66 (0)2 345-1000
Fax: + 66 (0)2 345-1296 -99
E-mail: information@fti.or.th
Internet: www.fti.or.th

Foreign Banks' Association
Sathorn Thani Building 2 (19th Floor),
92/55 North Sathorn Road, Bangrak,
Bangkok, 10500.
Tel: + 66 (0)2 236-6070 -2
Fax: + 66 (0)2 236-6069
E-mail: btathai@truemail.co.th
Internet: www.fba.or.th

Foreign Workers' Administration Office
Department of Employment
Ministry of Labour
Mit-Maitree Road, Din Daeng,
Bangkok, 10400.
Tel: + 66 (0)2 245-2745

Immigration Bureau
Tel: + 66 (0)2 287-3101 -10
Fax: + 66 (0)2 287-1310
Internet: www.immigration.go.th

Industrial Estates Authority of Thailand (IEAT)
Tel: + 66 (0)2 253-0561
Fax: + 66 (0)2 253-4086
Internet: www.ieat.go.th

Intellectual Property Institute
Internet: www.ip-institute.org

Investor Club Association (ICA)
TP & T Tower (16th Floor),
1 Soi 19, Vipawadee-Rangsit Road,
Bangkok.
Tel: + 66 (0)2 936-1429 -40
E-mail: investor@ic.or.th
Internet: www.ic.or.th

ICA is a private members club, part of the Board of Investment (BOI), which serves as a networking organization for BOI members. ICA members have access to the Customs Department tracking system for raw materials and machinery.

Land Development Department
Tel: + 66 (0)2 57-0111
E-mail: cit_1@ldd.go.th
Internet: www.ldd.go.th

Lawyers' Council of Thailand
Tel: + 66 (0)2 629-1430
Fax: + 66 (0)2 282-9907
Internet: www.lawyerscouncil.or.th

Ministry of Commerce (MOC)
44/100 Sanam Bin Nam-Nonthaburi Road,
Amphur Muang,
Nonthaburi, 11000.
Tel: + 66 (0)2 507-8000
Fax: + 66 (0)2 507-7717
E-mail: webmaster@moc.go.th
Internet: www.moc.go.th
Business registration.

Ministry of Finance (MOF)
Rama IV Road, Samsen,
Phayathai,
Bangkok, 10400.
Tel: + 66 (0)2 273-9021
Fax: + 66 (0)2 293-9408
Internet: www.mof.go.th

Ministry of Foreign Affairs
Sri Ayuthya Road,
Bangkok, 10400.
Tel: + 66 (0)2 643-5000
Fax: + 66 (0)2 643-5180
E-mail: consular@mfa.go.th
Internet: www.mfa.go.th
Visa information: www.mfa.go.th/web/12.php

Ministry of Industry (MOI)
Rama IV Road, Rachathewi,
Bangkok, 10400.
Tel: + 66 (0)2 202-3000
Fax: + 66 (0)2 202-3048
E-mail: pr@m-industry.go.th
Internet: www.m-industry.go.th

National Economic & Social Development Board (NESDB)
Tel: + 66 (0)2 280-4085
Fax: + 66 (0)2 281-3938
Internet: www.nesdb.go.th

National Electronics & Computer Technology Centre (NECTEC)
Ministry of Science, Technology, and the Environment
Tel: + 66 (0)2 564-6900 ext. 2346
E-mail: info@nectec.or.th
Internet: www.nectec.or.th

National Statistical Office
Internet: www.nso.go.th

Office of Industrial Economics
Tel: + 66 (0)2 202-4270
Fax: + 66 (0)2 644-7136
E-mail: verasak@oie.go.th
Internet: www.oie.go.th

One-Stop Service Centre For Visas and Work Permits
Krisada Plaza (3rd Floor),
207 Rachadapisek Road, Din Daeng,
Bangkok, 10400.
Tel: + 66 (0)2 693-9333 -9
Fax: + 66 (0)2 693-9352
E-mail: visawork@boi.go.th
Internet: www.boi.go.th
The centre can process visas and work permits in under three hours.

Revenue Department
90 Soi 7, Paholyothin Road,
Bangkok, 10400.
Internet: www.rd.go.th
Tax administration.

Securities and Exchange Commission (SEC)
Tel: + 66 (0)2 695-9999 ext. 6008
E-mail: info@sec.or.th
Internet: www.sec.or.th

Stock Exchange of Thailand (SET)
Tel: + 66 (0)2 229-2222
Internet: www.set.or.th/en/index.html

Thai Bankers' Association
Lake Rachada Office Complex, Building II (4th Floor),
195/5 Rachadapisek Road,
Bangkok, 10110.
Tel: + 66 (0)2 264-0883 -7
Fax: + 66 (0)2 264-0888
Internet: www.tba.or.th

Thai Industrial Standards Institute (TISI)
Tel: + 66 (0)2 202-3301 -4
Fax: + 66 (0)2 202-3415
E-mail: thaistan@tisi.go.th
Internet: www.tisi.go.th

Thailand Elite
Tel: + 66 (0)2 353-4000
+ 66 (0)2 352-3000 (members)
Fax: + 66 (0)2 353-4001
+ 66 (0)2 352-3001 (members)
E-mail: info@thailandelite.com
Internet: www.thailandelite.com
Benefits package includes a renewable, five-year multiple-entry visa.

Tourism Authority of Thailand (TAT)
Tel: + 66 (0)2 250-5500
Fax: + 66 (0)2 250-5511
E-mail: center@tat.or.th
Internet: www.tat.or.th

Treasury Department
Internet: www.treasury.go.th

Chambers Of Commerce

American Chamber of Commerce Thailand (AMCHAM)
Kian Gwan Building (7th Floor),
140 Wireless Road,
Bangkok, 10330.
Tel: + 66 (0)2 251-9266 -7
Fax: + 66 (0)2 651-4472 -4
Internet: www.amchamthailand.com; www.amcham-th.org

Australia-Thai Chamber of Commerce (AUSTCHAM)
202 Thai CC Tower (20th Floor),
889 South Sathorn Road, Yannawa,
Bangkok, 10120.
Tel: + 66 (0)2 210-0216 -7
Fax: + 66 (0)2 210-0218
Website: www.austchamthailand.com

Belgian-Luxembourg-Thai Chamber of Commerce
Tel: + 66 (0)2 231-0891 -2
E-mail: info@beluthai.org
Internet: www.beluthai.org

British Chamber of Commerce
208 Wireless Road (7th Floor),
Lumphini, Patumwan,
Bangkok, 10330.
Tel: + 66 (0)2 651-5350 -3
Fax: + 66 (0)2 651-5354
E-mail: greg@bccthai.com
Internet: www.bccthai.com

Canadian-Thai Chamber of Commerce
Tel: + 66 (0)2 231-0891 -2
Internet: www.tccc.or.th

Chambre de Franco-Thai
75/20 Soi 26, Sukhumvit Road,
Bangkok, 10110.
Tel: + 66 (0)2 261-8276 -7
Fax: + 66 (0)2 261-8278
E-mail: contact@francothaicc.com
Internet: francothaicc.com

Chinese Chamber of Commerce
233 South Sathorn Road,
Bangkok, 10330.
Tel: + 66 (0)2 211-8531
 + 66 (0)2 675-8574 -84
Fax: + 66 (0)2 211-8531
Internet: www.thaiccc.or.th

Danish-Thai Chamber of Commerce
Phayathai Building B (5th Floor),
34 Phayathai Road,
Bangkok, 10400.
Tel: + 66 (0)2 354-5220
Fax: + 66 (0)2 354-5221
E-mail: contact@dancham.or.th
Internet: www.dancham.or.th

Finnish-Thai Chamber of Commerce
Phayathai Building B (5th Floor),
34 Phayathai Road,
Bangkok, 10400.
Tel: + 66 (0)2 354-5215 -7
Fax: + 66 (0)2 354-5218
E-mail: tfcc@thaifin.or.th
Internet: www.thaifin.or.th

German-Thai Chamber of Commerce
195 South Sathorn Road,
Bangkok, 10120.
Tel: + 66 (0)2 670-0600
Fax: + 66 (0)2 670-0601
E-mail: info@gtcc.org
Internet: www.gtcc.org

Indian-Thai Chamber of Commerce
13 Soi Attakarnprasit, South Sathorn Road,
Bangkok, 10120.
Tel: + 66 (0)2 287-3001 -2
Fax: + 66 (0)2 679-7720
E-mail: info@itcc.or.th
Internet: www.itcc.or.th

Israel-Thai Chamber of Commerce
Tel: + 66 (0)2 672-7020
E-mail: ticc@thaisraelcc.or.th
Internet: www.thaisraelcc.or.th

Italian-Thai Chamber of Commerce
Vanit II Building (16th Floor),
1126/2 New Petchaburi Road,
Bangkok, 10400.
Tel: + 66 (0)2 253-9909
Fax: + 66 (0)2 253-9896
E-mail: ticc@loxinfo.co.th
Internet: www.thaitch.org

Japanese Chamber of Commerce
Amarin Tower (15th Floor),
500 Ploenchit Road,
Bangkok, 10330.
Tel: + 66 (0)2 256-9170 -3
Fax: + 66 (0)2 652-0931
E-mail: yon@jcc.or.th
Internet: www.jcc.or.th

Joint Foreign Chambers of Commerce in Thailand
Tel: + 66 (0)2 617-2075 ext. 402
Fax: + 66 (0)2 617-2089
E-mail: fcccc@inet.co.th
Internet: www.jfcct.com

Korea-Thai Chamber of Commerce
Tel: + 66 (0)2 233-1322 -3
+ 66 (0)2 266 6298
Fax: + 66 (0)2 653-2056
E-mail: tkcc@korchamthai.com
Internet: www.korchamthai.com

Malaysia-Thai Chamber of Commerce
Internet: www.mtcc.or.th

Netherlands-Thai Chamber of Commerce
Tel: + 66 (0)2 260-7501
Internet: www.ntccthailand.or.th

New Zealand-Thai Chamber of Commerce
ITF Tower (9th Floor),
140/26 Silom Road, Bangrak,
Bangkok, 10500.
Tel: + 66 (0)2 634-3283
Fax: + 66 (0)2 634-3004
E-mail: nztcc@loxinfo.co.th
Internet: www.nztcc.org

Norway-Thai Chamber of Commerce
Phayathai Building B (5th Floor),
34 Phayathai Road,
Bangkok, 10400.
Tel: + 66 (0)2 354-5229
Fax: + 66 (0)2 544-5232
E-mail: contact@norcham.com
Internet: www.norcham.com

Philippine-Thai Chamber of Commerce
Sethiwan Tower (21st Floor),
139 Pan Road, Bangrak,
Bangkok, 10300.
Tel/Fax: + 66 (0)2 266-6298

Singapore-Thai Chamber of Commerce
Tel: + 66 (0)2 260-8020 -41
E-mail: marketing@singaporethaicc.or.th
Internet: www.singaporethaicc.or.th

South Africa-Thai Chamber of Commerce
10-04 B Times Square Building,
246 Sukhumvit Road,
Bangkok, 10110.
Tel: + 66 (0)2 294-4747 -8
E-mail: satcc@satcc.net
Internet: www.satcc.net

Swedish Chamber of Commerce
Tel: + 66 (0)2 661-7761 -3
E-mail: secretary@swecham.com
Internet: www.swecham.com

Swiss-Thai Chamber of Commerce
Tel: + 66 (0)2 255-3767
E-mail: info@swissthai.com
Internet: www.swissthai.com

Thai Chamber of Commerce
150 Rajbopit Road,
Bangkok, 10200.
Tel: + 66 (0)2 622-1860 -76
Fax: + 66 (0)2 225-3372
Internet: www.tcc.or.th; www.thaiechamber.com

Business Brokers And Advisors

The Bizxchange
Head office: Bangkok
Tel: + 66 (0)2 636-7600
Fax: + 66 (0)2 636-7007
E-mail: info@businessmissionasia.com
Internet: www.thebizxchange.com

SEABS
Head office: Chiang Mai
Tel: + 66 (0)53 221-929 -31
Fax: + 66 (0)53 221-008
Internet: www.seabs.com

Sunbelt Asia
Head office: Bangkok
Tel: + 66 (0)2 642-0213
Fax: + 66 (0)2 641-1995
E-mail: info@sunbeltasia.com
Internet: www.sunbeltasia.com
Other offices in Chiang Mai, Koh Samui, Pattaya, and Phuket.

Thai Sunshine Business Advisors (TSBA)
Head office: Bangkok
Tel: + 66 (0)2 231-8190
Fax: + 66 (0)2 231-8121
E-mail: phil@tsba.info
Internet: www.tsba.info

Regional Export Promotion Centres

Chanthaburi
30/31-32 Trirat Road,
Chanthaburi, 22000.
Tel: + 66 (0)39 325-962 -3
Fax: + 66 (0)39 325-962

Chiang Mai
29/19 Singharaj Road,
Chiang Mai, 50200.
Tel: + 66 (0)53 216-350 -1
Fax: + 66 (0)53 215 307

Hat Yai
7-15 Jootee-Uthit 1 Road,
Hat Yai,
Songkhla, 90110.
Tel: + 66 (0)74 234-349
Fax: + 66 (0)74 234-329

Khon Kaen
68/4 Kiang Muang Road,
Khon Kaen, 40000.
Tel: + 66 (0)43 221-472
Fax: + 66 (0)43 221-476

Surat Thani
148/59 Surat-Nakhonsri Road,
Bang Kung,
Surat Thani, 84000.
Tel: + 66 (0)77 286-916
Fax: + 66 (0)77 288-632

Other Useful Contacts

Communications Authority of Thailand
99 Chaeng-Wattana Road,
Bangkok, 10002.
Tel: + 66 (0)2 573-0099
Internet: www.cat.or.th

General Post Office
Tel: + 66 (0)2 233-1050
Internet: www.ptd.go.th

Industrial Finance Corporation of Thailand
1770 New Petchaburi Road,
Bangkok, 10500.
Tel: + 66 (0)2 253-7111
Fax: + 66 (0)2 253-9677
Internet: www.ifet.co.th

Metropolitan Electrical Authority
30 Soi Chidlom, Ploenchit Road,
Patumwan,
Bangkok, 10330.
Tel: + 66 (0)2 254-9550
Fax: + 66 (0)2 253-1424
Internet: www.mea.or.th

Metropolitan Waterworks Authority
400 Prachachuen Road, Laksi,
Bangkok, 10210.
Tel: + 66 (0)2 504-0123
Fax: + 66 (0)2 503-9490

Provincial Electrical Authority
200 Ngam Wongwan Road, Chatuchak,
Bangkok, 10900.
Tel: + 66 (0)2 589-0100 -1
Fax: + 66 (0)2 589-4850 -1
Internet: www.pea.or.th

Provincial Waterworks Authority
72 Chaeng-Wattana Road, Don Muang,
Bangkok, 10210.
Tel: + 66 (0)2 551-1020
Fax: + 66 (0)2 551-1239

Telephone Organization of Thailand
89/2 Moo 3, Chaeng-Wattana Road, Don Muang,
Bangkok, 10002.
Tel: + 66 (0)2 505-1000
Fax: + 66 (0)2 574-9533
Internet: www.tot.or.th

Chapter 13
Appendices

Thailand Salary Survey

Selected Salaries		
	Monthly	
Position	**Baht**	**US Dollars**
Plant Manager	71,351	1,820
Personnel Manager	67,123	1,715
Office Manager	49,995	1,275
Executive Secretary	34,834	890
Engineer	18,620	475
Researcher (Thai)	24,032	615
Sales	22,806	580
Office Staff	15,030	385
Driver	8,150	210
Housekeeper	7.011	180

Notes: Bonus conditions vary from business to business, although one to two months extra salary a year is average.

These figures are based on the results of an informal survey conducted of selected businesses in Bangkok.

IT Positions	Monthly Baht	US Dollars
IT Manager	90,000-100,000	2,300-2,550
Web Designer	27,000-38,000	690-970
PC Programmer	24,000-27,000	610-690
System Analyst	40,000-55,000	1,020-1,400
Network Security Administrator (With vendor certifications)	65,000-85,000	1,650-2,170
LAN Manager	65,000-85,000	1,650-2,170

IT salaries are courtesy of ISM Technology Recruitment Ltd. and assume reasonable command of English and experience.

Entry-Level Salaries For Selected Job Positions	Monthly Baht	US Dollars
Accounting Manager	20,000	510
Civil Engineer	26,000	665
Electrical Engineer	17,500	450
Mechanical Engineer	27,500	700
Chemical Engineer	13,000	330
Architect	25,000	640
Accountant	16,250	415
Graphic Designer	9,750	250
Customer Service	7,630	195
System Analyst	18,000	460
Computer Programmer	14,000	360
Human Resources Manager	22,500	575
Sales And Marketing Manager	18,500	475
Public Relations Manager	18,000	460

Note: Salaries are subject to four percent social security fund contribution and one percent workmans compensation contribution (for the first 15,000 baht per month of salary'). For more information, refer to "Red Tape, Customs, And Procedures."

Source: Ministry of Labour and Social Welfare (July 13, 2005)

Overtime Regulations	
Overtime performed on regular working days	Time and a half
Regular work on public holidays	Double time
Overtime performed on public holidays	Triple time
Daily workers working more than eight hours	Time and a half

Severance Payment Entitlements	
Workers employed for:	
More than 120 days but less than one year	30 days severance pay
More than one year but less than three years	90 days severance pay
More than three years but less than six years	180 days severance pay
More than six years but less than ten years	240 days severance pay
Ten years and up	300 days severance pay

Source: Ministry of Labour and Social Welfare (www.mol.go.th).

Bonuses

The results of a remuneration survey conducted by Hewitt Associates (Thailand) in2006 indicated that local employers pay average guaranteed bonuses of 1.2 months salary. Variable bonuses average 2.5 months salary in Thailand during 2006. Eighty-nine percent of the organizations paid performance-related bonuses. In future, more firms are expected to pay performance-linked incentives.

Taxes In Thailand

Type Of Business	Personal Income Tax	Company Tax	With-Holding Tax	Value-Added Tax	Specific Business Tax	Stamp Duty
Sale of Household Goods	✔	✔		✔		
Business to Business Sales	✔	✔		✔		
Hardware and Software	✔	✔		✔		
Cars	✔	✔		✔		✔
Spare Parts	✔	✔		✔		

	Personal Income Tax	Company Tax	With-Holding Tax	Value-Added Tax	Specific Business Tax	Stamp Duty
Insurance	✔	✔	✔	✔		
House Rentals	✔	✔	✔			✔
Car Parking	✔	✔	✔	✔		
Construction	✔	✔	✔	✔		✔
Renting Land	✔	✔	✔			✔
Servicing Houses	✔	✔	✔	✔		✔
Broker / Agency	✔	✔	✔	✔		✔
Software Copyright	✔	✔	✔	✔		
Export	✔	✔		✔		
Consultancy	✔	✔	✔	✔		✔
Second-hand Car Sales	✔	✔	✔	✔		✔
Land and Houses	✔	✔	✔		✔	✔
Furniture	✔	✔	✔	✔		
Construction	✔	✔	✔	✔		✔
Financial Services and Loans	✔	✔	✔		✔	✔
Hotels	✔	✔		✔		
National Transmission	✔	✔	✔			
Internet	✔	✔	✔	✔		
Janitor, Security, Spa and Fitness	✔	✔	✔	✔		✔
Restaurant	✔	✔	✔	✔		
Ferry	✔	✔	✔	✔		
Advertising	✔	✔	✔	✔		✔
Photo Shop	✔	✔	✔	✔		✔

	Personal Income Tax	Company Tax	With-Holding Tax	Value-Added Tax	Specific Business Tax	Stamp Duty
Hospital	✔	✔	✔	✔		✔
Clinic	✔		✔			
Auditing		✔	✔			✔
Beauty Salon	✔	✔	✔	✔		✔
Book Store	✔	✔				
Motorcycle Repairs	✔	✔	✔	✔		✔
Car Rentals	✔	✔	✔	✔		
Factory	✔	✔		✔		
Debt Collection	✔	✔	✔	✔		✔
Investigation	✔	✔	✔	✔		✔
Pawn Broker	✔	✔			✔	✔
Mortgage	✔	✔			✔	✔
Golf Courses	✔	✔	✔	✔		
Rice Mill	✔	✔	✔			✔
Condominium	✔	✔	✔		✔	✔
Timber Mill	✔	✔	✔	✔		
Hire Purchase	✔	✔		✔		✔
Electricity and Water Supply	✔	✔		✔		
Tapped Water	✔	✔		✔		
Production of Drinks	✔	✔		✔		

Source: Revenue Department (www.rd.go.th)

English Version Of A Shop Rental Contract

Shop Rental Contract
Written at ....
Date .... Month ....Year.........

This contract is agreed by .... who has full authority over
this property which is located at .... Street....................................
Sub District.......................... District.................... Province ....
who will be referred to in this contract as the "the Landlord" with the Tenant whose name
is ....living at ...... Street ....Sub-District
.... District..................... Province.......................... referred to in this
contract as "the Tenant"

Both parties have agreed to enter this lease contract as following:

Section 1. The document agrees to allow another person, called the Tenant, to have the
use or possession of the property for a limited period of time and agrees to pay a rent.
The property is located at ....
....
covering the area of .... sq.m. The rental period of ....years from
.... to .... with the rental cost of .... baht
(...)
On the date of agreement the Tenant agrees to pay rent in advance for ....
months in amount of....................... baht (..) for the
letter and after this rental will be paid on ....of every month at ....

Section 2. The Tenant agrees to pay the utilities bills during the contract period

Section 3. The Tenant is bound to allow the Landlord or his agents to inspect the hired
property at reasonable times and intervals.

Section 4. The Tenant is bound to take as much care of the property hired as any
reasonable person would take of his own property, and maintain or repair the property as
required.

Section 5. The Tenant may not make alteration or addition to the property without the
Landlord's permission. If the hirer does so without such permission, the Tenant must, on
the request of the Landlord, restore the property to its former condition, and the Tenant
is liable to the Landlord for any loss or damage that may result from such alteration or
addition.

Section 6. The Tenant is not allowed to transfer the ownership.

Section 7. If the Tenant would like to extend the contract before the contract period, the
Tenant must notify the Landlord at least .... days in advance.

Section 8. The Tenant is liable for any loss or damage caused to the property hired by his
own fault or by the fault of a person living with him or being his sub-hirer.

Section 9. On the day of making the contract, the Tenant has brought .... Deposit
Rental Deposit in cash/ cheque .... baht (..)
given to the Landlord to ensure and guarantee the contract if the Tenant does not pay the

rent according to the contract. The Tenant is bound to allow the Landlord to deduct rent due from the property security deposit.

Section 10. When the contract has completed, the Tenant agrees to remove his or her possessions from the property rented and return the property to the Landlord in a proper condition within .... days of the end of contract date.

If the Tenant fails to comply with the agreement above, the Landlord may terminate the contract. This agreement is made for two contracts which are accurate and have the same context. Both parties have read and understood clearly. Both parties agree to sign their names in front of a witness and each of them will retain a copy of the contract

Signature .... Landlord   Signature ....Tenant

(..)   (..)

Signature .... witness   Signature ....,............. witness

(..)   (..)

Original Thai Version Of A Shop Rental Contract

สัญญาเช่าร้านค้า

เขียนที่...
วันที่............เดือน.......................พ.ศ..............

สัญญาฉบับนี้ทำขึ้นระหว่าง...โดย.............................
ผู้มีอำนาจกระทำการแทน สำนักงานตั้งอยู่ ณ...................................ตรอก/
ซอย.......................ถนน.......................ตำบล/แขวง......................
อำเภอ.......................จังหวัด.......................ซึ่งต่อไปในสัญญานี้เรียกว่า "ผู้ให้เช่า"
ฝ่ายหนึ่ง กับ
....อยู่บ้านเลขที่...................ตรอก/ซอย......................
ถนน.......................ตำบล/แขวง.......................อำเภอ.......................
จังหวัด.........................
ซึ่งต่อไปในสัญญานี้เรียกว่า "ผู้เช่า" ฝ่ายหนึ่ง
คู่สัญญาทั้งสองฝ่ายได้ตกลงทำสัญญาดังมีข้อความต่อไปนี้

ข้อ 1. ผู้เช่าตกลงให้เช่าและผู้เช่าตกลงเช่าสถานที่ภายในห้างสรรพสินค้าบริเวณชั้น...
.............เนื้อที่.......................ตารางเมตร หมายเลขที่.................มีกำหนด..............
ปี.......................เดือน ตั้งแต่วันที่.......................ถึงวันที่.........................
ณ ห้างสรรพสินค้า.......................ซึ่งอยู่เขต.......................
จังหวัด.......................ในอัตราค่าเช่าเดือนละ.......................บาท
(...) โดยในวันทำสัญญาฉบับนี้ผู้เช่าได้ชำระค่าเช่าล่วง
หน้าเป็นระยะเวลา.......................เดือน เป็นเงินจำนวน.......................บาท (..............
.......................)ให้แก่ผู้ให้เช่า และต่อไปจะชำระทุกวันที่.......................ของเดือน
ณ สำนักงานของผู้ให้เช่า

ข้อ 2. ผู้เช่าต้องชำระค่าน้ำประปาและค่าไฟฟ้าที่ใช้ในกิจการร้านค้าของผู้เช่าตามจำนวนที่
ปรากฏในมาตรวัด และต้องชำระค่าอำนวยความสะดวกอื่นๆ เช่น ยามรักษาการณ์ ค่าเก็บขยะ
เป็นต้น โดยผู้เช่าตกลงจะชำระค่าใช้จ่ายเหล่านี้ทุกวันที่.......................ของเดือน

ข้อ 3. ผู้ให้เช่าหรือตัวแทนของผู้ให้เช่ามีอำนาจในการควบคุมดูแลการดำเนินกิจการของผู้เช่า
ให้เป็นไปตามสัญญา ควบคุมด้านสาธารณูปโภคต่างๆ ให้ถูกต้องตามสุขลักษณะทั่วไป และอื่นๆ
(ถ้ามี) เพื่อให้การดำเนินกิจการของผู้เช่าเป็นไปในแนวทางเดียวกันกับกิจการอื่นๆ ที่ผู้เช่าเปิด
บริการไว้

ข้อ 4. ผู้เช่าต้องสงวนรักษาทรัพย์สินที่เช่านั้นเสมอกับวิญญูชนจะพึงสงวนรักษาทรัพย์สินของตน
และต้องบำรุงรักษาทั้งทำการซ่อมแซมเล็กน้อยด้วย

ข้อ 5. ผู้เช่าจะไม่ทำการแก้ไข เพิ่มเติม ดัดแปลงทรัพย์สินที่เช่า เว้นแต่จะได้รับอนุญาตเป็น
หนังสือจากผู้ให้เช่า บรรดาทรัพย์สินใด ที่ผู้เช่าได้ทำการแก้ไข เพิ่มเติม ดัดแปลงไปนั้น ผู้เช่า
ยินยอมให้ตกเป็นกรรมสิทธ์ของผู้ให้เช่าในทันทีที่สัญญาฉบับนี้สิ้นสุดลง และผู้เช่าจะไม่เรียกร้อง
เอาค่าใช้จ่ายและค่าตอบแทนใดๆ ทั้งสิ้น ทั้งนี้ หากผู้ให้เช่าไม่ต้องการทรัพย์สินดังกล่าวผู้เช่า
จะดำเนินการรื้อถอน ซ่อมแซมต่อไปให้ทรัพย์สินที่เช่าอยู่ในสภาพเดิมโดยผู้เช่าต้องเป็นผู้เสียค่า
ใช้จ่ายเองทั้งสิ้น

ข้อ 6. ผู้เช่าไม่มีสิทธิที่จะนำเอาทรัพย์สินที่เช่าตามสัญญานี้ออกให้เช่าช่วงไม่ว่าทั้งหมดหรือแต่
บางส่วน เว้นแต่จะได้รับอนุญาตจากผู้ให้เช่าเป็นหนังสือก่อนแล้ว

ข้อ 7. หากผู้เช่าประสงค์จะเลิกสัญญาเช่าก่อนกำหนดตามสัญญาฉบับนี้แล้ว ผู้เช่าต้องแจ้งเป็น
หนังสือไปยังผู้ให้เช่าทราบล่วงหน้าไม่น้อยกว่า.............วัน

ข้อ 8. ผู้เช่าต้องรับผิดชอบในบรรดาความเสียหาย สูญหาย หรือบุบสลายที่เกิดขึ้นกับทรัพย์สินที่
เช่าตามสัญญาฉบับนี้อันเกิดจากการกระทำของผู้เช่า หรือคนงาน หรือบริวารของผู้เช่า และผู้
เช่าต้องชดใช้ค่าเสียหายดังกล่าวให้แก่ผู้ให้เช่าและจัดการซ่อมแซมให้สามารถใช้ได้ดีดังเดิมด้วย
ค่าใช้จ่ายของผู้เช่าเอง ภายในเวลาที่ผู้ให้เช่าจะกำหนดต่อไป

ข้อ 9. ในวันทำสัญญาฉบับนี้ผู้เช่าได้นำ
....เป็นผู้ค้ำประกัน
หลักทรัพย์ประเภทหนังสือค้ำประกันจากธนาคาร/เงินสดจำนวน...............บาท
(..) ให้ไว้แก่ผู้ให้เช่าเพื่อเป็นการประกันการปฏิบัติตาม
สัญญา ถ้าผู้เช่าไม่ชำระหนี้ตามสัญญา ผู้เช่ายินยอมให้ผู้ให้เช่าเพื่อเป็นการประกันการปฏิบัติ
ตามสัญญา หรือเรียกเอากับผู้ค้ำประกันเหมือนอย่างเป็นลูกหนี้ร่วมกับผู้เช่าตามสัญญาฉบับนี้ได้
ทันทีเช่นกัน

ข้อ 10. เมื่อสัญญาเช่าสิ้นสุดลงไม่ว่ากรณีใดๆ ผู้เช่าจะต้องขนย้ายทรัพย์สินและบริวารออกจาก
ทรัพย์สินที่เช่า และส่งมอบทรัพย์สินที่เช่าคืนแก่ผู้ให้เช่าในสภาพที่เรียบร้อยภายในกำหนด.........
.........วัน นับแต่วันที่ทำสัญญาเช่าสิ้นสุดลง
หากผู้เช่าไม่ปฏิบัติตามความดังกล่าวข้างต้น ผู้เช่ายินยอมให้ผู้ให้เช่าจัดการหรือจ้างให้ผู้อื่นจัด
การแทน ทั้งนี้ โดยผู้เช่าจะต้องเป็นผู้ออกค่าใช้จ่ายอันพึงมีแทนผู้ให้เช่าทั้งสิ้น
สัญญานี้ถูกทำขึ้นเป็นสองฉบับมีข้อความถูกต้องตรงกัน คู่สัญญาทั้งสองฝ่ายได้อ่านและเข้าใจ
แล้ว จึงลงลายมือชื่อไว้ต่อหน้าพยานเป็นสำคัญ และเก็บสัญญาไว้ฝ่ายละฉบับ

ลงชื่อ.............................ผู้ให้เช่า   ลงชื่อ.............. ....ผู้เช่า
(.............................)   (.............................)

ลงชื่อ.............................พยาน   ลงชื่อ.............................พยาน
(.............................)   (.............................)

Visa Application Form

ROYAL THAI CONSULATE-GENERAL
87 Annerley Road,
South Brisbane 4102
Australia

Telephone: **(07) 3846 7771**
Fax: **(07) 3846 7772**
email: admin@thaiconsulate.org

❑ Transit Visa
❑ Tourist Visa
❑ Non-Immigrant Visa

Number of Entries ....
*(Please tick box to indicate the type
of visa required.)*

---

1 photograph must be submitted with **1** application form **PLEASE AFFIX PHOTO**

APPLICATION FOR VISA

Mr.
Mrs. ....
Miss   Family Name   Given Names

Former Name ....

Nationality ....

Nationality at birth ....

Birth place ....

Date of birth ....

Occupation ....

Present Address ....

....

....

Telephone ....

Permanent Address ....
(if different from above)

....

....

Names, dates places of birth of minor children
if accompanying you on same passport.

....

....

....

Passport No. ....

Issued at ....

Date of Issue ....

Expiry Date ....

Purpose of Visit ....

....

Date of previous visits to Thailand ....

Date of arrival in Thailand ....

Duration of stay ....

Proposed address in Thailand ....

....

Travelling by .... Flight No. ....

FOR NON-IMMIGRANT VISAS ONLY

Local guarantor and address ....

....

....

Guarantor and address in Thailand ....

....

....

**TOURISTS VISA APPLICANTS ACKNOWLEDGE
THAT WORK OF ANY KIND IS PROHIBITED
AND UNDERTAKEN NOT TO ENGAGE IN ANY
PROFESSION OR OCCUPATION WHATSOEVER
WHILE IN THAILAND**

Signature ....

Date ....

FOR OFFICIAL USE

Kind of Visa & No. ....

Date of Issue ....

NOTE:

Fee ....

Expiry date ....

Signature ....

CONSULAR OFFICER

Work Permit Application Form

แบบ ดท. ๑
FORM WP. 1

กระทรวงแรงงาน
MINISTRY OF LABOUR

คำขอรับใบอนุญาตทำงาน
ตามมาตรา ๑๐
APPLICATION FOR WORK PERMIT
ACCORDING TO SECTION 10

๑ ข้อความทั่วไป
    GENERAL STATEMENT

๑.๑ ชื่อผู้ยื่นคำขอ นาย/นาง/นางสาว...สัญชาติ.........................

Name of applicant Mr./Mrs./Miss   Nationality

เพศ.........................อายุ.........................ปี   เกิดวันที่........................เดือน.........................พ.ศ.........................

Sex   Age   Years   Date of birth   Month   Year

๑.๒ ที่อยู่ในประเทศไทย...

Address in Thailand

....รหัสไปรษณีย์..........................โทรศัพท์..........................

Post Code   Telephone

๑.๓ หนังสือเดินทางหรือเอกสารใช้แทนหนังสือเดินทาง เลขที่..

Passport or other travelling document No.

ออกให้วันที่...ออกให้ที่..........................

Date of Issue   Issued at

๑.๔ ตรวจลงตราประเภท..เลขที่.........................ออกให้วันที่..........................

Kind of Visa   No.   Date of Issue

เดือน.........................พ.ศ.........................ออกให้ที่..........................

Month   Year   Issued at

มีอายุใช้ได้ถึงวันที่.........................เดือน.........................พ.ศ.........................

Valid until   Month   Year

๑.๕ เดินทางมาถึงประเทศไทยเมื่อวันที่.........................เดือน.........................พ.ศ.........................

Entered Thailand on   Month   Year

ได้รับอนุญาตจากพนักงานเจ้าหน้าที่คนเข้าเมือง ณ ที่ทำการตรวจคนเข้าเมือง..........................

Permitted by Immigration officer of the Immigration office at

ให้อยู่มีกำหนด.........................ปี.........................เดือน.........................วัน

For   Year (s)   Month (s)   Day (s)

ครบกำหนดอนุญาตวันที่.........................เดือน.........................พ.ศ.........................

Expired on   Month   Year

Work Permit Application Form, page 2

๒

๒	นายจ้าง EMPLOYER STATEMENT

๒.๑ ชื่อนายจ้างหรือผู้จัดการ
Name of Employer or Manager
ที่อยู่ .... รหัสไปรษณีย์ .... โทรศัพท์ ....
Address   Post Code   Telephone

๒.๒ ชื่อสถานประกอบการ
Name of company
ที่อยู่ .... รหัสไปรษณีย์ .... โทรศัพท์ ....
Address   Post Code   Telephone

๒.๓ ประเภทกิจการหรือธุรกิจ
Type of activity or business

๓	การอนุญาตให้เข้ามาทำงานในราชอาณาจักร THE PERMISSION TO WORK IN THE KINGDOM

๓.๑ ได้รับอนุญาตให้เข้ามาทำงานโดย
Permission to work by

☐ คณะกรรมการส่งเสริมการลงทุน
Board of investment

☐ อื่นๆ
Others

เลขที่หนังสือ .... ลงวันที่ .... เดือน .... พ.ศ. ....
Document No.   Dated   Month   Year

๓.๒ ระยะเวลาที่ได้รับอนุญาต .... ปี .... เดือน .... วัน ....
Period of Permission   Year(s)   Month(s)   Day(s)

๓.๓ ได้รับอนุญาตถึง วันที่ .... เดือน .... พ.ศ. ....
Valid until   Month   Year

๓.๔ ตำแหน่งหน้าที่/อาชีพ/วิชาชีพ
Title/Occupation/Profession
รายละเอียดของงานที่จะทำ
Job description

....

....

....

....

....

Work Permit Application Form, page 3

๓.๔ ค่าจ้างหรือรายได้ เดือนละ/วันละ_____
Wage or income per month/day
ผลประโยชน์อื่นๆ เดือนละ /วันละ_____
Other benefits per month/day

ข้าพเจ้าขอรับรองว่า ข้อความข้างต้นนี้เป็นความจริงทุกประการ
I hereby certify that the above statements are true in every respect.

(ลายมือชื่อ)_____ ผู้ยื่นคำขอ
(Signature)   Applicant
วันที่_____ เดือน_____ พ.ศ._____
Date   Month   Year

---

๔. | คำรับรองของนายจ้าง
CONFIRMATION OF EMPLOYER

ข้าพเจ้าขอรับรองว่ามีความประสงค์จะจ้าง นาย/นาง/นางสาว_____
I hereby confirm that I intend to accept
_____ เป็นลูกจ้างในสถานประกอบการ
To be an employee in the company according

ตามข้อ ๓.๔ เป็นระยะเวลา_____ ปี_____เดือน_____วัน
To item 3.4 for   Year(s)   Month(s)   Day(s)
นับตั้งแต่วันที่_____เดือน_____พ.ศ._____
Commence on   Month   Year

(ลายมือชื่อ)_____ นายจ้าง
(Signature)   Employer
วันที่_____ เดือน_____ พ.ศ._____
Date   Month   Year

Company Registration Form in English

Form Bor Or Jor 1

Request No. ....   Registration Office for Partnership Company
Received Date ....

Limited Company Registration Request form

Company .... Limited
Registration Number ....
I would like to register a limited company according to the civil and commercial law as follows:

♣ Prospectus   ♣ Amendment on prospectus before forming company No.
....
♣ Forming a company   ♣ Merging companies (........... Company Limited,
♣ Special approval to (increase/decrease capital/merge company)   Registration No. .... to be merged with .... Company
♣ Increasing capital/Decreasing capital   Limited, Registration No.........................)
♣ Amendment on prospectus No. 1 (company's name) ♣ Amendment on prospectus No. 3 (company's objectives)
♣ Amendment on prospectus No. 2 (company's office) ♣ Amendment on regulations No. ....
♣ Amendment on prospectus No. 5 (capital /stock/value) ♣ Amendment on numbers or names of board of directors
♣ Board of Directors (in .... persons) (out .... persons) ♣ Amendment on company's seal
♣ Amendment on the location of the head office and/or branch office
♣ Other items which the public should know are ....
Attached are all the required items for registration in the total of .... pages
I, a member of the board of directors who is requesting this registration, certify that this registration is processed completely and correctly
according to the law and regulations. The following has been performed.

♣ Submitting a letter to inform the forming of the company/regular/special meeting to stock holders Meeting Number
.... on (date) .... and/or ♣ Announcing the regular/special meeting to stock holders Meeting
Number............................ in .... Newspaper on (date) ....
♣ Meeting's conclusion ....Meeting Number. ....on (date) ....at (time)
.... at (address)..
There are .... BOD/stock holders attending with the total of .... stocks (number of stocks)
Presided the meeting by .... according to the meeting period Number ....
♣ Letter of resignation of a board of director...
dated .... Effective date ....
♣ Others ....
... and that all items and documents on this request form are true and correct.

                                                  Signature of the registration petitioner/BOD
                                                  ....
        (Company's seal)   (....)
                                                  ....
                                                  (....)

I certify that the person who is requesting the registration   Registrar's Note
has signed in my presence on (date)   Registration received on (date) ....
....   (Signature) .... Registrar
(.....................................)   (.....................................)
Registrar /.................................   Position Seal

Warning: Anyone who produces false information to officer is subject to criminal code Section 137, 267 and 268.

Company Registration Form in Thai

แบบ บอจ.1

คำขอที่.................

รับวันที่.................

สำนักงานทะเบียนหุ้นส่วนบริษัท
....

คำขอจดทะเบียนบริษัทจำกัด

บริษัท...จำกัด

ทะเบียนเลขที่.................

ข้าพเจ้าขอจดทะเบียนบริษัทจำกัด ตามประมวลกฎหมายแพ่งและพาณิชย์ ดังต่อไปนี้

☐ หนังสือบริคณห์สนธิ

☐ จัดตั้งบริษัท

☐ มติพิเศษให้ (เพิ่มทุน / ลดทุน / ควบบริษัท)

☐ เพิ่มทุน / ลดทุน

☐ แก้ไขเพิ่มเติมหนังสือบริคณห์สนธิ ข้อ 1. (ชื่อบริษัท)

☐ แก้ไขเพิ่มเติมหนังสือบริคณห์สนธิ ข้อ 2. (สำนักงานของบริษัท)

☐ แก้ไขเพิ่มเติมหนังสือบริคณห์สนธิ ข้อ 5. (ทุน / หุ้น / มูลค่าหุ้น)

☐ กรรมการ (เข้า.................คน) (ออก.................คน)

☐ แก้ไขเพิ่มเติมที่ตั้งสำนักงานแห่งใหญ่ และ/หรือ สำนักงานสาขา

☐ รายการอย่างอื่นซึ่งเห็นสมควรจะให้ประชาชนทราบ คือ.................

☐ แก้ไขเพิ่มเติมหนังสือบริคณห์สนธิก่อนการจัดตั้งบริษัท ข้อ.................

☐ ควบบริษัท (บริษัท.................

.................จำกัด ทะเบียนเลขที่.................

ได้ควบเข้ากันกับบริษัท.................

.................จำกัด ทะเบียนเลขที่.................)

☐ แก้ไขเพิ่มเติมหนังสือบริคณห์สนธิ ข้อ 3. (วัตถุประสงค์ของบริษัท)

☐ แก้ไขเพิ่มเติมข้อบังคับ ข้อ.................

☐ แก้ไขเพิ่มเติมจำนวนหรือชื่อกรรมการลงชื่อผูกพันบริษัท

☐ แก้ไขเพิ่มเติมตราของบริษัท

ได้แนบรายการจดทะเบียน และเอกสารประกอบคำขอมาครบถ้วนตามที่ระเบียบสำนักงานทะเบียนหุ้นส่วนบริษัทกลางฯ กำหนดแล้ว รวม.................แผ่น

ข้าพเจ้ากรรมการผู้ขอจดทะเบียนขอรับรองว่า การขอจดทะเบียนครั้งนี้ได้ดำเนินการถูกต้องครบถ้วนตามกฎหมายและข้อบังคับของบริษัทได้เป็นไปตาม

☐ ได้มีหนังสือบอกกล่าวนัดประชุมตั้งบริษัท / สามัญ / วิสามัญผู้ถือหุ้น ครั้งที่.................เมื่อวันที่.................และ

ครั้งที่.................เมื่อวันที่.................และ/หรือ ได้ประกาศในหนังสือพิมพ์ และ ได้ประกาศในหนังสือพิมพ์.................ฉบับลงวันที่.................และครั้งที่.................

ลงในหนังสือพิมพ์.................ฉบับลงวันที่.................

☐ มีมติที่ประชุม.................ครั้งที่.................เมื่อวันที่.................เวลา.................น.

ณ บ้านเลขที่.................

มีกรรมการ/ผู้ถือหุ้นเข้าประชุมจำนวน.................คน นับจำนวนหุ้นได้.................หุ้น โดย.................เป็นประธาน

ที่ประชุม ตามวาระการประชุมที่.................และมีมติที่ประชุมสามัญ/วิสามัญผู้ถือหุ้นครั้งที่.................เมื่อวันที่.................

เวลา.................น.ณ บ้านเลขที่.................

มีผู้ถือหุ้นเข้าประชุมจำนวน.................คน นับจำนวนหุ้นได้.................หุ้น โดย.................เป็นประธานที่ประชุม

ตามวาระการประชุมที่.................

☐ หนังสือลาออกจากตำแหน่งกรรมการของ.................

ลงวันที่.................โดยให้มีผลในวันที่.................

☐ อื่นๆ.................

และรายการที่ระบุในคำขอจดทะเบียนและเอกสารประกอบถูกต้องตรงตามความเป็นจริงทุกประการ

ลงลายมือชื่อผู้เริ่มก่อการผู้ขอจดทะเบียน/กรรมการผู้มีอำนาจผูกพันบริษัท

....

(.................)

(ประทับตราบริษัท)

....

(.................)

ขอรับรองว่าผู้ขอจดทะเบียนได้ลงลายมือชื่อต่อหน้าข้าพเจ้าจริง

เมื่อวันที่.................

....

(.................)

นายทะเบียน /.................

บันทึกนายทะเบียน

รับจดทะเบียน ณ วันที่.................

(ลงลายมือชื่อ).................นายทะเบียน

(.................)

ประทับตราตำแหน่ง

คำเตือน ผู้ใดแจ้งข้อความอันเป็นเท็จแก่เจ้าหน้าที่พนักงานมีความผิดตามประมวลกฎหมายอาญา มาตรา 137, 267 และ 268

Registration Form for Limited Partnership in English

Written at   Registration Office for Partnership Company

....

Letter of Certification

       I certify that this company has registered as a juristic person according to the civil and commerce law in the category of "limited company." Registration number .... on (date) .... The details appear on the registration documents on the date of issue are as follows

1. Company name "... Company Limited"
2. There are .... members on the Board of Directors as follows
   - (1) .... (2) ....
   - (3) .... (4) ....
   - (5) .... (6) ....
   - (7) .... (8) ....
   - (9) .... (10) ....
   - (11) .... (12) ....
   - (13) .... (14) ....
   - (15) .... (16) ....
3. Numbers or names of the Board of Directors who have signed their names to be committed to the company

   ....
   ....
   ....
4. Capital amount for registration .... baht
5. Head office located at ....
   ....
6. There are ......objectives for the company as attached along with this letter of certification for.............. pages.

With the signature of registrar certifying this letter and company's seal

Issued on (date) ....

....

(....)

Registrar

Registration Form for Limited Partnership in Thai

สำนักงานทะเบียนหุ้นส่วนบริษัท

ที่..

หนังสือรับรอง

ขอรับรองว่าบริษัทนี้ ได้จดทะเบียนตามประมวลกฎหมายแห่งและพาณิชย์ เป็นนิติบุคคลประเภท บริษัทจำกัด

ทะเบียนเลขที่...เมื่อวันที่..ปรากฏข้อความในรายการตามเอกสารทะเบียน

ณ วันออกหนังสือนี้ ดังนี้

1. ชื่อบริษัท "บริษัท...จำกัด"

2. กรรมการของบริษัท มี....................คน ตามรายชื่อ ดังต่อไปนี้

    (1)..   (2)..

    (3)..   (4)..

    (5)..   (6)..

    (7)..   (8)..

    (9)..   (10)..

    (11)..   (12)..

    (13)..   (14)..

    (15)..   (16)..

3. จำนวนหรือชื่อกรรมการซึ่งลงชื่อผูกพันบริษัทได้ คือ

    ....

    ....

    ....

    ....

4. ทุนจดทะเบียน กำหนดไว้เป็นจำนวนเงิน...................................บาท

5. สำนักงานแห่งใหญ่ตั้งอยู่เลขที่..

    ....

6. วัตถุประสงค์ของบริษัท มี....................ข้อ ดังปรากฏในสำเนาเอกสารแนบท้ายหนังสือรับรองนี้ จำนวน...................แผ่น

โดยมีลายมือชื่อนายทะเบียนซึ่งรับรองเอกสารและประทับตราสำนักงานทะเบียนหุ้นส่วนบริษัทเป็นสำคัญ

ออกให้ ณ วันที่...

....

(..)

นายทะเบียน

Shareholder Registration Form in English

Form Bor Or Jor 2

PROSPECTUS

.... Company Limited

Registration Number Bor Kor...............

Company's prospectus includes the following items

1) Company Name "..Company Limited"
Written in Roman alphabet as ....

2) Company's head office is located at ....Province

3) Company's objectives include .... items as shown in

♣ Attached Form W.   ♣ Objective form from the central registration office.   Subject: Company's objectives
requesting registration dated ....Form ¶ W.1   ¶ W.2   ¶ W.3   ¶ W.4

4) Company's stock holders are liable for no more than their unpaid stock value

....
(The Company's Board of Directors can be liable for unlimited amount if it so state. If not, assign to "........")

5) Company's capital is .... baht (..)
(letter)   (number)

In the total of .... stocks (................) Value per stock .... baht (.................)

6) Company's founders' names, addresses, occupations, signatures and number of stocks for each person. Total
.... persons as follows:

(1) ....Occupation .... Age ....
Address: House Number ...... Moo ...... Road .... Sub-District .... District ....
Province .... Number of stocks purchased: .... stocks
(Signature) ....

(2) ....Occupation .... Age ....
Address: House Number ...... Moo ...... Road .... Sub-District .... District ....
Province .... Number of stocks purchased: .... stocks
(Signature) ....

(3) ....Occupation .... Age ....
Address: House Number ...... Moo ...... Road .... Sub-District .... District ....
Province .... Number of stocks purchased: .... stocks
(Signature) ....

(4) ....Occupation .... Age ....
Address: House Number ...... Moo ...... Road .... Sub-District .... District ....
Province .... Number of stocks purchased: .... stocks
(Signature) ....

(5) ....Occupation .... Age ....
Address: House Number ...... Moo ...... Road .... Sub-District .... District ....
Province .... Number of stocks purchased: .... stocks
(Signature) ....

(6) ....Occupation .... Age ....
Address: House Number ...... Moo ...... Road .... Sub-District .... District ....
Province .... Number of stocks purchased: .... stocks
(Signature) ....

(7) ....Occupation .... Age ....
Address: House Number ...... Moo ...... Road .... Sub-District .... District ....
Province .... Number of stocks purchased: .... stocks
(Signature) ....

Signature .... Company's founder requesting the registration

(....)

Page .... of ....   Signature .... Registrar
Supplementary document for request number ..../......   (....................................)

Witness Signature Certification

I ...., Age ....,
Residing at ....

I ...., Age ....,
Residing at ....

Certify that all the company founders have signed their names in my presence.

(Signature) .... Witness
(..........................)

(Signature) .... Witness
(..........................)

This prospectus was made on (date) ....

Affix stamp
200 baht for original
5 baht for each copy

Signature .... Company's founder requesting the registration
(....)

Page .... of .... Company Limited
Supplementary document for request number ..../......   Signature .... Registrar
(...................................)

Shareholder Registration Form in Thai

แบบ บอจ.2

หนังสือบริคณห์สนธิ

บริษัท..จำกัด

ทะเบียนเลขที่ บค...................

หนังสือบริคณห์สนธิของบริษัท มีรายการดังต่อไปนี้

ข้อ 1 ชื่อบริษัท "บริษัท..จำกัด"

เขียนเป็นอักษรโรมัน ดังนี้

ข้อ 2 สำนักงานของบริษัทจะตั้งอยู่ ณ จังหวัด...

ข้อ 3 วัตถุที่ประสงค์ทั้งหลายของบริษัท มี...................ข้อ ดังปรากฏใน

☐ แบบ ว.ที่แนบ ☐ แบบวัตถุที่ประสงค์ตามประกาศสำนักงานทะเบียนหุ้นส่วนบริษัทกลาง เรื่อง กำหนด

แบบวัตถุที่ประสงค์ประกอบคำขอจดทะเบียน ลงวันที่...แบบ ◯ว.1 ◯ว.2 ◯ว.3 ◯ว.4

ข้อ 4 ผู้ถือหุ้นของบริษัทนี้ต่างรับผิดจำกัดเพียงไม่เกินจำนวนเงินใช้ไม่ครบมูลค่าหุ้นที่ตนถือ

....
(ถ้าจะให้ควบรวมการรับผิดโดยไม่จำกัดก็ได้ โดยให้นอกลงความรับผิดเช่นนั้นไว้ด้วย ถ้าไม่มีให้ "...........")

ข้อ 5 ทุนของบริษัท กำหนดไว้เป็นจำนวน.................................บาท (.............................)
         (ตัวอักษร)   *(ตัวเลข)*

แบ่งออกเป็น...........................หุ้น (.............................) มูลค่าหุ้นละ...............................บาท (.............................)

ข้อ 6 ชื่อ สำนัก อาชีวะ ลายมือชื่อ และ จำนวนหุ้นที่แต่ละคนได้เข้าชื่อซื้อไว้ของผู้เริ่มก่อการ รวม...................คน
มีดังนี้

(1) ....อาชีวะ.........................อายุ...............ปี
อยู่บ้านเลขที่.............หมู่ที่.........ถนน...................แขวง/ตำบล.................เขต/อำเภอ...............
จังหวัด..............................ได้เข้าชื่อซื้อหุ้นไว้แล้ว...................หุ้น (ลงลายมือชื่อ)................

(2) ....อาชีวะ.........................อายุ...............ปี
อยู่บ้านเลขที่.............หมู่ที่.........ถนน...................แขวง/ตำบล.................เขต/อำเภอ...............
จังหวัด..............................ได้เข้าชื่อซื้อหุ้นไว้แล้ว...................หุ้น (ลงลายมือชื่อ)................

(3) ....อาชีวะ.........................อายุ...............ปี
อยู่บ้านเลขที่.............หมู่ที่.........ถนน...................แขวง/ตำบล.................เขต/อำเภอ...............
จังหวัด..............................ได้เข้าชื่อซื้อหุ้นไว้แล้ว...................หุ้น (ลงลายมือชื่อ)................

(4) ....อาชีวะ.........................อายุ...............ปี
อยู่บ้านเลขที่.............หมู่ที่.........ถนน...................แขวง/ตำบล.................เขต/อำเภอ...............
จังหวัด..............................ได้เข้าชื่อซื้อหุ้นไว้แล้ว...................หุ้น (ลงลายมือชื่อ)................

(5) ....อาชีวะ.........................อายุ...............ปี
อยู่บ้านเลขที่.............หมู่ที่.........ถนน...................แขวง/ตำบล.................เขต/อำเภอ...............
จังหวัด..............................ได้เข้าชื่อซื้อหุ้นไว้แล้ว...................หุ้น (ลงลายมือชื่อ)................

(6) ....อาชีวะ.........................อายุ...............ปี
อยู่บ้านเลขที่.............หมู่ที่.........ถนน...................แขวง/ตำบล.................เขต/อำเภอ...............
จังหวัด..............................ได้เข้าชื่อซื้อหุ้นไว้แล้ว...................หุ้น (ลงลายมือชื่อ)................

(7) ....อาชีวะ.........................อายุ...............ปี
อยู่บ้านเลขที่.............หมู่ที่.........ถนน...................แขวง/ตำบล.................เขต/อำเภอ...............
จังหวัด..............................ได้เข้าชื่อซื้อหุ้นไว้แล้ว...................หุ้น (ลงลายมือชื่อ)................

(ลงลายมือชื่อผู้)..ผู้เริ่มก่อการผู้ขอจดทะเบียน

(..)

หน้า.............ของจำนวน.................หน้า   (ลงลายมือชื่อ).........................นายทะเบียน

เอกสารประกอบคำขอที่............./.............   (...)

คำรับรองลายมือชื่อของพยาน

ข้าพเจ้า...อายุ.................ปี

อยู่บ้านเลขที่...

ข้าพเจ้า...อายุ.................ปี

อยู่บ้านเลขที่...

ขอรับรองว่าผู้เริ่มก่อการตั้งบริษัทนี้ทุกคน ได้ลงลายมือชื่อต่อหน้าข้าพเจ้า

(ลงลายมือชื่อ)...พยาน

(...)

(ลงลายมือชื่อ)...พยาน

(...)

หนังสือบริคณห์สนธิฉบับนี้ ทำขึ้นเมื่อวันที่...

ผนึกอากรแสตมป์
ต้นฉบับ 200 บาท
คู่ฉบับ 5 บาท

(ลงลายมือชื่อ)...ผู้เริ่มก่อการผู้ขอจดทะเบียน

(...)

หน้า..............ของจำนวน.....................หน้า บริษัท...จำกัด

เอกสารประกอบคำขอที่................/................ (ลงลายมือชื่อ)...นายทะเบียน

(...)

Partnership Registration Form in English

Form Hor Sor 1

Request No. ....
Received Date ....

Registration Office for Partnership Company
....

Partnership Registration Request Form

(Name of) Partnership ....

Registration No. ....

I would like to register a limited partnership company as a juristic person according to the civil and commercial law as follows:

- ♣ Establishing a limited partnership as a juristic person
- ♣ Merging partnerships (...............Partnership, Registration No. ....
  to be merged with ....Partnership, Registration No. ....)
- ♣ Amendment on the name of the partnership
- ♣ Amendment of the objectives of the partnership
- ♣ Amendment on the location of the head office and/or branch office
- ♣ Amendment on details of partnership (in .... persons) (out .... persons)
  (Increasing/Decreasing capital .... persons) (Changing items used for investing .... persons)
  (Changing number of partners .... persons)
- ♣ Amendment on managing partners
- ♣ Amendment on the limitation of power of managing partners
- ♣ Amendment on partnership's seal
- ♣ Other items which the public should know are ....
  Attached are all the required items for registration in the total of .... pages

I, a partner who is requesting this registration, certify that this registration is processed completely and correctly according to the law and regulations and according to

- ♣ Every partner's contract dated .... Effective date ....
- ♣ Order/Court Order .... Case name .... Case No. ....
  Date .... and the case has been followed through.

... and that all items and documents in this request form are true and correct.

(Seal of the Limited Partnership)   Signature of Managing Partner

                                           ....
                                           (....)

                                           ....
                                           (....)

I certify that the person who is requesting the registration   Registrar's Note
has signed in my presence on (date)   Registration received on (date) ....
....   (Signature) ....
Registrar
(.....................................)
(...................................)
Registrar /.............................   Position Seal

Warning: Anyone who produces false information to officer is subject to criminal code Section 137, 267 and 268.

Partnership Registration Form in Thai

แบบ หส. 1

คำขอที่.................................
รับวันที่.................................

สำนักงานทะเบียนหุ้นส่วนบริษัท
....

คำขอจดทะเบียนห้างหุ้นส่วน

ห้างหุ้นส่วน...

ทะเบียนเลขที่...

ข้าพเจ้าขอจดทะเบียนห้างหุ้นส่วน สามัญนิติบุคคล / จำกัด ตามประมวลกฎหมายแพ่งและพาณิชย์ ดังต่อไปนี้

❏ จัดตั้งห้างหุ้นส่วนสามัญนิติบุคคล / จำกัด

❏ ควบห้างหุ้นส่วน (ห้างหุ้นส่วน...ทะเบียนเลขที่..................

ได้ควบเข้ากันกับ ห้างหุ้นส่วน...ทะเบียนเลขที่..................)

❏ แก้ไขเพิ่มเติมชื่อห้างหุ้นส่วน

❏ แก้ไขเพิ่มเติมวัตถุที่ประสงค์ของห้างหุ้นส่วน

❏ แก้ไขเพิ่มเติมที่ตั้งสำนักงานแห่งใหญ่ และ / หรือ สำนักงานสาขา

❏ แก้ไขเพิ่มเติมผู้เป็นหุ้นส่วน (หุ้นส่วนเข้า.................คน) (หุ้นส่วนออก.................คน)

(เพิ่มทุน / ลดทุน.................คน) (เปลี่ยนสิ่งที่นำมาลงหุ้น.................คน) (เปลี่ยนจำพวกหุ้นส่วน.................คน)

❏ แก้ไขเพิ่มเติมหุ้นส่วนผู้จัดการ

❏ แก้ไขเพิ่มเติมข้อจำกัดอำนาจหุ้นส่วนผู้จัดการ

❏ แก้ไขเพิ่มเติมตราของห้างหุ้นส่วน

❏ รายการอื่น ๆ ที่เห็นสมควรจะให้ประชาชนทราบ คือ...

ได้แนบรายการจดทะเบียน และเอกสารประกอบคำขอครบถ้วนตามที่ระเบียบสำนักงานทะเบียนหุ้นส่วนบริษัททกลางฯ

กำหนดแล้ว รวม.................แผ่น

ข้าพเจ้าหุ้นส่วนผู้จัดการผู้ขอจดทะเบียน ขอรับรองว่า การขอจดทะเบียนครั้งนี้ได้ดำเนินการถูกต้องครบถ้วนตามกฎหมาย

โดยเป็นไปตาม

❏ สัญญาของผู้เป็นหุ้นส่วนทุกคน เมื่อวันที่.................................มีผลใช้บังคับวันที่.................................

❏ คำสั่ง / คำพิพากษาของศาล.................................ตามคดี.................หมายเลข.................

เมื่อวันที่.................................และคดีถึงที่สุดแล้ว

และรายการที่ระบุในคำขอจดทะเบียนและเอกสารประกอบถูกต้องตรงความเป็นจริงทุกประการ

(ประทับตราของห้างหุ้นส่วน) ลงลายมือชื่อหุ้นส่วนผู้จัดการ

....

(...)

....

(...)

บันทึกนายทะเบียน

รับจดทะเบียน ณ วันที่.................................

ขอรับรองว่าผู้ขอจดทะเบียนได้ลงลายมือชื่อต่อหน้าข้าพเจ้าจริง

เมื่อวันที่.................................

.... (ลงลายมือชื่อ).................................นายทะเบียน

(...) (...)

นายทะเบียน /... ประทับตราตำแหน่ง

┌───┐

คำเตือน ผู้ใดแจ้งข้อความอันเป็นเท็จแก่เจ้าหน้าที่พนักงานมีความผิดตามประมวลกฎหมายอาญา มาตรา 137,267 และ 268

└───┘

Letter of Certification in English

Written at   Registration Office for Partnership Company

                                              ....

Letter of Certification

          I certify that this (limited) partnership has registered as a juristic person according to the civil and commerce law in the category of "partnership." Registration number .... on (date) .... The details appear on the registration documents on the date of issue are as follows:

1. Name of Partnership " ....Partnership"
2. There are .... partners as follows:
    - (1) .... investing with money/assets/labor .... baht
    - (2) .... investing with money/assets/labor .... baht
    - (3) .... investing with money/assets/labor .... baht
    - (4) .... investing with money/assets/labor .... baht
    - (5) .... investing with money/assets/labor .... baht
    - (6) .... investing with money/assets/labor .... baht
    - (7) .... investing with money/assets/labor .... baht
3. There are .... managing partners as follow:
    - (1) .... (2) ....
    - (3) .... (4) ....
4. There are limitations in the managing partners' power as follows:

    ....

    ....

    ....
5. Head office located at ....

    ....
6. There are .... objectives for the partnership as attached to this letter of certification in the total of .... pages with a signature of registrar and the seal of the registration office.

Issued on (date) ....

....

(....)

Registrar

Registrar can withdraw this registration if later it is found that this registration is not done properly.

Registration Request in English

(Official Use Only)

Commercial Registration Central Office
Commercial Registration office
  District: ....
  Province: ....

Received No. ....
Received Date ....

Original Request No. ....
Registration No.

Types of Request
* * Business Registration (Fill out *1* - *8* /and *9* - *12* are optional)
* * Item Change Registration * ** ** ** * from (date) .... are as follows (Fill out only
  items that need to be changed.)
* * Business Termination Registration from (date) .... (Fill out only *1* *2* and *5*)

1 **Entrepreneur's Name** .... Age ...... Race .... Nationality ....
      Residing at .... Moo .... Soi .... Road .... Sub-District ....
      District .... Province .... Telephone .... Fax ....

2 **Business Name**: Thai Language ....
                  Foreign Language (if any) ....

3 **Types of Business**   Code for
Officer

    (1) ....

    (2) ....

    (3) ....

    (4) ....

4 **Capital Used for Business Purposes** Amount .... Baht (...............)
5 **Company's Head Office** Address No. .... Moo .... Soi
....
      Road .... Sub-District .... District ....
      Province .... Telephone .... Fax ....

6 **Manager's Name** .... Age .... Nationality ....
      Address No. .... Moo .... Soi .... Road ....
      Sub-District .... District .... Province ....
      Telephone .... Fax ....

7 **Date of Starting Business in Thailand**. from (date) ....

8 **Date of Requesting for Registration**
....

9 **Business Has Been Transferred from** .... Nationality ....
    Address No. ....Moo .... Soi .... Road .... Sub-District
    .... District .... Province .... Telephone .... Fax ....
    Name used in doing business .... Date of Transfer ....
    Reason for the Transfer ....

10 **Branch Office Location** No. .... Moo .... Soi
....
      Road .... Sub-District .... District ....
      Province .... Telephone .... Fax ....

Registration Request in English (continued)

Warehouse Location No. .... Moo ....… Soi ....
Road .... Sub-District .... District ....
Province .... Telephone .... Fax ....

Business Representative is ....Address No. .... Moo ....
Soi .... Road .... Sub-District ....….
District .... Province .... Telephone .... Fax ....

11 <u>**Name, Age, Race, Nationality, Address, Business Partner's Capital and Company's Capital**</u>
The total number of existing partners/new partners are .... as follows:
(1) .... Age .... Race .... Nationality ....
Address No. .... Moo .... Soi .... Road ....… Sub-District ....
District ....…... Province .... Telephone .... Fax ....
Invested with .... Total .... Baht (Signature) ....
(2) .... Age .... Race .... Nationality ....
Address No. .... Moo .... Soi .... Road ....… Sub-District ....
District ....…... Province .... Telephone .... Fax ....
Invested with .... Total .... Baht (Signature) ....
(3) .... Age .... Race .... Nationality ....
Address No. .... Moo .... Soi .... Road ....… Sub-District ....
District ....…... Province .... Telephone .... Fax ....
Invested with .... Total .... Baht (Signature) ....

12 <u>**Capital, Stock and Value of the Limited Company. Number and Stock Value for Each Person**</u>
<u>**Categorized by Nationality**</u>
Registered capital ....Baht   Total ...... Stocks   Value per Stock .... Baht
Nationality .... Holding .... Stocks, Nationality .... Holding .... Stocks
Nationality .... Holding .... Stocks, Nationality .... Holding .... Stocks

13 <u>**Partners Quit or Die**</u> Total .... Persons as follows: (In case that there are changes in No. 11.)
(1) .... Age .... Race .... Nationality ....
Address No. .... Moo ...... Soi .... Road ....…... Sub-District ....
District .... Province .... Telephone .... Fax ....
Invested with................... Total .... Baht (Signature) ....
(2) .... Age .... Race .... Nationality ....
Address No. .... Moo ...... Soi .... Road ....…... Sub-District ....
District .... Province .... Telephone .... Fax ....
Invested with................... Total .... Baht (Signature) ....

14 <u>**Others**</u> ....
....

I certify that the above items are all true and correct.

(Signature) .... Entrepreneur
(..........................…...)

<u>**Registrar's Record**</u>

Received Registration on (date) ....…....

(Signature) .... Registrar
(..........................…...)

Registration Request in Thai

แบบ ทพ.

[ ] สำนักงานกลางทะเบียนพาณิชย์
[ ] สำนักงานทะเบียนพาณิชย์
อำเภอ_____
จังหวัด_____

คำขอจดทะเบียน

(เฉพาะเจ้าหน้าที่)
เลขรับที่_____
รับวันที่_____

เลขที่คำขอเดิม_____
ทะเบียนเลขที่_____

ประเภทคำขอ

[ ] จดทะเบียนพาณิชย์ (ให้กรอก [1] - [8] ส่วน [9] - [12] ให้เลือกกรอกตามแต่กรณี)
[ ] จดทะเบียนเปลี่ยนแปลงรายการ [ ] [ ] [ ] [ ] ตั้งแต่วันที่_____เป็นดังนี้ (ให้กรอกเฉพาะรายการซึ่งประสงค์จะขอเปลี่ยนแปลง)
[ ] จดทะเบียนเลิกประกอบพาณิชยกิจ ตั้งแต่วันที่_____(ให้กรอกรายการเฉพาะใน [1] [2] และ [5])

[1] **ชื่อผู้ประกอบพาณิชยกิจ**_____อายุ___ปี เชื้อชาติ_____สัญชาติ_____
    ที่อยู่เลขที่_____หมู่ที่_____ตรอก/ซอย_____ถนน_____ตำบล/แขวง_____
    อำเภอ/เขต_____จังหวัด_____โทรศัพท์_____โทรสาร_____

[2] **ชื่อที่ใช้ในการประกอบพาณิชยกิจ** ภาษาไทย_____
    ภาษาต่างประเทศ (ถ้ามี)_____

[3] **ชนิดแห่งพาณิชยกิจ**

รหัสสำหรับเจ้าหน้าที่

    (1)_____

    (2)_____

    (3)_____

    (4)_____

[4] **จำนวนเงินทุนที่นำมาใช้ในการประกอบพาณิชยกิจเป็นประจำ** จำนวน_____บาท (_____)

[5] **ที่ตั้งสำนักงานแห่งใหญ่** เลขที่_____หมู่ที่_____ตรอก/ซอย_____
    ถนน_____ตำบล/แขวง_____อำเภอ/เขต_____
    จังหวัด_____โทรศัพท์_____โทรสาร_____

[6] **ชื่อผู้จัดการ**_____อายุ___ปี สัญชาติ_____ที่อยู่เลขที่_____
    หมู่ที่_____ตรอก/ซอย_____ถนน_____ตำบล/แขวง_____
    อำเภอ/เขต_____จังหวัด_____โทรศัพท์_____โทรสาร_____

[7] **วันที่เริ่มต้นประกอบพาณิชยกิจในประเทศไทย** ตั้งแต่วันที่_____

[8] **วันที่ขอจดทะเบียนพาณิชย์**_____

[9] **รับโอนพาณิชยกิจนี้จาก**_____สัญชาติ_____ที่อยู่เลขที่_____
    หมู่ที่_____ตรอก/ซอย_____ถนน_____ตำบล/แขวง_____
    อำเภอ/เขต_____จังหวัด_____โทรศัพท์_____โทรสาร_____
    ชื่อใช้ในการประกอบพาณิชยกิจ_____โอนเมื่อวันที่_____
    สาเหตุที่โอน_____

[10] **ที่ตั้งสำนักงานสาขา** เลขที่_____หมู่ที่_____ตรอก/ซอย_____
    ถนน_____ตำบล/แขวง_____อำเภอ/เขต_____
    จังหวัด_____โทรศัพท์_____โทรสาร_____
    ที่ตั้งโรงเก็บสินค้า เลขที่_____หมู่ที่_____ตรอก/ซอย_____
    ถนน_____ตำบล/แขวง_____อำเภอ/เขต_____
    จังหวัด_____โทรศัพท์_____โทรสาร_____

ตัวแทนค้าต่าง คือ_____ ที่อยู่เลขที่_____หมู่ที่_____
ครอก/ซอย_____ถนน_____ตำบล/แขวง_____
อำเภอ/เขต_____จังหวัด_____โทรศัพท์_____โทรสาร_____

[11] ชื่อ อายุ เชื้อชาติ สัญชาติ ตำบลที่อยู่ และจำนวนหุ้นของผู้เป็นหุ้นส่วน และจำนวนเงินทุนของห้างหุ้นส่วน
ผู้เป็นหุ้นส่วนของห้างหุ้นส่วน/ผู้เป็นหุ้นส่วนเข้าใหม่ มีจำนวน_____คน ดังนี้

(1)_____ อายุ_____ปี เชื้อชาติ_____สัญชาติ_____
ที่อยู่เลขที่_____หมู่ที่_____ครอก/ซอย_____
ถนน_____ตำบล/แขวง_____อำเภอ/เขต_____
จังหวัด_____โทรศัพท์_____โทรสาร_____
ลงหุ้นด้วย_____จำนวน_____บาท (ลงลายมือชื่อ)_____

(2)_____ อายุ_____ปี เชื้อชาติ_____สัญชาติ_____
ที่อยู่เลขที่_____หมู่ที่_____ครอก/ซอย_____
ถนน_____ตำบล/แขวง_____อำเภอ/เขต_____
จังหวัด_____โทรศัพท์_____โทรสาร_____
ลงหุ้นด้วย_____จำนวน_____บาท (ลงลายมือชื่อ)_____

(3)_____ อายุ_____ปี เชื้อชาติ_____สัญชาติ_____
ที่อยู่เลขที่_____หมู่ที่_____ครอก/ซอย_____
ถนน_____ตำบล/แขวง_____อำเภอ/เขต_____
จังหวัด_____โทรศัพท์_____โทรสาร_____
ลงหุ้นด้วย_____จำนวน_____บาท (ลงลายมือชื่อ)_____

[12] จำนวนเงินทุน จำนวนหุ้น และมูลค่าหุ้นของบริษัทจำกัด จำนวนและมูลค่าหุ้นที่บุคคลแต่ละสัญชาติถืออยู่
ทุนจดทะเบียน_____บาท แบ่งออกเป็น_____หุ้น มูลค่าหุ้นละ_____บาท
สัญชาติ_____ถือหุ้น_____หุ้น สัญชาติ_____ถือหุ้น_____หุ้น
สัญชาติ_____ถือหุ้น_____หุ้น สัญชาติ_____ถือหุ้น_____หุ้น

[13] ผู้เป็นหุ้นส่วนออกหรือตาย จำนวน_____คน ดังนี้ (ใช้กรณีของจดทะเบียนเปลี่ยนแปลงรายการตามข้อ 11)
(1)_____ อายุ_____ปี เชื้อชาติ_____สัญชาติ_____
ที่อยู่เลขที่_____หมู่ที่_____ครอก/ซอย_____
ถนน_____ตำบล/แขวง_____อำเภอ/เขต_____
จังหวัด_____โทรศัพท์_____โทรสาร_____
(2)_____ อายุ_____ปี เชื้อชาติ_____สัญชาติ_____
ที่อยู่เลขที่_____หมู่ที่_____ครอก/ซอย_____
ถนน_____ตำบล/แขวง_____อำเภอ/เขต_____
จังหวัด_____โทรศัพท์_____โทรสาร_____

[14] อื่น ๆ_____
_____
ข้าพเจ้าขอรับรองว่ารายการข้างต้นถูกต้องและเป็นความจริงทุกประการ

(ลงลายมือชื่อ)_____ผู้ประกอบการพาณิชยกิจ
(_____)

บันทึกนายทะเบียนพาณิชย์

รับจดทะเบียน ณ วันที่_____

(ลงลายมือชื่อ)_____นายทะเบียนพาณิชย์
(_____)

Power of Attorney

Power of Attorney
หนังสือมอบอำนาจ

Written at
ทำที่ ....

Date   Month   B.E.
วันที่ .... เดือน .... พ.ศ. ....

I.   Mr./Mrs./Miss.
ข้าพเจ้า นาย/นาง/นางสาว ....

hereby authorize and appoint Mr./Mrs./Miss.   at present working
ขอมอบอำนาจให้ นาย/นาง/นางสาว .... ปัจจุบันทำงานใน

In the position of   at the office of
ตำแหน่ง .... ตั้งอยู่ที่สำนักงานชื่อ ....

Tel.   Located on   Soi/Lane
โทร. .... ตั้งอยู่เลขที่ .... ซอย ....

Rd.   Sub-District   District
ถนน .... แขวง .... เขต ....

Province   to be lawful and legal attorney for the purpose concerning with work permit,
จังหวัด .... มีอำนาจดำเนินการเกี่ยวกับการขออนุญาตทำงาน ลงนามในเอกสารประกอบการ

sign any documents on behalf of myself including changing words on the related documents.
ขออนุญาตแทนข้าพเจ้าได้ทุกฉบับ รวมทั้งเปลี่ยนแปลงแก้ไขข้อความในเอกสารดังกล่าวด้วย

What has been done by   will remain in full force
การใดที่นาย/นาง/นางสาว .... ได้กระทำไปให้ถือเสมือนว่า

and effect as it has been done by myself.
ข้าพเจ้าได้กระทำเองทุกประการ

Signed   Grantor
ลงชื่อ .... ผู้มอบอำนาจ
          (...)

Signed   Grantee
ลงชื่อ .... ผู้รับมอบอำนาจ
          (...)

Signed   Witness
ลงชื่อ .... พยาน
          (...)

Signed   Witness
ลงชื่อ .... พยาน
          (...)

หมายเหตุ หากผู้มอบอำนาจประสงค์จะจำกัดขอบการมอบอำนาจเป็นอย่างอื่น ย่อมกระทำได้ โดยไม่ต้องใช้เนื้อความตามนี้
Remark In case grantor perfer to limit the authorization giving to the grantee it could be done by using the other
forms of power of attorney.

Non Immigrant Visa Specimen Sponsorship Letter

Business Letterhead Of ABC Co., Ltd.
Name and Address Of Business Sponsor
Telephone, Fax, And E-Mail Address
Registered Company Number

Visa Section
Royal Thai Consulate General
Name of City
Name of Country

Date of Application

Honorable Excellency,

Application for a Non-Immigrant visa (one-year, multiple entry, Type B)
    ABC Co., Ltd. is a company registered in Thailand under Registration Number (4) 445/2542 since (date of registration). (Company Details): We have over 100 titles published and distributed in Thailand since the establishment of the company. We produce and publish high-quality, user-friendly guidebooks, audio and other materials that help people to communicate and make new friends while travelling and living in this region of the world. Our products are sold in book stores throughout Thailand, through online and phone orders from our office in the US and our distributors in Europe.
    This is to certify that (Name of Applicant), a (Nationality) citizen with passport (number) has been requested to help our company (develop our range of business publications). (Name of Applicant) is a (details of profession, training, and experience). (Name of Applicant) is researching and planning a joint-venture project in Thailand; therefore he needs a visa for the purposes of research and investment in Thailand.
    We would be most grateful if you could issue a one-year multiple entry Non-Immigrant visa to (Name of Applicant), before he returns to Thailand. Since he will continue to travel in and out of Thailand, a multiple entry visa is requested.

Please find (Name of Applicant's) passport details below:

Name:
Date of Birth:
Passport Number:
Date of Issue:
Date of Expiry:
Place of Issue:

Thank you very much for your attention.

Yours sincerely,

(Name of Director/Sponsor)
(Name of Sponsoring Company)

Apply Company Seal

Prohibited Businesses For Foreigners

Foreign Business Act BE 2542 (1999)
(Source: www.dbd.go.th/eng/law)

List One: The Businesses Not Permitted For Foreigners To Operate Due To Special Reasons:

(1) Newspaper business, radio broadcasting or television station business. (2) Rice farming, farming, or gardening. (3) Animal farming. (4) Forestry and wood fabrication from natural forest. (5) Fishery for marine animals in Thai waters and within Thailand specific economic zones. (6) Extraction of Thai herbs. (7) Trading and auctioning Thai antiques or national historical objects. (8) Making or casting Buddha images and monk alms bowls. (9) Land trading.

List Two: The Businesses Related To National Safety Or Security Or Affecting Arts And Culture, Tradition, Folk Handicraft Or Natural Resources And The Environment.

Group 1: The businesses related to the national safety or security: (1) Production, selling, repairing, and maintenance of (a) firearms, ammunition, gun powder, explosives; (b) Accessories of firearms, ammunition, and explosives; (c) Armaments, ships, aircraft or military vehicles; (d) Equipment or components, all categories of war materials. (2) Domestic land, waterway or air transportation, including domestic airline business. Group 2: The businesses affecting arts and culture, traditional and folk handicrafts: (1) Trading antiques or art objects being Thai arts and handicrafts. (2) Production of carved wood. (3) Silkworm farming, production of Thai silk yarn, weaving Thai silk or Thai silk pattern printing. (4) Production of Thai musical instruments. (5) Production of goldware, silverware, nielloware, bronzeware or lacquerware. (6) Production of crockery of Thai arts and culture. Group 3: The businesses affecting natural resources or the environment: (1) Manufacturing sugar from sugarcane. (2) Salt farming, including underground salt. (3) Rock salt mining. (4) Mining, including rock blasting or crushing. (5) Wood fabrication for furniture and utensil production.

List Three: The Businesses Which Thai Nationals Are Not Yet Ready To Compete With Foreigners:

(1) Rice milling and flour production from rice and farm produce. (2) Fishery, specifically marine animal cultures. (3) Forestry from forestation. (4) Production of plywood, veneer board, chipboard or hardboard. (5) Production of lime. (6) Accounting service business. (7) Legal service business. (8) Architecture service business. (9) Engineering service business. (10) Construction, except for: (a) Construction rendering basic services to the public in public utilities or transport requiring special tools, machinery, technology or construction expertize having the foreigners minimum capital of 500 million baht or more; (b) Other categories of construction as prescribed by the ministerial regulations. (11) Broker or agent business, except: (a) Being broker or agent for underwriting securities or services connected with future trading of commodities or financing instruments or securities; (b) Being broker or agent for trading or procuring goods or services necessary for production or rendering services amongst affiliated enterprises; (c) Being broker or agent for trading, purchasing or distributing or seeking both domestic and foreign markets for selling

domestically manufactured or imported goods in the manner of international business operations having the foreigners' minimum capital of 100 million baht or more; (d) Being broker or agent of other categories as prescribed by the ministerial regulations. (12) Auction, except: (a) Auction in the manner of international bidding, not being the auction of antiques, historical artifacts or art objects which are Thai works of arts, handicrafts or antiques or having historical value; (b) Other categories of auction as prescribed by the ministerial regulations. (13) Internal trade connected with native products or produce not yet prohibited by law. (14) Retailing all categories of goods having a total minimum capital of less than 100 million baht or having a minimum capital of each shop less than 20 million baht. (15) Wholesaling all categories of goods having minimum capital of each shop less than 100 million baht. (16) Advertising business. (17) Hotel business, except for hotel management service. (18) Guided tour. (19) Selling food or beverages. (20) Plant cultivation and propagation business. (21) Other categories of service business except that prescribed in the ministerial regulations.

Chapter 14
Glossary Of Terms

Asset Sale   When a business ceases to trade, the seller cannot charge a   premium for goodwill; instead the basis of business valuation is the perceived value of the second-hand tangible assets.

Buyer   The person buying a business.

Commission   The fee payable to the introducer, intermediary or broker.

Completion   The final stage of business transfer when the buyer legally owns the business.

Depreciation   The hypothetical expense of using fixed assets. Usually fixed assets are amortised linearly over their estimated economic life (e.g. a 30,000-baht computer depreciated linearly over three years would result in an annual depreciation charge of 10,000 baht).

Due Diligence   The verification of information provided by the seller to the buyer. Due diligence, which is the buyer's responsibility, includes validation of the seller's financial statements and accounts.

Fixed Assets   All tangible items (including fixtures, fittings, furniture, computers, and equipment) for use in the business, with an economic life exceeding one year.

Franchisee   An independent businessperson who has been granted by the franchisor the right to duplicate its entire business format at a particular location and for a specified period, under terms and conditions set forth in the franchise agreement.

Franchise Fee   The initial fee paid to the franchisor. This fee usually includes the license, training, site selection and support, and the rights to use the franchisor's trademark and business systems.

Franchisor   The legal entity (individual, partnership or limited company) which sells the franchise license to the franchisee for a specific territory.

Freehold   Legal ownership of the land or property that is registered in the owner's name at the Land Office. The alternative to freehold property is a long lease.

Going Concern   An actively trading business. The buyer of a going concern would usually expect to earn a profit immediately after transfer of business ownership.

Goodwill   An intangible business asset that includes the value of trademarks, contacts, future orders placed by customers, good location, specialist knowledge, and business systems.

Gross Profit   The profit percentage, taking into account only the direct material and labour costs of production, but not the fixed overheads (including rent and administration costs).

Lessee   The business owner who leases the premises.

Lessor   The landlord (or property owner) who leases the property to the lessee (or tenant).

Net Book Value   The cost of a fixed asset (e.g. equipment) less accumulated depreciation (to allow for wear and tear of the asset).

Net Profit   The real earnings of the business, after allowing for the wear and tear of fixed assets and remuneration paid to employees.

Offer to Purchase   The offer made by the buyer to the seller for a business. If an intermediary (or broker) is involved, the buyer must pay a deposit (usually at least ten percent of the offer value).

Payback Period   The estimated period of time (in years) for the buyer to recover his total investment in the business

Royalty   The fee paid to the franchisor for the continuing use of the franchisor's trademark and ongoing support services. Royalties are usually based on a percentage of the franchise's sales (e.g. ten percent of sales turnover, typically payable monthly or quarterly).

Security Deposit   The lessee is usually required to pay the landlord of the business premises a security deposit to cover possible damage to the landlord's fixtures and fittings. The deposit, which is governed by the lease agreement, is usually two or three months' rent.

Seller   The person (or legal entity) selling their business.

T-Money   Or 'transfer money' is the fee payable by the seller to the landlord when the business is transferred to a new buyer. This fee, which is ultimately paid by the buyer, covers the cost of preparing a new lease.

Total Investment The price paid for the business plus any additional costs of remodelling the premises, replacement of fixed assets, legal fees, security deposit, and any other costs of establishing a profitable business.

Turnkey The business is fully operational and profitable from the date of transfer of business ownership to the buyer.

Glossary Of Thai Words

amphur sub-division of a province (e.g. '*amphur* Chiang Mai' refers to the city area itself)

chanote title/deed document to a property

rai a land division (similar usage to an 'acre' or a 'hectare') = 1,600 square meters

ramwong traditional Thai folk dancing

sa paper made from barks of the mulberry tree

sala a traditional wooden pavilion, almost like a gazebo

sanuk fun, having fun

tuk-tuk three-wheeled, open-sided motor vehicle with a canopy roof

wai Thai way of greeting and paying respect by bringing hands together and slightly bending the head

Useful Business Words

accountant	นักบัญชี	nák-ban-chii
account	บัญชี	ban-chii
advertising	การโฆษณา	gaan-koo-sa-naa
agent	ตัวแทน	dtua-tɛɛn
agreement	ข้อตกลง	kɔ̂ɔ-dtòk-long
appeal (v.)	อุทธรณ์	ùt-tɔɔn
application	การสมัคร	gaan-sa-màk
application form	ใบสมัคร	bai sa-màk
asset	ทรัพย์สิน	sáp-sǐn
association	สมาคม	sa-maa-kom
bank account	บัญชีธนาคาร	ban-chii ta-naa-kaan
benefit	สวัสดิการ	sa-wàt-di-gaan
Bill of Lading	ใบตราส่งสินค้า	bai dtraa-sòng sǐn-káa
Board of Directors	กรรมการ	gaam-ma-gaan
bond	พันธบัตร	pan-tá-bàt
boss	เจ้านาย	jâo-nai

broker	นายหน้า	naai-nâa
business	ธุรกิจ	tú-ra-gìt
businessperson	นักธุรกิจ	nák-tú-ra-gìt
business owner	เจ้าของธุรกิจ	jâo-kɔ̌ɔng tú-ra-gìt
capital	เงินทุน	ngən-tun
cash	เงินสด	ngən-sòt
check/cheque	เช็ค	chék
commercial invoice	ใบกำกับสินค้า	bai-gam-gàp-sǐn-káa
concept	ข้อคิดเห็น	kɔ̂ɔ-kít-hěn
confidentiality	การรักษาความลับ	gaan-rák-sǎa-kwaam-láp
contract	สัญญา	sǎn-yaa
contractor	ผู้รับเหมา	pûu-ráp-mǎo
credit	สินเชื่อ	sǐn-chɨ̂a
credit note	ใบลดหนี้	bai-lót-nîi
custom	ธรรมเนียม	tam-niam
customer	ลูกค้า	lûuk-káa
customs	ศุลกากร	sǔn-lá-gaa-gɔɔn
debit note	ใบเพิ่มหนี้	bai-pɔ̂əm-nîi
Department of Labour	กรมแรงงาน	grom rɛɛng-ngaan
deposit (v.)	ฝาก	fàak
director	ผู้อำนวยการ	pûu-am-nuai-gaan
discount (v.)	ลดราคา	lót-raa-kaa
document	เอกสาร	èek-ga-sǎan
dual pricing	มีสองราคา	mii sɔ̌ɔng raa-kaa
equipment	อุปกรณ์	ùp-bpa-gɔɔn
employee	พนักงาน	pa-nák-ngaan
employer	นายจ้าง	naai-jâang
estate tax	ภาษีมรดก	paa-sǐi mɔɔ-ra-dòk
estimate	ตีราคา	dtii-raa-kaa
evaluation	การประเมินค่า	gaan-bpra-məən-kâa
existing business	ธุรกิจที่มีอยู่แล้ว	tú-ra-gìt tîi-mii yùt-lɛ́ɛo
expense	ค่าใช้จ่าย	kâa-chái-jàai
export	ส่งออก	sòng-ɔ̀ɔk
finance	ไฟแนนซ์	fai-nɛ́ɛn
financial statement	ใบแจ้งยอดเงิน	bai-jɛ̂ɛng yɔ̂ɔt-ngən
fee	ค่าธรรมเนียม	kâa-tam-niam
foreign	ต่างชาติ	dtàang-châat
foreigner	ชาวต่างชาติ	chaao-dtàang-châat
franchise	แฟรนไชซ์	frɛɛn-cháai
gross sale	ยอดขายรวม	yɔ̂ɔt-kǎai-ruam
ID card	บัตรประจำตัว	bàt bpra-jam-dtua
income	รายได้	raai-dâai
income tax	ภาษีเงินได้	paa-sǐi ngən-dâai
import	นำเข้า	nam-kâo

inheritance	มรดก	mɔɔ-ra-dòk
installment	การติดตั้ง	gaan-dtǐt-dtâng
insure	ประกัน	bpra-gan
insurance	การประกัน	gaan-bpra-gan
interpreter	ล่าม	lâam
invest	ลงทุน	long-tun
investment	การลงทุน	gaan-long-tun
investor	นักลงทุน	nák-long-tun
invoice	ใบแจ้งหนี้	bai-jɛ̂ɛng-nîi
land	ที่ดิน	tîi-din
landlord	เจ้าของที่ดิน	jâo-kɔ̌ɔng tîi-din
land office	สำนักงานที่ดิน	sǎm-nák-ngaan tîi-din
law	กฎหมาย	gòt-mǎai
lawyer	ทนายความ	tá-naai-kwaam
lease	เช่าซื้อ	châo-súu
lease agreement	สัญญาเช่า	sǎn-yaa châo
leasing land	เช่าที่ดิน	châo tîi-din
legal	ถูกกฎหมาย	tùuk-gòt-mǎai
Letter of Credit	หนังสือประกันสินเชื่อ	nǎng-sǔu bpra-gan-sǐn-chûa
liability	การรับผิดชอบ	gaan-ráp-pǐt-chɔ̂ɔp
license	ใบอนุญาต	bai-a-nu-yâat
limited company	บริษัทจำกัด	bɔɔ-ri-sàt jam-gàt
limited partnership	ห้างหุ้นส่วนจำกัด	hâang-hûn-sùan jam-gàt
loan	เงินกู้	ngən-gûu
location	สถานที่	sa-tǎan-tîi
management	การจัดการ	gaan-jàt-gaan
manager	ผู้จัดการ	pûu-jàt-gaan
manufacture	การผลิต	gaan-pa-lìt
meeting	การประชุม	gaan-bpra-chum
method	วิธี	wí-tii
minimum wage	ค่าแรง	kâa-rɛɛng
Ministry of Labour	กระทรวงแรงงาน	gra-suan rɛɛng-ngaan
morale	ขวัญ, กำลังใจ	kwǎn, gam-lang-jai
net profit	กำไรสุทธิ	gam-rai sùt-tí
offer (n.)	ข้อเสนอ	kɔ̂ɔ-sa-nɔ̌ə
ownership	การเป็นเจ้าของ	gaan-bpen-jâo-kɔ̌ɔng
partner	หุ้นส่วน	hûn-sùan
partnership	ห้างหุ้นส่วน	hâang-hûn-sɔ̀an
personal income tax	ภาษีรายได้ส่วนบุคคล	paa-sǐi raai-dâai sùan-bùk-kon
plan (n.)	การวางแผน	gaan-waang-pɛ̌ɛn
premises	สิ่งปลูกสร้าง	sǐng-bplùuk-sâang

premium	เบี้ยประกัน	bîa-bpra-gan
presentation	การนำเสนอ	gaan-nam-sa-nǒ̌
product	สินค้า	sǐn-káa
prohibited occupation	อาชีพต้องห้าม	aa-chîip dtôɔng-hâam
profit	กำไร	gam-rai
property	ทรัพย์สิน	sáp-sǐn
proprietor	ผู้ถือกรรมสิทธิ์	pûu-tǔu-gam-ma-sìt
purchase order	ใบสั่งสินค้า	bai-sàng-sǐn-káa
receipt	ใบเสร็จ	bai-sèt
referral	การแนะนำ	gaan-né-nam
referral fee	ค่าแนะนำ	kâa-né-nam
refund (v.)	คืนเงิน	kʉʉn-ngən
registration	การจดทะเบียน	gaan-jòt-ta-bian
registration office	สำนักงานทะเบียน	sam-nák-ngaan ta-bian
rent (v.)	เช่า	châo
rent (n.)	ค่าเช่า	kâa-châo
representative	ตัวแทน	dtua-tɛɛn
restriction	ข้อจำกัด	kɔ̂ɔ-jam-gàt
Revenue Department	กรมสรรพากร	grom-sǎn-paa-gɔɔn
right (n.)	สิทธิ	sìt, sìt-tí
salary	เงินเดือน	ngən-dʉan
sales	การขาย	gaan-kǎai
schedule	การกำหนดเวลา	gaan-gam-nòt-wee-laa
secretary	เลขา	lee-kǎa
security deposit	ค่ามัดจำ	kâa-mát-jam
service	บริการ	bɔɔ-ti-gaan
share holder	ผู้ถือหุ้น	pûu-tǔu-hûn
social	สังคม	sǎng-kom
social insurance	ประกันสังคม	bpra-gan sǎng-kom
start-up company	บริษัทที่เริ่มใหม่	bɔɔ-ri-sàt tîi-rə̂əm-mài
stock	หุ้น	hûn
supplier	ผู้จัดส่งสินค้า	pûu-jàt-sòng-sǐn-káa
tax	ภาษี	paa-sǐi
total investment	การลงทุนทั้งหมด	gaan-long-tun táng-mòt
transfer (v.)	โอน	oon
translation	การแปลเอกสาร	gaan-bplɛɛ eèk-ga-sǎan
trustworthy	ไว้วางใจได้	wái-waang-jai-dâai
value added tax (VAT)	ภาษีมูลค่าเพิ่ม	paa-sǐi mun-la-kâa-pɔ̂əm
venture	เงินลงทุน	ngən-long-tun
visa regulation	กฎระเบียบวีซ่า	gòt-ra-bǐap-wii-sâa
wage	ค่าแรง	kâa-rɛɛng
withholding tax	การหักภาษี ณ ที่จ่าย	gaan-hàk-paa-sǐi ná tîi-jàai
work permit	ใบอนุญาตทำงาน	bai-a-nú-yâat tam-ngaan

Recommended Books

Business Guide To Thailand
Christopher Seline
Barnes and Noble (www.bn.com)

The Complete Guide To Business Brokerage
Tom West
Business Brokerage Press (www.businessbookpress.com)

Culture Shock: Thailand: A Survival Guide To Customs And Etiquette
Robert Cooper and Nanthapa Cooper
Graphic Arts Centre Publishing Company

Doing Business In Thailand
Baker and McKenzie
(www.bakernet.com)

Franchising: The Science Of Reproducing Success
Gaurav Marya
Franchise India Holdings Ltd.

How To Buy Land And Build A House In Thailand
Philip Bryce
Paiboon Publishing (www.paiboonpublishing.com)

Retiring In Thailand
Philip Bryce and Sunisa Wongdee Terlecky
Paiboon Publishing (www.paiboonpublishing.com)

Speak Like A Thai (Volume 1, 2, 3, 4 and 5)
Benjawan Poomsan Becker
Paiboon Publishing (www.paiboonpublishing.com)

Start Up And Stay Up
Roy Tomizawa
Alpha Research Co., Ltd.

Thailand In Figures
Alpha Research Co., Ltd. (www.alpharesearch.co.th)

Thailand Fever: A Road Map For Thai-Western Relationships
Chris Pirazzi and Vitida Vasant
Paiboon Publishing (www.paiboonpublishing.com)

About The Author

Philip Wylie was born in Liverpool, England. He is a Fellow of the Institute of Chartered Accountants in England and Wales and has a masters degree (MBA) in management science from Imperial College, London. Philip worked with Price Waterhouse Cooper's London office specializing in independently-owned businesses. He has worked with numerous SMEs across all industrial sectors.

Author Photo © 2007 Asia Pacific Media Services

Philip also worked with Ernst & Young International in the Middle East as an advisor and technical writer. He was director of an information services company, and director and company secretary of an offshore private bank. In Thailand he has worked as a franchise manager, business broker, and advisor. Philip is currently engaged with research and writing as well as promoting investment in Asia.

Acknowledgements

Philip is grateful to everyone who has contributed to this publication, especially Benjawan, Nicholas, Gordon, and Mo at Paiboon Publishing, and to the successful businesspeople profiled in the book. Also to Pick for assistance with accounting regulations, and Jakkapan and Atiphat for valuable research material.

Contact Information

If you have questions or comments about this book, or about investing in Asia, contact Philip using the contact form on www.advisaweb.com.

Index

Titles from Paiboon Publishing

Title: **Thai for Beginners**
Author: Benjawan Poomsan Becker ©1995
Description: Designed for either self-study or classroom use. Teaches all four language skills- speaking, listening (when used in conjunction with the cassette tapes), reading and writing. Offers clear, easy, step-by-step instruction building on what has been previously learned. Used by many Thai temples and institutes in America and Thailand. Cassettes & CD available. Paperback. 270 pages. 6" x 8.5"

Book	US$12.95	Stock # 1001B
Two CDs	US$20.00	Stock # 1001CD

Title: **Thai for Travelers** (Pocket Book Version)
Author: Benjawan Poomsan Becker ©2006
Description: The best Thai phrase book you can find. It contains thousands of useful words and phrases for travelers in many situations. The phrases are practical and up-to-date and can be used instantly. The CD that accompanies the book will help you improve your pronunciation and expedite your Thai language learning. You will be able to speak Thai in no time! Full version on mobile phones and PocketPC also available at www.vervata.com.

Book & CD	US$15.00	Stock # 1022BCD

Title: **Thai for Intermediate Learners**
Author: Benjawan Poomsan Becker ©1998
Description: The continuation of Thai for Beginners . Users are expected to be able to read basic Thai language. There is transliteration when new words are introduced. Teaches reading, writing and speaking at a higher level. Keeps students interested with cultural facts about Thailand. Helps expand your Thai vocabulary in a systematic way. Paperback. 220 pages. 6" x 8.5"

Book	US$12.95	Stock # 1002B
Two CDs	US$15.00	Stock # 1002CD

Title: **Thai for Advanced Readers**
Author: Benjawan Poomsan Becker ©2000
Description: A book that helps students practice reading Thai at an advanced level. It contains reading exercises, short essays, newspaper articles, cultural and historical facts about Thailand and miscellaneous information about the Thai language. Students need to be able to read basic Thai. Paperback. 210 pages. 6" x 8.5"

Book	US$12.95	Stock # 1003B
Two CDs	US$15.00	Stock # 1003CD

Title: **Thai-English, English-Thai Dictionary for Non-Thai Speakers**
Author: Benjawan Poomsan Becker ©2002
Description: Designed to help English speakers communicate in Thai. It is equally useful for those who can read the Thai alphabet and those who can't. Most Thai-English dictionaries either use Thai script exclusively for the Thai entries (making them difficult for westerners to use) or use only phonetic transliteration (making it impossible to look up a word in Thai script). This dictionary solves these problems. You will find most of the vocabulary you are likely to need in everyday life, including basic, cultural, political and scientific terms. Paperback. 658 pages. 4.1" x 5.6"
Book   US$15.00 Stock # 1008B

Title: **Improving Your Thai Pronunciation**
Author: Benjawan Poomsan Becker ©2003
Description: Designed to help foreigers maximize their potential in pronouncing Thai words and enhance their Thai listening and speaking skills. Students will find that they have more confidence in speaking the language and can make themselves understood better. The book and the CDs are made to be used in combination. The course is straight forward, easy to follow and compact. Paperback. 48 pages. 5" x 7.5" + One-hour CD
Book & CD   US$15.00 Stock # 1011BCD

Title: **Thai for Lovers**
Author: Nit & Jack Ajee ©1999
Description: An ideal book for lovers. A short cut to romantic communication in Thailand. There are useful sentences with their Thai translations throughout the book. You won't find any Thai language book more fun and user-friendly.
Rated R! Paperback. 190 pages. 6" x 8.5"
Book   US$13.95 Stock #: 1004B
Two CDs   US$17.00 Stock #: 1004CD

Title: **Thai for Gay Tourists**
Author: Saksit Pakdeesiam ©2001
Description: The ultimate language guide for gay and bisexual men visiting Thailand.   Lots of gay oriented language, culture, commentaries and other information. Instant sentences for convenient use by gay visitors. Fun and sexy. The best way to communicate with your Thai gay friends and partners! Rated R! Paperback. 220 pages. 6" x 8.5"
Book   US$13.95 Stock # 1007B
Two Tape Set   US$17.00 Stock # 1007T

Title: **Thailand Fever**
Authors: Chris Pirazzi and Vitida Vasant ©2005
Description: A road map for Thai-Western relationships.   The must-have relationship guidebook which lets each of you finally express complex issues of both cultures. Thailand Fever is an astonishing, one-of-a-kind, bilingual expose of the cultural secrets that are the key to a smooth Thai-Western relationship. Paperback. 258 pages. 6" x 8.5"
Book   US$15.95 Stock # 1017B

Title: **Thai-English, English-Thai Software Dictionary**
         for Palm OS PDAs With Search-by-Sound
Authors: Benjawan Poomsan Becker and Chris Pirazzi ©2003
Description: This software dictionary provides instant access to 21,000 English, Phonetic and Thai Palm OS PDA with large, clear fonts and everyday vocabulary. If you're not familiar with the Thai alphabet, you can also look up Thai words by their sounds. Perfect for the casual traveller or the dedicated Thai learner. Must have a Palm OS PDA and access to the Internet in order to use this product.
Book & CD-ROM   US$39.95   Stock # 1013BCD-ROM

Title: **Thai for Beginners Software**
Authors: Benjawan Poomsan Becker and Dominique Mayrand ©2004
Description: Best Thai language software available in the market! Designed especially for non-romanized written Thai to help you to rapidly improve your listening and reading skills! Over 3,000 recordings of both male and female voices. The content is similar to the book Thai for Beginners, but with interactive exercises and much more instantly useful words and phrases. Multiple easy-to-read font styles and sizes.   Super-crisp enhanced text with romanized transliteration which can be turned on or off for all items.
Book & CD-ROM   US$40.00   Stock # 1016BCD-ROM

Title: **Lao-English, English-Lao Dictionary for Non-Lao Speakers**
Authors: Benjawan Poomsan Becker & Khamphan Mingbuapha ©2003
Description: Designed to help English speakers communicate in Lao.   This practical dictionary is useful both in Laos and in Northeast Thailand. Students can use it without having to learn the Lao alphabet.   However, there is a comprehensive introduction to the Lao writing system and pronunciation. The transliteration system is the same as that used in Paiboon Publishing's other books. It contains most of the vocabulary used in everyday life, including basic, cultural, political and scientific terms. Paperback. 780 pages. 4.1" x 5.6"
Book   US$15.00 Stock # 1010B

Title: **Lao for Beginners**
Authors: Buasawan Simmala and Benjawan Poomsan Becker ©2003
Description: Designed for either self-study or classroom use. Teaches all four language skills- speaking, listening (when used in conjunction with the audio), reading and writing. Offers clear, easy, step-by-step instruction building on what has been previously learned. Paperback. 292 pages. 6" x 8.5"
Book   US$12.95 Stock # 1012B
Three CDs   US$20.00 Stock # 1012CD

Title: **Cambodian for Beginners**
Authors: Richard K. Gilbert and Sovandy Hang ©2004
Description: Designed for either self-study or classroom use. Teaches all four language skills- speaking, listening (when used in conjunction with the CDs), reading and writing. Offers clear, easy, step-by-step instruction building on what has been previously learned. Paperback. 290 pages. 6" x 8.5"
Book   US$12.95 Stock # 1015B
Three CDs   US$20.00 Stock # 1015CD

Title: **Burmese for Beginners**
Author: Gene Mesher ©2006
Description: Designed for either self-study or classroom use. Teaches all four language skills- speaking, listening (when used in conjunction with the CDs), reading and writing. Offers clear, easy, step-by-step instruction building on what has been previously learned. Paperback. 320 pages. 6" x 8.5"
Book   US$12.95 Stock # 1019B
Three CDs   US$20.00 Stock # 1019CD

Title: **Vietnamese for Beginners**
Authors: Jake Catlett and Huong Nguyen ©2006
Description: Designed for either self-study or classroom use. Teaches all four language skills- speaking, listening (when used in conjunction with the CDs), reading and writing. Offers clear, easy, step-by-step instruction building on what has been previously learned. Paperback. 292 pages. 6" x 8.5"
Book   US$12.95 Stock # 1020B
Three CDs   US$20.00 Stock # 1020CD

Title: **Tai Go No Kiso**
Author: Benjawan Poomsan Becker ©2002
Description: Thai for Japanese speakers. Japanese version of Thai for Beginners. Paperback. 262 pages. 6" x 8.5"
Book   US$12.95 Stock # 1009B
Three Tape Set US$20.00 Stock # 1009T

Title: **Thai fuer Anfaenger**
Author: Benjawan Poomsan Becker ©2000
Description: Thai for German speakers. German version of Thai for Beginners.
Paperback. 245 pages. 6" x 8.5"
Book   US$13.95   Stock # 1005B
Two CDs   US$20.00   Stock # 1005CD

Title: **Practical Thai Conversation DVD Volume 1**
Author: Benjawan Poomsan Becker ©2005
Description: This new media for learning Thai comes with a booklet and a DVD.
You will enjoy watching and listening to this program and learn the Thai language
in a way you have never done before. Use it on your TV, desktop or laptop. The
course is straight forward, easy to follow and compact. A must-have for all Thai
learners! DVD and Paperback, 65 pages 4.8" x 7.1"
Book & DVD   US$15.00   Stock # 1018BDVD

Title: **Practical Thai Conversation DVD Volume 2**
Author: Benjawan Poomsan Becker ©2006
Description: Designed for intermediate Thai learners! This new media for
learning Thai comes with a booklet and a DVD. You will enjoy watching and
listening to this program and learn the Thai language in a way you have never
done before. Use it on your TV, desktop or laptop. The course is straight forward,
easy to follow and compact. DVD and Paperback, 60 pages 4.8" x 7.1"
Book & DVD   US$15.00   Stock # 1021BDVD

Title: **A Chameleon's Tale - True Stories of a Global Refugee -**
Author: Mohezin Tejani ©2006
Description: A heart touching real life story of Mo Tejani, a global refugee who
spends thirty four years searching five continents for a country he could call
home. Enjoy the ride through numerous countries in Asia, Africa, North and
South America. His adventurous stories are unique – distinctly different from
other travelers' tales. Recommended item from Paiboon Publishing for avid
readers worldwide. Paperback. 257 pages. 5" x 7.5"
Book   US$19.95   Stock #1024B

Title: **Thai Touch**
Author: Richard Rubacher ©2006
Description: The good and the bad of the Land of Smiles are told with a comic touch. The book focuses on the spiritual and mystical side of the magical kingdom as well as its dark side. The good and the bad are told with a comic touch. The Sex Baron, the Naughty & Nice Massage Parlors, the "Bangkok haircut" and Bar Girls & the Pendulum are contrasted with tales of the Thai Forrest Gump, the Spiritual Banker of Thailand and the 72-year old woman whose breasts spout miracle milk. Paperback. 220 pages. 5" x 7.5"
Book   US$19.95   Stock #1024B

Title: **How to Buy Land and Build a House in Thailand**
Author: Philip Bryce ©2006
Description: This book contains essential information for anyone contemplating buying or leasing land and building a house in Thailand. Subjects covered: land ownership options, land titles, taxes, permits, lawyers, architects and builders. Also includes English/Thai building words and phrases and common Thai building techniques. Learn how to build your dream house in Thailand that is well made, structurally sound and nicely finished. Paperback. 6" x 8.5"
Book   US$19.95   Stock #1025B

Title: **Retiring in Thailand**
Authors: Philip Bryce and Sunisa Wongdee Terlecky ©2006
Description: A very useful guide for those who are interested in retiring in Thailand. It contains critical information for retirees, such as how to get a retirement visa, banking, health care, renting and buying property, everyday life issues and other important retirement factors.   It also lists Thailand's top retirement locations. It's a must for anyone considering living the good life in the Land of Smiles. 6" x 8.5"
Book   US$19.95   Stock #1026B

Title: **How to Establish a Successful Business in Thailand**
Author: Philip Wylie ©2007
Description: This is the perfect book for anyone thinking of starting or buying a business in Thailand. This book will save readers lots of headaches, time and money. This guide is full of information on how to run a business in Thailand including practical tips by successful foreign business people from different trades, such as guest house, bar trade, e-commerce, export and restaurant. This is an essential guide for all foreigners thinking of doing business - or improving their business - in Thailand.
Book   US$19.95   Stock #1031B

Title: **Speak Like A Thai Volume 1**
           -Contemporary Thai Expressions-
Author: Benjawan Poomsan Becker ©2007
Description: This series of books and CDs is a collection of numerous words
and expressions used by modern Thai speakers. It will help you to understand
colloquial Thai and to express yourself naturally. You will not find these phases
in most textbooks. It's a language course that all Thai learners have been waiting
for. Impress your Thai friends with the real spoken Thai. Lots of fun. Good for
students of all levels.
Book & CD   US$15.00   Stock # 1028BCD

Title: **Speak Like A Thai Volume 2**
           -Thai Slang and Idioms-
Author: Benjawan Poomsan Becker ©2007
Description: This volume continues the fun of learning the real Thai
language. It can be used independently. However, you should be comfortable
speaking the Thai phrases from the first volume before you use this one. You will
not find these words and phases in any textbooks. It's a language course that all
Thai learners have been waiting for. Impress your Thai friends even more. Lots of
fun. Good for students of all levels.
Book & CD   US$15.00   Stock # 1029BCD

Title: **Speak Like A Thai Volume 3**
           -Thai Proverbs and Sayings-
Author: Benjawan Poomsan Becker ©2007
Description: The third volume is an excellent supplementary resource for all
Thai learners. Common Thai proverbs and sayings listed in the book with the
literal translations will help you understand Thai ways of thinking that are different
from yours. You can listen to these proverbs and sayings over and over on the
CD. Sprinkle them here and there in your conversation. Your Thai friend will be
surprised and appreciate your insight into Thai culture. Good for intermdiate and
advanced students, but beginners can use it for reference.
Book & CD   US$15.00   Stock # 1030BCD

Title: **Speak Like a Thai Volume 4**
          -Heart Words-
Author: Benjawan Poomsan Becker ©2007
Description: "Heart" Words contains 300 common contemporary "heart" words
and phrases. They are recorded on the CD and explained in the booklet with a
brief translation, a literal translation and used in a sample phrase or sentence.
More than a hundred bonus "heart" words are included in the booklet for your
reference. Listen and learn how Thai people express their feelings and thoughts.
You will gain significant insight about the Thai people and their social contexts.
Book & CD   US$15.00   Stock # 1033BCD

Title: **Speak Like a Thai Volume 5**
          -Northeastern Dialect-
Author: Benjawan Poomsan Becker ©2007
Description: *Northeastern Dialect* contains 500 Isaan words and phrases which
have been carefully chosen from real life situations. They are recorded on the CD
and explained in the booklet with a brief translation and a literal translation when
needed. Throughout the book there are also lists of many Isaan words that are
different from standard Thai. This is a fun program that will bring a smile to the
face of your Isaan friends.
Book & CD   US$15.00   Stock # 1034BCD